RAF Bomber Command Profiles

619 Squadron

RAF Bomber Command Profiles

619 Squadron

Chris Ward

www.bombercommandbooks.com

This edition first published 2021 by Mention the War Ltd., 25 Cromwell Street, Merthyr Tydfil, CF47 8RY.

Copyright 2021 © Chris Ward.

The right of Chris Ward to be identified as Author of this work is asserted by him in accordance with the Copyright, Designs and Patents Act 1988.

The original Operational Record Book of 619 Squadron and the Bomber Command Night Raid Reports are Crown Copyright and stored in microfiche and digital format by the National Archives. Material is reproduced under Open Licence v. 2.0.

All rights reserved. No part of this publication may be reproduced, stored in a retrieval system, transmitted in any form or by any means, electronic, mechanical or photocopied, recorded or otherwise, without the written permission of the copyright owners.

This squadron profile has been researched, compiled and written by its author, who has made every effort to ensure the accuracy of the information contained in it. The author will not be liable for any damages caused, or alleged to be caused, by any information contained in this book. E. & O.E.

Cover design: Topics - The Creative Partnership www.topicsdesign.co.uk

Photos and captions: Clare Bennett

A CIP catalogue reference for this book is available from the British Library.

ISBN 9781911255864

Also by Chris Ward from Bomber Command Books:

Casualty of War: Letters Home from Flight Lieutenant Bill Astell DFC

Dambuster Deering: The Life and Death of an Unsung Hero

Dambusters : The Complete WWII History of 617 Squadron
(with Andy Lee and Andreas Wachtel)

Other RAF Bomber Command Profiles:

10 Squadron (with Ian MacMillan)
35 (Madras Presidency) Squadron
44 (Rhodesia) Squadron
50 Squadron
75(NZ) Squadron (with Chris Newey)
83 Squadron
101 Squadron
103 Squadron (with David Fell)
106 Squadron (with Herman Bijlard)
115 Squadron
138 Squadron (with Piotr Hodyra)
207 Squadron (with Raymond Glynne-Owen)
300 Squadron (with Grzegorz Korcz)
467 Squadron RAAF
514 Squadron (with Simon Hepworth)
617 Squadron

Contents

Dedication 9
Introduction 10
Narrative History 12
June 1943 15
July 1943 21
August 1943 28
September 1943 37
October 1943 43
November 1943 48
December 1943 53
January 1944 73
February 1944 79
March 1944 83
April 1944 89
May 1944 96
June 1944 104
July 1944 111
August 1944 119
September 1944 128
October 1944 135
November 1944 140
December 1944 144
January 1945 174
February 1945 178
March 1945 184
April 1945 190
Stations 211

Commanding Officers	211
Aircraft	211
Operational Record	211
Aircraft Histories	212
Roll of Honour	216
Key to Abbreviations	228

Dedication

This 619 Squadron WWII history is dedicated to Wing Commander John Bell MBE, DFC, L.d'H, who, at the time of writing, is a venerable 98-year-old and an inspiration to us all.

He served with distinction as a bomb-aimer in the crew of F/Sgt, later, F/L "Bob" Knights, first in 619 Squadron and then in 617 Squadron, participating in many operations including attacks on V-Weapon sites. In his retirement years, John became President of the 617 Squadron Association, which he also served honourably and with great dignity.

Introduction

RAF Bomber Command Squadron Profiles first appeared in the late nineties and proved to be very popular with enthusiasts of RAF Bomber Command during the Second World War. They became a useful research tool, particularly for those whose family members had served and were no longer around. The original purpose was to provide a point of reference for all of the gallant men and women who had fought the war, either in the air, or on the ground in a support capacity, and for whom no written history of their unit or station existed. I wanted to provide them with something they could hold up, point to and say, "this was my unit, this is what I did in the war". Many veterans were reticent to talk about their time on bombers, partly because of modesty, but perhaps mostly because the majority of those with whom they came into contact had no notion of what it was to be a "Bomber Boy", to face the prospect of death every time they took to the air, whether during training or on operations. Only those who shared the experience really understood what it was to go to war in bombers, which is why reunions were so important. As they approached the end of their lives, many veterans began to speak openly for the first time about their life in wartime Bomber Command, and most were hurt by the callous treatment they received at the hands of successive governments with regard to the lack of recognition of their contribution to victory. It is sad that this recognition in the form of a national memorial and the granting of a campaign medal came too late for the majority. Now this inspirational, noble generation, the like of which will probably never grace this earth again, has all but departed from us, and the world will be a poorer place as a result.

RAF Bomber Command Squadron Profiles are back. The basic format remains, but, where needed, additional information has been provided. Squadron Profiles do not claim to be comprehensive histories, but rather detailed overviews of the activities of the squadron. There is insufficient space to mention as many names as one would like, but all aircraft losses are accompanied by the name of the pilot. Fundamentally, the narrative section is an account of Bomber Command's war from the perspective of the bomber group under which the individual squadron served, and the deeds of the squadron are interwoven into this story. Information has been drawn from official records, such as group, squadron and station Operations Record Books (ORBs), and from the many, like me, amateur enthusiasts, who dedicate much of their time to researching individual units, and become unrivalled authorities on them. I am grateful for their generous contributions, and their names will appear in the appropriate Profiles. The statistics quoted in this series are taken from *The Bomber Command War Diaries*, that indispensable tome written by Martin Middlebrook and Chris Everitt, and I am indebted to Martin for his kind permission to use them.

Finally, let me apologise in advance for the inevitable errors, for no matter how hard I and other authors try to write "nothing but the truth", there is no such thing as a definitive account of history, and there will always be room for disagreement and debate. Official records are notoriously unreliable tools, and yet we have little choice but to put our faith in them. It is not my intention to misrepresent any person or Bomber Command unit, and I ask my readers to understand the enormity of the task I have undertaken. It is relatively easy to become an authority on single units or even a bomber group, but I chose to write about them all, idiot that I am, which means 128 squadrons serving operationally in Bomber Command at some time between the 3rd of September 1939 and the 8th of May 1945. I am dealing with eight bomber groups, in which some 120,000 airmen served, and I am juggling around 28,000 aircraft serial numbers, code letters and details of provenance and fate. I ask not for your sympathy, it was, after all, my choice, but rather your understanding if you should find something with which you disagree. My thanks to you, my readers, for making the original series of RAF Bomber Command Squadron Profiles so popular, and I hope you receive this new incarnation equally enthusiastically.

My thanks are due, as always, to my gang members, Andreas Wachtel, photo editor, Clare Bennett, Steve Smith and Greg Korcz for their unstinting support, without which my Profiles would be the poorer. My gratitude also to Anne Grimshaw, Linda Cannon, Jane Knox and others associated in some way with the 619 Squadron Association for their eagerness to help with photos and to Thorpe Camp Visitors Centre for providing access to its photograph archive. Finally, my appreciation to my publisher, Simon Hepworth of Mention the War Publications, for his belief in my work, untiring efforts to promote it, and for the stress I put him through to bring my books to publication.

Chris Ward. Skegness, Lincolnshire. August 2021.

Narrative History

Formed at Woodhall Spa in Lincolnshire on the 18th of April 1943 in the middle of the Ruhr campaign, 619 Squadron was part of the expansion of Bomber Command during the spring of that year. It was born into 5 Group, and, unlike all but the recently formed and soon to be famous 617 Squadron among its fellow units, it was brand new and had no previous history or tradition. Sadly, it would never officially be awarded a badge or a motto to commemorate its existence. As a squadron of the line in 5 Group, it would operate Lancasters, and inherited its first three crews, those of F/L Bell DFC, F/O Harrison DFM and Sgt McLeod, from 97 Squadron, which left them behind, apparently, surplus to requirements, when departing 5 Group on that day to join the Path Finders. Fortunately, each was a battle-hardened crew, around which the squadron would be built over the ensuing weeks. Wing Commander I J McGhie was posted in from Scampton to command, and he was joined by F/O Burdett from 17 O.T.U to fulfil the vital role of squadron adjutant. The squadron would be the twenty-first unit in the Command to receive the Lancaster, but it would have to wait until the 29th before taking on charge the first two examples. Acting F/L Churcher DFC and F/O Dampier-Crossley were posted in from 1660 Conversion Unit on the 22nd, each with a crew, the former to be elevated immediately to acting squadron leader rank to enable him to take command of A Flight. F/L Dampier-Crossley RAAF, who was actually a Kiwi, had completed a tour with 50 Squadron, before a posting to 61 Squadron's Conversion Flight on the 4th of October 1942 to lend his experience to the training of new crews arriving from training establishments. Thereafter, he served the almost mandatory spell as an instructor, in his case at 1660 Conversion Unit, until teaming up again at 619 Squadron with former 50 Squadron colleague, acting F/L Taylor, who came directly from 50 Squadron at Skellingthorpe. F/O Walmsley was recruited on the same day from 1654 Conversion unit to be appointed bombing leader.

A further four crews were added to squadron strength from 1660 Conversion Unit on the 23rd, and, while those of Sgts Jordan, McCulloch, Metcalfe and Coombes had completed only a few operations between them, the adjutant recorded that they would benefit from the tutelage of their commanding officer and their more experienced colleagues. A steady stream of technical and support personnel passed through the main gates as the squadron attempted to fill all of the vacancies to enable it to achieve operational status, and 107 were on strength by the end of the 24th. The aircrew officers would find themselves billeted in the beautiful Petwood Hotel, situated on the Stixwould road heading north on the outskirts of the nearby town of Woodhall Spa. The grounds had been carved out of the favourite (pet) wood belonging to the wealthy heiress, Baroness Grace van Eckhardstein, and a lavish Tudor/Jacobean-style residence built, beginning in 1905. In 1933, it became a hotel, and in 1942 was taken over by the RAF to accommodate the first residents from the RAF station, while the rest of the squadron and station staff were accommodated in Thorpe camp in Nissen hut-type accommodation opposite the airfield. P/O Henderson was posted in from 57 Squadron at Scampton on the 26th, Easter Monday, as the navigation leader, while F/O Howard arrived on the following day on posting from 1485 Bombing and Gunnery Unit to become gunnery leader. 617 Squadron donated Lancasters W4921 and W4929 on the 29th, having itself acquired them from 106 and 61 Squadron's respectively, but some brand new examples would arrive from the Avro Woodford assembly plant in due course. With the arrival of F/L Gilmour as signals leader on the 29th, all of the senior crew trade positions had been filled, and strength at the end of April stood at two Lancasters, ten complete crews, thirty-one WAAFs and 202 other ranks. With five holders of the DFC and four of the DFM, the consensus was that the squadron possessed a nucleus capable of developing into an efficient fighting unit.

The Ruhr campaign had begun on the night of the 5/6th of March at the industrial powerhouse of Essen in the heart of the Ruhr conurbation. The home of the giant armaments-producing Krupp empire had been Harris's nemesis thus far and, for the first time since the war began, the Command would have at its disposal a device which would negate the industrial haze that had been the city's, and indeed, the region's protector. The magnificent pioneering work by W/C Hal Bufton and his crews at 109 Squadron in marrying Oboe to the Mosquito was about to bear fruit in spectacular fashion, and the towns and cities of Germany's arsenal would suffer destruction on an unprecedented scale. The system involved radio signals from two transmitters, which would be picked up by a transponder in the aircraft and rebroadcast back to provide a precise range with a margin of error of around five hundred yards. The target aircraft would fly along the radius of a circle until receiving a signal to bomb when over the aiming point, and would, thus, achieve, what at an urban target, amounted to pinpoint accuracy. The Krupp organisation had been the largest manufacturer of weapons in Europe since before the Great War, and had a hand in all aspects of German war production from tanks to artillery and ship and U-Boot construction, and was given a controlling share in all major heavy engineering companies in Germany and the Occupied Countries. It also built manufacturing sites in other parts of Germany, many situated close to concentration camps, and employed vast numbers of forced workers in all of its factories. Once known as "Die Waffenschmiede des Reichs", the weapon-forge of the realm, its manufacturing sites in Essen included the Friedrich Krupp steelworks, the Friedrich Krupp locomotive and general engineering works, six coal mines and ten coke-oven plants, the Altenberg zinc works, the Presswerk plastics factory, and the Goldschmidt non-ferrous metals smelting plant, all situated either within or close to the four Borbeck districts, located in a segment radiating out from near the city centre to the Rhein-Herne Canal on the north-western boundary as far as the banks of the Emscher River. The steel and engineering works, alone, employed in the region of eighty thousand people, and the company's sites covered an area of more than two thousand acres, of which three hundred acres were occupied by factories and workshops. All of that required massive rail and canal access in the form of marshalling yards and its own harbour, and energy from at least four nearby power stations.

Post-raid reconnaissance from this opening salvo of the Ruhr offensive revealed 160 acres of devastation and damage to fifty-three buildings within the Krupp district, and the success of the operation was confirmed by local reports of 3,018 houses destroyed and more than two thousand others seriously damaged. The operation cost the Command an acceptable fourteen aircraft, and it was a most encouraging start to what would become a five-month-long campaign. It would be a further week before round two was mounted, and, in the meantime, Harris turned his attention upon southern Germany, beginning with Nuremberg on the 8th, followed by Munich on the 9th and Stuttgart on the 11th. All were beyond the range of Oboe, which was limited by the curvature of the earth and the height at which Mosquitos could fly, and relied upon the recently introduced H2S ground-mapping radar to provide the necessary accuracy. H2S was carried initially by 35 Squadron Halifaxes and 7 Squadron Stirlings of the Path Finder Force, and consisted of a rotating scanner housed in a cupola aft of the bomb bay, linked to a cathode-ray tube in the navigator's compartment. The navigator's challenging task was to interpret the jumble of images moving across his screen and guide the aircraft to the aiming point, and this would require much practice, particularly with the early version of the system. Despite the inherent difficulty of establishing a position over an urban sprawl like a major city, the first two mentioned operations enjoyed moderate success, while the last produced disappointing results.

Round two of the Ruhr campaign took place on the night of the 12/13th, and was directed once more at Essen, where further extensive damage was inflicted upon Krupp sites, after which, operational activity slackened, and the third Ruhr operation did not take place until the final week of the month, with Duisburg as the target. Oboe equipment failure was responsible for the raid failing to achieve its aims, and Duisburg would continue to lead something of a charmed life for a few weeks more. Two attacks on Berlin closed the month of March, and Essen opened April, but the new month would prove to be one of underachievement as the majority of operations took place beyond Oboe's range.

May would bring a return to winning ways with some spectacular successes, but the month would pass with 619 Squadron still working towards operational status. The third Lancaster was taken on charge on the 2nd, the day on which the first training flight took place in the hands of Sgt Jordan and his crew, but what would be quite a protracted journey to join the war still had six weeks to run. The largest force to be assembled since the three "thousand bomber raids" against Cologne, Essen and Bremen a year earlier, consisting of 596 aircraft, was dispatched to Dortmund at the eastern end of the Ruhr on the night of the 4/5th, and scored a major success by destroying twelve hundred buildings. S/L Scorer was posted in from Fiskerton, home of 49 Squadron, to take command of B Flight on the 6th, and three days later the squadron boasted sufficient numbers of personnel for W/C McGhie to hold a parade, with the purpose of bringing together all officers, men and WAAFs to engender a squadron spirit. All around, the war continued, and those at Woodhall Spa would have been aware of the heavy raids drawing large numbers of Lancasters into the air from other 5 Group stations in southern Lincolnshire, although nearby Coningsby was silent and undergoing a major upgrade with the laying of concrete runways. One of the routes to the northern and central Ruhr and the north-western ports and manufacturing centres like Hamburg, Bremen and Wilhelmshaven, began at the Lincolnshire coast anywhere from Skegness to Mablethorpe, and the drone of aircraft engines would pass within earshot of Woodhall Spa as they headed to their targets, and again some five or six hours later as the survivors came home.

There was a degree of despondency at the slow progress caused by the lack of training aircraft and miserable weather conditions, but the mood lightened somewhat on the 13th when seven brand new Lancaster IIIs arrived to be crawled over immediately by fitters and riggers preparing them for the rigours of life ex-factory. Duisburg had succumbed to a heavy assault on the previous night, and it would be the turn of Bochum that night for one force, while 5 Group attempted unsuccessfully to redress the previous month's failure to destroy the Skoda armaments works at Pilsen in Czechoslovakia. On the night of the 16/17th, 617 Squadron wrote its page in history with its attack on the dams under Operation Chastise, which made front page news, and, no doubt, had the 619 Squadron crews champing at the bit to have a go at Hitler. Further new Lancasters arrived in ones and twos over the ensuing days, and, on the 22nd, W/C McGhie led a formation over Boston for "Wings for Victory Week". On the following night, Dortmund hosted its second heavy raid of the month, this time by a new record non-one thousand force, which, at take-off, had numbered 813 Lancasters, Halifaxes and Stirlings and thirteen Mosquitos. This was a demonstration of the Command's massive expansion since the earlier raid, and, this time, two thousand buildings were reduced to rubble and the Hoesch steelworks was among a number of important war industry casualties. The Ruhr offensive continued at Düsseldorf, Essen again and the Barmen half of the Wuppertal conurbation during the final week of the month. Unimaginable destruction was visited upon the last-mentioned, which left a thousand acres of devastation and reduced to rubble almost four thousand houses and five of the six largest factories, while killing an estimated 3,400 of its inhabitants.

June 1943

By the start of June, 619 Squadron was ready to go to war, as was confirmed by a visit on the 2nd from the Air Officer Commanding 5 Group, AVM Sir Ralph Cochrane, in company with W/C "Darky" Hallows, formerly of 97 Squadron and a veteran of the epic daylight Augsburg raid in April 1942. The squadron was officially welcomed into the group, and would have begun operations immediately, had there not been a general stand-down because of the moon period. 5 Group stations were alerted on most of the first ten days, but no operations actually took place, and this kept the Path Finder and main force crews kicking their heels on the ground and becoming increasingly bored and frustrated. The squadron suffered its first loss on the 9th, when EE113 failed to return from an air-test, and its nine occupants, captained by Sgt Shirley, were presumed lost at sea. Finally, on the 11th, Düsseldorf was briefed out to 783 crews, 326 of them on Lancaster stations, while, for the first time, more than two hundred 4 and 6 Group Halifaxes would operate. 5 Group was responsible for 162 of the Lancasters and 619 Squadron a dozen, which were loaded with a cookie, four 500 pounders and ten SBCs each at Woodhall Spa, while the crews of W/C McGhie, S/Ls Churcher and Scorer, F/Ls Bell, Dampier-Crossley, Harrison and Taylor, P/O Jones, F/Sgt McLeod and Sgts Coomber, Jordan and Metcalfe attended briefing for this momentous occasion of the squadron's operational debut. They took off in two elements, the first between 22.34 and 22.43, and the second between 23.16 and 23.36, but lost the services of F/Sgt McLeod and crew almost immediately to instrument failure. The others had to contend with static and lightning conditions in towering ten-tenths cloud that extended as high as 23,500 feet as they made their way across the North Sea, but this dissipated to leave just small amounts at 2,000, 5,000 and 10,000 feet, dependent upon their time of arrival on final approach to the target. Those in the vanguard of the main force were drawn on by yellow tracking flares from 01.05, and red skymarkers with green stars at 01.16, while those a little further back in the bomber stream were guided on by red and green skymarkers. They carried out time-and-distance runs to the aiming point five minutes away, noting that fires were beginning to build and join together. The Paramatta marking (ground-marking TIs) did not seem to appear until these crews were turning away, but they were clearly visible to those in the rear-guard, who described a sea of flames covering a massive area and columns of smoke rising through 21,000 feet. The 619 Squadron effort was spread throughout the duration of the raid, and the bombing was carried out from 18,000 to 22,000 feet between 01.21 and 02.17. Ten Lancasters returned to Woodhall Spa and their crews passed on their impressions to the Intelligence Section at debriefing, but absent was the crew of F/L Taylor, whose ED978 had been shot down by a night-fighter to crash at Tongeren in Belgium. The pilot managed to retain his freedom, while his crew fell into enemy hands, and, as a previously unknown squadron, some or all of them would have spent time at the Luftwaffe Interrogation Centre at

Oberursel, near Frankfurt. It had been an expensive night for the Command, which had lost thirty-eight aircraft, a figure that equalled the heaviest loss of the Ruhr offensive to date. Post-raid reconnaissance revealed an area of fire across central districts measuring eight by five kilometres, and local reports confirmed 8,882 individual fire incidents. More than seventy war-industry factories suffered a complete or partial loss of production, 140,000 people were bombed out of their homes and 1,292 lost their lives. Had it not been for an errant Oboe marker attracting a proportion of the bombing onto open country some fourteen miles to the north-east, the destruction would have been greater.

Bochum would face its second heavy visitation of the campaign on the 12th, and a force of 503 aircraft was made ready for the purpose. 5 Group contributed 165 Lancasters, of which a dozen were provided by 619 Squadron, and they departed Woodhall Spa between 22.12 and 22.53 with W/C McGhie and both flight commanders leading from the front. Sgt Coomber had reached a position some twenty miles from the Frisian island of Texel when his oxygen supply failed and he became unconscious. He was revived by his crew, but was not in the best condition to continue, and the decision was taken to jettison the bombs and head for home, where a safe landing was carried out at Bardney. The remaining 619 Squadron crews carried on to the target, passing over central Holland and entering Germany to the west of Münster, before turning south for a direct run on Bochum, situated between Essen to the west and Dortmund to the east. It is believed that night-fighters were waiting over Dutch airspace and the frontier region, and a number of bombers fell victim at this stage of the operation. According to the superb book, *The Bomber Command War Diaries*, by Martin Middlebrook and Chris Everitt, Bochum was completely covered by ten-tenths cloud, but, according to many 5 Group crew reports, they encountered three to six-tenths patchy cloud, and many described almost clear skies and good visibility. The 5 Group crews carried out time-and-distance runs from yellow tracking markers, and those from 619 Squadron had green or red TIs in the bombsights as they let their loads go from 20,000 to 25,000 feet between 01.18 and 01.58. Returning crews reported concentrated fires, the glow from which was visible for up to a hundred miles into the return flight. Photo-reconnaissance revealed 130 acres of devastation, and this was backed up by local reports that 449 buildings had been destroyed and more than nine hundred severely damaged. The success had been achieved at a cost to the Command of twenty-four aircraft, at least nine of which had fallen victim to night-fighters. F/L Harrison finished his second tour on this night, while Sgt Baker of F/Sgt McLeod's crew completed his first.

Following a night's rest, the Ruhr offensive continued at Oberhausen, a major centre of oil production situated between Duisburg to the west and Essen to the east. An all-Lancaster heavy force numbering 197 aircraft contained 108 of the type provided by 5 Group, of which six represented 619 Squadron. They departed Woodhall Spa between 22.34 and 23.15 with S/L Churcher the senior pilot on duty, and set course for the Scheldt estuary to bypass Antwerp on their way to the Belgian/German frontier. They reached the target area to find three to ten-tenths cloud with tops in places as high as 18,000 feet and the entire panorama bathed in very bright moonlight. Tracking flares were drifting above the target area, from which the crews would carry out a "time-and-distance" run, and the 619 Squadron crews aimed at reds with green stars and white skymarkers dropped by the six Oboe Mosquitos and the backing-up 8 Group heavy brigade. Their loads of a cookie, four 500 pounders and incendiaries were dropped from between 14,000 and 21,000 feet between 01.15 and 01.26 in the face of intense heavy flak, which continued to chase them out of the target area into the guns of night-fighters, and between them, the defences accounted for seventeen Lancasters, 8.4% of the force. The low bombing height was that of Sgt Jordan and crew, who were running in on the aiming point at 20,000 feet, when they were coned by searchlights, and shed height rapidly to break free before releasing their load. There was one empty dispersal at Woodhall Spa, which should have been occupied by ED980 and had not been heard from since take-off. It had fallen victim to the night-fighter of Hptm Hans-Dieter Frank of I./NJG1 while outbound, and had crashed at 00.56 at Schijndel in southern Holland with fatal consequences for the crew of P/O McCulloch. Local reports confirmed that the Wanganui flares had been right over the city centre, where 267 buildings had been destroyed and 584 seriously damaged.

On the 16th, 1, 5 and 8 Group stations were notified that Cologne was to be the target for that night, for which a force of 202 Lancasters and ten Halifaxes was made ready. They learned at briefings that there would be no Oboe Mosquitos on hand to mark the target, as that role was to be undertaken by the Path Finder Halifax element and six Lancasters employing H2S. 619 Squadron was not invited to contribute to the 5 Group element of eighty Lancasters, which were to carry out a time-and-distance run to the aiming point from tracking flares. The Path Finders were late on target, and problems with some of the H2S sets led to sparse and scattered marking with solid white flares and reds with green stars. A number of crews witnessed a large, orange explosion at 01.08, although, generally, they were unable to assess the outcome. The impression was that a proportion of the bombing had been concentrated where intended, but that some crews had been lured away by dummy markers. Local reports suggesting that only around a hundred aircraft had been involved, tended to support this view. Residential districts bore the brunt of the raid, and 401 houses were destroyed, with 13,000 others sustaining damage to some extent, mostly lightly, while sixteen industrial premises and nine railway stations were hit, along with public and utility buildings.

The recent successes in the Ruhr had been aided by the sheer size of the urban areas below, which all but guaranteed that the bombs would hit something useful, even after smoke had obscured the aiming point TIs. It was a different matter at a small or precision target, however, which would rapidly be enveloped in smoke from the first bombs before the rest of the attacking force had a chance to draw a bead on the aiming point. When, on the 20th, therefore, an attack was prepared under the codename Operation Bellicose against the production site of the Würzburg radar sets, which the enemy was employing very successfully to warn of and intercept Bomber Command raids, a plan was already in place to combat the problem by adopting the oft-used and still-under-development 5 Group "time-and-distance" method. Briefings actually took place on the day before, when crews learned that the factory was housed in the old Zeppelin sheds at Friedrichshafen, situated on the shore of Lake Constance (Bodensee) on the frontier with Switzerland, and represented a very small target. The plan was to use a designated "Master of Ceremonies" to direct the bombing, much in the manner of Gibson at the Dams, and the officer chosen was the highly experienced G/C Len Slee, the former 49 Squadron commanding officer, with the popular W/C Cosme Gomm, commanding officer of 467 Squadron RAAF, as his deputy. 5 Group was to provide the main force element of fifty-six Lancasters, five of them from 619 Squadron, with four others from 8 Group's 97 Squadron to provide the marking for the selected crews at the head of the stream. The plan called for the Channel to be crossed at a standard altitude, before descending gradually to 10,000 feet by the time that Orleans was reached, and, thereafter, to fly at between 2,500 and 3,000 feet all the way to a point on the Rhine. After crossing the Rhine, they were to climb to their briefed bombing height of between 5,000 and 10,000 feet for the rendezvous over the north-western shore of Lake Constance, and then circle until receiving the start signal.

The Woodhall Spa quintet took off between 21.44 and 21.52 with S/L Scorer the senior pilot on duty, and all would make it to the target on a rare night when not a single aircraft from the entire force turned back, despite encountering electrical storms in the Orleans region and having to adjust the briefed course. That said, G/C Slee lost an engine over France, and was forced to drop back into the formation and hand over the lead to W/C Gomm, who, on arrival at the target under clear skies and in bright moonlight, became concerned about the hostility of the searchlight and light flak defences. In order to reduce the very real risk of heavy casualties, he decided to add five thousand feet to the bombing height, where, unknown to him, the wind was stronger and would push the bombing towards the north-east. The Path Finder element also had little time to climb to the new height, and this caused a slight delay in the opening of the attack. The first TI fell wide of the aiming point, but the second one was assessed by W/C Gomm to be accurate, upon which he called in the first crews, whose high explosives and incendiaries created the expected smoke and obscured the target. He decided that another TI on the aiming point might still provide a reference for some crews, but the Path Finders were driven off by the searchlights and light flak and abandoned the attempt. They were then ordered to drop flares along the shore of Lake Constance, to enable the remaining crews to begin their runs from a pre-determined landmark, fly across the lake to the opposite shore, pick up another landmark 2,000 yards from the target, and continue at a constant speed for the requisite number of seconds to cover the distance to bomb release. The 619 Squadron crews carried out their attacks on cascading green TIs from 9,000 to 13,500 feet between 02.45 and 02.58, and observed explosions and fires, some of which remained visible for eighty miles into the onward flight to landing grounds in North Africa, in what was the first official shuttle operation of the war. Post-raid reconnaissance revealed that a proportion of the bombs had hit the target, causing extensive damage, and there had been no losses among the attacking force. Sadly, F/Sgt McLeod's bomb-aimer, Sgt May, was killed by shrapnel from flak, which caused damage to a bomb door and electrical feeds to the front and rear turrets, but it is not clear if this occurred over the target.

While the above crews were absent from England, a hectic round of four major operations to the Ruhr in the space of five nights began at Krefeld on the 21st, for which a force of 705 aircraft was assembled. 5 Group contributed ninety-two Lancasters, of which seven represented 619 Squadron, and they departed Woodhall Spa between 23.10 and 00.04 with S/L Churcher the senior pilot on duty. From this point on it would be standard practice to carry propaganda leaflets (nickels) in addition to bomb loads, and dispense them over Germany at some time during the operation. Sgt Hughes and crew turned back early on when the pilot's compass revealed itself to be unreliable and the rear gunner's electrically heated suit failed. The others reached the target, situated a short distance to the south-west of Duisburg, and on the opposite side of the Rhine, where conditions were found to be ideal with small amounts of thin cloud between 6,000 and 10,000 feet and bright moonlight. The Path Finders delivered a near-perfect marking performance, their red TIs falling in concentrated fashion to clearly identify the city centre aiming point for the main force crews. Those from 619 Squadron carried out their attacks from 20,000 to 22,000 feet between 01.36 and 02.15, and described a sea of red fire giving off masses of smoke, with one particular jet-black column rising through 18,000 feet as they turned away. All were convinced of the success of the operation, and one crew likened it to the Wuppertal-Barmen raid. There was no hint of troublesome flak or night-fighters, and yet, forty-four aircraft failed to return, the heaviest casualties of the campaign to date, and many of these were lost to the Nachtjagd. Remarkably, only three 5 Group Lancasters were among the missing, but one of these was 619 Squadron's EE198, which crashed six miles south-south-east of Helmond in southern Holland, killing Sgt Jordan and his crew. 35 (Madras Presidency) Squadron of the Path Finders lost six of its nineteen Halifaxes. Three-quarters of the bombing photos were plotted within three miles of the aiming point, and the 2,306 tons of bombs wiped out by fire an estimated 47% of the built-up area. 5,517 houses were destroyed, the largest number to date at a single target, and more than a thousand people lost their lives.

The medium-sized town of Mülheim-an-der-Ruhr, a close neighbour of Duisburg, Oberhausen and Essen, lies around a dozen miles to the north-east of Krefeld, and it was here that the red ribbon terminated on the target wall maps at briefings across the Command on the 22nd. A force of 557 aircraft was prepared, of which ninety of the Lancasters were provided by 5 Group, five of them representing 619 Squadron. They departed Woodhall Spa between 22.39 and 22.45 with P/O Jones the only commissioned pilot, and made their way via the Scheldt through the Cologne corridor to arrive at the target over small amounts of cumulostratus cloud at between 5,000 and 10,000 feet. Red and green TIs were clearly visible and defining the aiming point as the 619 Squadron crews bombed from 19,000 to 21,300 feet between 01.20 and 01.25, and they witnessed the development of a concentrated area of fire, which was visible from the Dutch coast homebound. Returning crews commented on the intense searchlight and flak response, and the number of night-fighters, and reported that Krefeld was still burning from the night before. Local reports confirmed that the town had suffered severe damage, particularly in the northern districts, where 1,135 houses had been destroyed and more than 12,000 others damaged to some extent. The road and telephone communications to Oberhausen had been cut, preventing any passage out of the town other than on foot, and, in fact, some of the bombing had spilled into the eastern districts of Oberhausen, which was linked to Mülheim for air-raid purposes. It was another expensive night for the Command, however, which registered the loss of thirty-five aircraft, with the Halifaxes and Stirlings representing two-thirds of them, and suffering a respective loss rate of 7.7% and 11.8%.

While the Path Finder and main force units were enjoying a night off on the 23rd and girding their loins for the next round of the Ruhr offensive, fifty of the 5 Group Lancasters that had landed in North Africa following the Friedrichshafen raid took off with two 97 Squadron Path Finder aircraft to bomb the docks at La Spezia on the way home to England. The 619 Squadron crews of S/L Scorer, F/Ls Bell and Dampier-Crossley, F/O Jones and F/Sgt McLeod took off from Blida in Algeria between 19.23 and 20.00, and arrived in the target area to find clear skies but hazy conditions made worse by a smoke-screen. There appeared to be a degree of confusion in getting the raid started, but a lucky hit on an oil storage facility resulted in a large explosion at 23.41 just as the main force was running-in, and most crews were able to identify the target visually, thereafter, and by red, green and white Path Finder flares. Bombing was carried out by the 619 Squadron quintet on instructions from a Master Bomber from 8,000 to 14,500 feet between 23.45 and 00.09, and all returned safely home to moan about the length of time it had taken for the raid to develop, and the poor communications with the raid controller. The authorities seemed happy to claim the destruction of the oil depot and an armaments store, and declared the operation to be a success.

Having destroyed the Barmen half of Wuppertal at the end of May in one of the most devastating attacks to date, it was time to visit the same catastrophe upon the western half, Elberfeld, for which a force of 630 aircraft was made ready on the 24th. 5 Group supported the operation with 103 Lancasters, nine of which were provided by 619 Squadron, and they departed Woodhall Spa between 22.25 and 23.01 with F/O Bell (not to be confused with F/L Bell) the senior pilot on duty. He and his crew were soon contending with a series of issues, including an overheating starboard-outer engine and an unserviceable rear turret and intercom system, which persuaded them to turn back. The others ran the usual gauntlet of searchlights and flak from the Cologne and Düsseldorf defence zones, the crews of which were aided by the formation of condensation trails at between 18,000 and 21,000 feet to advertise the presence of the bomber stream. There seemed to be fewer guns firing at them over the target, where small amounts of cloud with tops at 17,000 feet were insufficient to obscure the ground. The 5 Group crews carried out time-and-distant runs from yellow tracking flares until observing cascading red and green TIs, the 619 Squadron element bombing from 19,000 to 23,000 feet between 01.06 and 01.40. Those arriving at the tail end of the attack, when the built-up area was well-alight, described thick columns of smoke already passing through 19,000 feet and the glow of fires visible from the Dutch coast. Post-raid reconnaissance revealed another massively concentrated and accurate attack, which had reduced to rubble an estimated 90% of Elberfeld's built-up area, including three thousand houses and 171 industrial premises. It had also severely damaged 2,500 houses and dozens of important factory buildings, and the fact that more buildings had been destroyed than damaged, provided a telling commentary on the conditions on the ground. The number of fatalities stood at around eighteen hundred, and some of the survivors might have been cheered to know that thirty-four bombers, containing 240 of their tormentors, would not be returning to England that night. Remarkably, only two of these belonged to 5 Group.

114 Lancasters were made ready on 5 Group stations on the 25th as part of an overall force of 473 aircraft, which were to attack the Ruhr city of Gelsenkirchen, where a number of synthetic oil refineries, including the Gelsenkirchener Bergwerke A.G plant, otherwise known as Nordstern or Gelsenberg, and the Hydrierwerke-Scholven plant, were supporting the German war effort. At Woodhall Spa, seven Lancasters were loaded with a cookie, four 500 pounders and thirteen SBCs of incendiaries each, and were dispatched between 22.45 and 23.39 with F/L Dampier-Crossley the senior pilot on duty. F/O Jones and crew got away very late, and then experienced an oxygen supply problem, which prevented them from climbing to operational height and forced them to abandon their sortie. When they landed, they found Sgt Pearce and crew already on the ground having lost the use of their port-outer engine. The others reached the target area to find ten-tenths stratus lying over the region with tops at 10,000 to 15,000 feet, which would not have been a problem for Oboe, had five of the twelve participating Mosquitos not suffered equipment failures. This caused tracking flares to be late and to drop in the wrong order in a somewhat scattered manner, at a time when the crews were contending with an intense flak barrage. Searchlights illuminated the cloud as those from 619 Squadron bombed on red flares with green stars from 18,500 to 21,000 feet between 01.25 and 01.34. A large explosion was witnessed at 01.43, and the glow from the target was visible from the Dutch coast, to which the returning bombers were chased by a large deployment of enemy night-fighters. Post-raid reconnaissance and local reports confirmed that the operation had failed to achieve accuracy and concentration, and, in an echo of the past, bombs had been sprayed all over the Ruhr, leaving Gelsenkirchen largely untouched.

Thirty aircraft were missing, and, this time, eight of them were from 5 Group, four alone from 106 Squadron.

A series of three operations against Cologne would span the turn of the month, and began on the night of the 28/29th, when 608 aircraft took off in the late evening to deliver what would be the Rhineland capital's greatest ordeal of the war to date. 5 Group contributed 131 Lancasters, the 619 Squadron element of twelve departing Woodhall Spa between 22.39 and 23.58 with S/Ls Churcher and Scorer the senior pilots on duty. There were no early returns to deplete the squadron's impact, and they reached the target area to encounter ten-tenths cloud below them at 8,000 to 10,000 feet, with good visibility above. The main force crews were unaware that five of the Oboe Mosquitos had turned back and a sixth was unable to drop its skymarkers, leaving just six to do so, and these were behind schedule by seven minutes and could manage only intermittent flares. The omens for a successful attack were not good, particularly as skymarking was the least reliable method because of drift, but the Path Finder heavy element had released green tracking flares to aid a time-and-distance run, and the Woodhall Spa crews delivered their attacks on red and white flares and red TIs from 18,000 to 21,000 feet between 01.45 and 02.04. They deduced from the glow beneath the clouds and the presence of smoke rising through them that they had contributed to a successful operation, and this was confirmed by post-raid reconnaissance and local reports, which provided details of forty-three industrial buildings and 6,374 others completely destroyed, and a further fifteen thousand sustaining damage to some extent. The death toll was put at 4,377, the greatest by far from a Bomber Command attack, and 230,000 others had lost their homes for varying periods. By recent standards, the figure of twenty-five missing aircraft could be considered moderate, but that was no consolation to the individual stations with an empty dispersal. F/Sgt Murphy and crew failed to return to Woodhall Spa in ED979, having been shot down homebound by Major Günter Radusch of 1./NJG1, and crashing at 02.14 without survivors three miles south of Eindhoven in southern Holland. This was one of four bombers, two Lancasters and two Halifaxes, claimed by Radusch on this night.

One of the new crews to join the squadron during the month was that of Sgt Hubert "Nick" Knilans, an American from Delavan, Wisconsin, who had been conscripted into the United States Army in April 1941, but wanted to fly and absconded across the border to Canada, where he joined the RCAF. He sailed to England on board Queen Elizabeth, and joined 619 Squadron to begin an illustrious career in Bomber Command. At around the same time, F/Sgt "Bob" Knights and crew arrived to begin their operational careers, and among them was bomb-aimer, Sgt John Bell, which meant that there would be three Bells in the Squadron. The Knilans and Knights crews would carry out their first sorties on the same night and eventually find their way to 617 Squadron, the Knilans gang more by default than planning. During the course of the month the squadron participated in ten operations and dispatched eighty sorties for the loss of five Lancasters and their crews.

July 1943

One of the Command's most effective campaigns, referred to as "gardening", involved the mining of the sea lanes used by the enemy. The first "planting" of parachute mines had been carried out by 5 Group Hampdens in mid-April 1940 during the ill-fated Norwegian campaign, and it had been expanded massively since with all heavy groups becoming involved. The entire network of enemy shipping lanes from the Pyrenees in the south-west to what is now the Baltic port of Kaliningrad in the north-east, the whole of the western Baltic between Denmark, Germany and Sweden, western and southern Norway and even the northern coast of Italy, was divided into regions known as gardens, each with a horticultural or marine biological codename, and systematically and regularly topped up with mostly 1,500lb mines, referred to as vegetables. By war's end, this monumental effort by Bomber Command would have destroyed and damaged more enemy ships than the Royal Navy, and, although often a dangerous undertaking, it would be employed as a gentle way to introduce new crews to operations. Initially, mines had been dropped from very low level, typically from between 400 and 800 feet after carrying out a time-and-distance run from a selected pinpoint, but high-level gardening operations would become standard during 1943. The delivery of each mine was planned meticulously to create a lethal net in which to ensnare enemy vessels.

5 Group began the new month by sending a dozen Lancasters to mine the waters around the Frisians on the 1st. The Frisian islands form a chain from Texel, situated off the Den Helder peninsula in the south-west to Wangerooge at the mouth of Jade Bay off Germany's north-western coast, and they were sectioned into three gardens, Nectarine I from Texel to Ameland, Nectarine II from Schiermonnikoog to Juist and Nectarine III from Norderney to Wangerooge. 619 Squadron made ready six Lancasters to send to Nectarine I on the 1st, and launched them from Woodhall Spa with freshman crews on board between 22.27 and 22.39. Among them was the crew of P/O O'Shaughnessy, who were embarking on an operational career that would take them later in the year to 617 Squadron and for some members, an untimely end. They arrived in the target area to encounter ten-tenths low cloud with tops at 1,500 to 2,000 feet, and established their positions by Gee-fix (also known as TR). The vegetables were delivered into the briefed locations from 4,000 to 6,000 feet between 00.01 and 00.12, and all returned safely from uneventful sorties.

The second operation of the series against Cologne was posted on the 3rd, and a force of 653 aircraft assembled, of which 141 Lancasters were provided by 5 Group. At Woodhall Spa, 619 Squadron's armourers winched the standard city busting load of a 4,000lb cookie and SBCs (small bomb cases, containers or canisters) of incendiaries into eleven of their Lancasters, and they took off between 22.27 and 23.07 with W/C McGhie the senior pilot on duty. Sgt Firth and crew were outbound at 20,000 feet, when the navigator became ill, almost certainly as a result of oxygen starvation, and it was discovered that they were heading across the North Sea towards the Frisians rather than on the southerly route via the Scheldt estuary. The navigator recovered, but they were too far behind schedule to catch up and abandoned their sortie. The others pressed on in favourable conditions to reach the target, which they found clearly visible under two to three-tenths cloud at 8,000 feet, and protected by many searchlight cones and a moderate flak defence. Green tracking flares guided the first wave crews to the aiming point, which the Path Finders marked with red skymarkers with green stars and red and green ground markers (TIs), achieving great accuracy and concentration, while later crews were drawn on for the final one hundred miles by the sight of the city already burning fiercely. The 619 Squadron crews bombed on red TIs from 18,000 to 22,000 feet between 01.15 and 01.58, and reported the city to be a mass of flames, the glow from which remained visible for 170 miles into the return journey.

Some crews commented on the presence of day fighters over the target, and this was clear evidence of a new tactic being employed by the Luftwaffe. The newly formed JG300 was operating for the first time, employing the Wilde Sau (Wild Boar) tactics, which was the brainchild of former bomber pilot, Major Hans-Joachim (Hajo) Herrmann. The unit had been formed in June with borrowed standard BF109 and FW190 single-engine day fighters to operate directly over a target, seeking out bombers silhouetted against the fires and TIs. On this night, the unit would claim twelve victories, but would have to share them with the flak batteries, which claimed them also. Unaccustomed to being pursued by fighters over a target, it would take time for the bomber crews to work out what was happening, and, until they did, friendly fire would often be blamed for damage incurred by unseen causes. Post-raid reconnaissance and local reports confirmed another stunningly accurate and concentrated attack, in which twenty industrial premises and 2,200 houses had been destroyed, and 72,000 people bombed out of their homes at a cost to the Command of thirty aircraft.

The series against Cologne would be completed on the 8th by an all-Lancaster heavy force of 282 aircraft drawn from 1, 5 and 8 Groups, with six Oboe Mosquitos to carry out the initial marking. 5 Group provided 151 Lancasters, of which thirteen were made ready at Woodhall Spa, and they took off between 22.16 and 22.40 with W/C McGhie the senior pilot on duty and first away. They flew through the top of a towering bank of cumulonimbus cloud as they made their way across the North Sea, and F/O Bell and crew had reached the mid-point when frozen instruments forced them to turn back. They were greeted at the target by ten-tenths cloud at around 10,000 feet, which concealed the ground from view, and the main force crews had to rely on tracking flares to guide them to the aiming point. The release-point flares were late in going down, and some crews bombed on e.t.a before they were deployed. The 619 Squadron crews carried out their attacks from 18,000 to 21,500 feet between 01.16 and 01.30 in the face of an intense flak barrage, and a very large orange explosion was witnessed at 01.23. Post-raid reconnaissance and local reports revealed another highly successful operation, which had caused extensive damage in north-western and south-western districts, where nineteen industrial premises and 2,381 houses had been destroyed. The success cost a modest seven Lancasters, five of them from 5 Group. When the dust had settled over Cologne, the local authorities catalogued the destruction over the three raids of more than eleven thousand buildings, and a death toll of almost 5,500 people, with a further 350,000 rendered homeless.

The Ruhr campaign was winding down by the time that Gelsenkirchen was posted across Lancaster and Halifax stations as the target on the 9th, for which a heavy force of 408 aircraft was made ready supported by ten Oboe Mosquitos. Eight 619 Squadron Lancasters were among the 112 representing 5 Group, and they departed Woodhall Spa between 22.24 and 22.36 with the newly promoted F/L Jones the senior pilot on duty. F/Sgt Taylor and crew turned back early because of generator issues, leaving the remainder to make their way to the target above ten-tenths cloud, which stretched over the Ruhr at around 16,000 feet and topped out in places at 20,000 feet. The Path Finder skymarkers were several minutes late, partly as a result of a 50% failure rate of the Oboe equipment, while a sixth Mosquito dropped its markers ten miles to the north. The Woodhall Spa crews timed their runs from red and green tracking flares, and were over the aiming point between 01.10 and 01.16 to deliver their bombs from 18,000 to 21,300 feet onto the Wanganui markers as they drifted into the cloud. Some explosions were reflected in the cloud, one particularly large one at 01.40 lighting up the area like day, long after the 619 Squadron participants had turned for home. However, the general impression offered at debriefings was that the raid had fallen short of the recent outstanding successes, and this was confirmed by local reports. To those on the ground, it appeared that the attack had been meant for Bochum and Wattenscheid, which received more bombs than Gelsenkirchen, where limited damage occurred in southern districts.

Although two more operations to the region would be launched late in the month, Harris was already planning his next attempt to shorten the war by bombing, and was buoyed by the success of the spring offensive. He could look back on the past four and a half months with genuine satisfaction at the performance of his squadrons, and, as a champion of technological innovation, take particular pride in the performance of Oboe, which had been the decisive factor. Although losses had been grievously high, and the Ruhr's reputation as "Happy Valley" well earned, its most important towns and cities had suffered catastrophic destruction. In Britain, the aircraft factories had more than kept pace with the rate of attrition, while the training units both at home and overseas continued to pour eager new crews into the fray to fill the gaps. Among new crews arriving at 619 Squadron during the month were those of F/L Pullen from 1661 Conversion Unit on the 7th, F/O Morrison and P/O Rayment from 1660 Conversion Unit on the 9th, and the experienced F/L Aytoun, formerly of 106 Squadron, for whom a headless crew was posted in from 207 Squadron on the 14th. With confidence high in the ability of his Command to destroy almost any target at will, Harris prepared for his next major campaign, the erasure from the map of a prominent German city in a short, sharp series of maximum effort raids to be launched during the final week of the month.

In the meantime, 1, 5 and 8 Groups were alerted to prepare for a trip to Italy to attack the city of Turin, home to Fiat's Lingotto and Mirafiori car plants, the Lancia motor works, the Arsenale army munitions factory, the Nebioli foundry and plants belonging to the Westinghouse company, for which 295 Lancasters were made ready on the 12th. 5 Group put up 130 aircraft, eleven of them representing 619 Squadron, and they departed Woodhall Spa between 22.27 and 22.37 with W/C McGhie and S/L Scorer the senior pilots on duty. There were no early returns to diminish the squadron's presence, despite having to negotiate poor weather conditions over France, including icing, and they were greeted at the target by clear skies and good visibility, and defences up to their usual poor standard, characterised by ineffective searchlights and inaccurate light flak rising to 15,000 feet. The marking was punctual, accurate and concentrated, inviting the bombing by the 619 Squadron crews to be carried out from 14,500 to 19,000 feet between 01.56 and 02.12, and a column of black smoke was observed rising through 12,000 feet as they withdrew. The return route involved a low-level circumnavigation of the Brest peninsula, and many of the thirteen missing Lancasters disappeared without trace into the sea after running into enemy night-fighters in this area. At debriefing, F/L Jones and crew claimed a Ju88, credited to the skill of Sgt Cook in the mid-upper turret and P/O Cartwright DFM in the rear, and it was a small consolation for the losses. 44 (Rhodesia) Squadron's celebrated commanding officer, W/C Nettleton VC, disappeared without trace with his crew, and it was always a sobering moment when someone of his stature was lost. If it could happen to him, then what chance did everyone else have? Little information came out of Turin, other than a death toll of almost eight hundred people, which was the highest from the ten major attacks on the city.

Hamburg, had been a regular target for the Command throughout the war to date, and had been attacked, amongst other occasions, during the final week of July in 1940, 1941 and 1942. It had been spared by the weather from hosting the first "One Thousand" bomber raid at the end of May 1942, but Harris now identified it as the ideal candidate for destruction under Operation Gomorrah, the intention of which was to cause the maximum impact to the enemy's morale in a short, sharp campaign, employing ten thousand tons of bombs. Hamburg's political status was second only to that of Berlin, and its value to the war effort in terms of ship and U-Boot construction and other war production was undeniable, but, it suited Harris's criteria also in other respects. Its location close to a coastline aided navigation and made it accessible from the North Sea without the need to spend time over hostile territory, and its relatively short distance from the bomber stations enabled a force to approach and retreat during the few hours of darkness afforded by mid-summer. Finally, lying beyond the range of Oboe, which had proved so decisive at the Ruhr, Hamburg boasted the wide River Elbe and the Binnen and Aussen-Alster Lakes to provide a solid H2S signature for the navigators high above.

The campaign would begin on the night of the 24/25th, for which a force of 791 aircraft was assembled, 143 of the Lancasters provided by 5 Group, and sixteen of these by 619 Squadron. The crews would be aided by the first operational use of "Window", tinfoil-backed strips of paper of precise length, which, when released in bundles into the airstream at a predetermined point, would drift down slowly in vast clouds to swamp the enemy night-fighter, searchlight and gun-laying radar with false returns and render it blind. The device had actually been available for a year, but its use had been vetoed in case the enemy copied it for use against Britain. It was not realised that Germany had, in fact, already developed its own version called Düppel, which it had withheld for the same reason. The Woodhall Spa crews took off between 22.20 and 22.58 with W/C McGhie the senior pilot on duty and F/L Pullen flying as his second pilot, and there were operational debuts for the crews of Sgt Knilans and F/Sgt Knights. The Lancaster squadrons had not operated since Turin, leaving the crews well-rested and the aircraft on top-line, and this was reflected by the absence of early returns among the 619 Squadron element. After climbing out, they headed for the North Sea to rendezvous with the rest of the force and form into an elongated bomber stream that would take the better part of an hour to pass over the target city. Having reached a predetermined point, the designated crew member, generally, the wireless operator, began to dispense Window, beginning shortly after 00.30, and the effects appeared to be immediate as few fighters rose to meet the approaching bombers. A number of aircraft were shot down over the sea during the outward flight, two of them 103 Squadron Lancasters, but these were off course and outside of the protection of the bomber stream, and may well have been returning early with technical difficulties.

The efficacy of Window was made more apparent in the target area, where the crews noticed an absence of the usually efficient co-ordination between the searchlights and flak batteries, and defence appeared random and sporadic. This offered the Path Finders the opportunity to mark the target by visual reference and H2S virtually unmolested, and, although the red and green TIs were a little misplaced and scattered, they landed in sufficient numbers close to the city centre to provide the main force crews with ample opportunity to deliver a massive blow. The 619 Squadron crews were guided in by yellow tracking flares and red and green skymarkers, and delivered their loads of a cookie, four 500 pounders and thirteen SBCs of incendiaries each from 18,000 to 21,300 feet onto red TIs between 01.05 and 01.44, before returning home to report a successful operation that had left part of the city ablaze with a column of smoke rising through 20,000 feet. Post-raid reconnaissance revealed that a six-mile-long creep-back had developed, which cut a swathe of destruction from the city centre along the line of approach, out across the north-western districts, and into open country, where a proportion of the bombing had been wasted. In fact, less than half of the force had bombed within three miles of the city centre during the fifty-minute-long raid, in which 2,284 tons of bombs had been delivered, but, despite that, the city had suffered a telling blow, and fifteen hundred of its inhabitants lay dead. For the Command it was an encouraging start to the campaign, particularly in the light of just twelve missing aircraft, for which Window was largely responsible.

On the following night, and in the expectation that Hamburg would be covered by smoke, Harris switched his force to Essen, where he could take advantage of the body blow dealt to the enemy defensive system by Window. A force of 705 aircraft included 136 Lancasters of 5 Group, the fifteen at Woodhall Spa taking off between 22.05 and 22.35 with F/Ls Jones and Pullen the senior pilots on duty. *(The ORB entries are heavily corrupted and difficult to read)*. There were seventeen early returns from the 5 Group, but none among the 619 Squadron contingent, which arrived in the target area to find clear skies with just the usual ground haze to spoil the vertical visibility. Yellow tracking flares guided them to the aiming point, which was marked by red and green TIs, and they bombed from 18,000 to 21,000 feet between 00.35 and 01.12, before returning to report concentrated fires around the aiming point in a one-and-a-half-square-mile area of the city. Two large, red explosions were witnessed at 00.36 and 00.39, and a column of smoke was rising through 20,000 feet as they withdrew to the west. Post-raid reconnaissance confirmed the raid to be another outstanding success against this important war materials producing city, with more than 2,800 houses destroyed, while the complex of Krupp manufacturing sites suffered its heaviest damage of the war to date. Twenty-six aircraft failed to return, just two of them from 5 Group, and 619 Squadron came through unscathed.

After a night's rest, a force of 787 aircraft was made ready for round two of Operation Gomorrah, for which 619 Squadron bombed-up and fuelled fourteen Lancasters as part of 5 Group's contribution of 155. They departed Woodhall Spa between 22.11 and 22.53 with W/C McGhie the senior pilot on duty and the station commander, G/C "Sam" Patch, flying as second pilot with S/L Scorer. There were no early returns among the Woodhall Spa element, which pushed on towards Hansastadt (Ancient Free Trade City) Hamburg, crossing the coast over the Schleswig-Holstein peninsula to the north, not one of them with any concept of the events that were to follow their arrival. A previously unknown and terrible phenomenon was about to present itself to the world and introduce a new word "firestorm" into the English language. A number of factors would conspire on this night to seal the fate of this great city and its hapless inhabitants in an orgy of destruction quite unprecedented in air warfare. An uncharacteristically hot and dry spell of weather had left the city a tinderbox, and the spark to ignite it came with the Path Finders' H2S-laid red and green TIs, which fell with almost total concentration some two miles to the east of the intended city-centre aiming point, and into the densely populated working-class residential districts of Hamm, Hammerbrook and Borgfeld. To compound this, the main force, which had been drawn on to the target by yellow release-point flares, bombed with rare precision and almost no creep-back, and deposited much of its 2,300 tons of bombs into this relatively compact area. The 619 Squadron crews carried out their attacks from 18,000 to 21,000 feet between 01.01 and 01.40, and observed many explosions and a sea of flames developing below. Those bombing towards the later stages of the raid observed a pall of smoke rising through 20,000 feet, and the glow of fires was reported to remain visible for up to two hundred miles into the return journey.

On the ground, individual fires began to join together to form one giant conflagration, a meteorological phenomenon, which sucked in oxygen from surrounding areas at hurricane speeds to feed its voracious appetite. Trees were uprooted and flung bodily into the inferno, along with debris and people, and temperatures at the seat of the flames exceeded one thousand degrees Celcius. The defences were overwhelmed, and the fire service unable to pass through the rubble-strewn streets to gain access to the worst-affected areas. Even had they done so, they could not have entered the firestorm area, and, only after all of the combustible material had been consumed, did the flames subside. By this time, there was no-one alive to rescue, and an estimated forty thousand people died on this one night alone. A mass exodus from the city, which would ultimately exceed one million people, began on the following morning, and this undoubtedly saved many from the ravages of the next raid, which would come two nights later. Seventeen aircraft failed to return, reflecting the enemy's developing response to the advantage gained by the Command through Window. No gain was ever permanent, and the balance of power would continue to shift from one side to the other for the next year. For a change, it was the Lancaster brigade that sustained the highest numerical casualties on this night of eleven, six of them belonging to 5 Group.

Bomber Command's heavy brigade stayed at home on the following night, while four Mosquitos carried out a nuisance raid on Hamburg, to ensure that the residents' sleep was disturbed. A force of 777 aircraft was put together to continue Hamburg's torment on the 29th, and, this time, 5 Group contributed 148 Lancasters, of which a dozen would represent 619 Squadron. They departed Woodhall Spa between 22.11 and 22.54 with S/L Churcher the senior pilot on duty, and all reached the target, which they found under clear skies and protected only by slight ground haze. The plan was to approach from due north to hit the northern and north-eastern districts, which had, thus far, escaped serious damage, but the Path Finders strayed two miles to the east of the intended track, and dropped their markers just to the south of the already devastated firestorm area. A four-mile creep-back rescued the situation for the Command, by spreading along the line of approach into the residential districts of Wandsbek and Barmbek, and parts of Uhlenhorst and Winterhude. The 619 Squadron crews bombed on yellow, red and green TIs from 18,000 to 22,000 feet between 00.45 and 01.32, and reported smoke rising through 17,000 feet and fires visible for two hundred miles into the return journey. It was another massive blow against this proud city, but, as the defenders began to recover from the effects of Window, so the bomber losses began to creep up, and twenty-eight aircraft failed to return home on this night, five of them from 5 Group.

Before the final round of Operation Gomorrah took place, the curtain on the Ruhr offensive was brought down with a raid on the town of Remscheid, situated on the southern edge of the region, about six miles south of Wuppertal, where the main industries were mechanical engineering and tool-making. Up until this point, only twenty-six people had lost their lives in this town as a result of stray bombs, but it was now to face a modest force of 273 aircraft consisting of roughly equal numbers of Lancasters, Halifaxes and Stirlings with nine Oboe Mosquitos to mark out the aiming point. 5 Group put up thirty-nine Lancasters, four of which were loaded with a cookie and seventeen SBCs of various incendiaries at Woodhall Spa, and sent on their way between 21.58 and 22.03 bearing aloft the crews of W/C McGhie, F/Os O'Shaughnessy and Sandison and P/O O'Leary. They all reached the target area to find clear skies and good visibility, and bombed on red TIs from 10,000 to 19,800 feet between 01.02 and 01.10, observing the burst of many cookies and a pall of smoke rising through 5,000 feet. They returned home with a red glow in the sky behind them, that remained visible as they crossed the enemy coast homebound and gave promise of another Ruhr town left devastated. It would be left to a post-war bombing survey to establish that a mere 871 tons of bombs had laid waste to around 83% of Remscheid's built-up area, destroying 107 industrial buildings and 3,117 houses. Three months war production was lost, and the town's industry never recovered fully. Fifteen aircraft failed to return, and the Stirling brigade suffered 10% casualties.

During the course of the month the squadron participated in ten operations and dispatched 110 sorties without loss.

August 1943

Briefings for the final act of Operation Gomorrah took place on the 2nd, and a force of 740 aircraft was made ready, 128 of the Lancasters provided by 5 Group. 619 Squadron detailed fourteen Lancasters, which departed Woodhall Spa between 23.15 and 00.05 with S/Ls Churcher and Scorer the senior pilots on duty. Sgt Goddard and crew were a hundred miles out from the Lincolnshire coast when the rear turret became unserviceable and ended their interest in proceedings, leaving the others to press on in initially good weather conditions until they reached 7 degrees East, where a towering bank of ice-bearing cumulonimbus cloud was encountered, which could not be circumnavigated, and stretched upwards to 20,000 feet and beyond. Upon entering it, aircraft were thrown around by violent electrical storms, and it was a hugely terrifying experience beyond anything that most crews had ever experienced, with enormous flashes of lightning, thunder, electrical discharges and instruments going haywire. F/Sgt Mason and crew were unable to maintain height because of icing, and had reached a position some fifteen miles north-east of Bremen when they jettisoned their bombs "live" from 17,000 feet at 02.15. Many other crews simply abandoned their sorties and also jettisoned their bombs live over Germany or safe into the sea, and among them were the 619 Squadron crews of S/L Churcher and F/O Joss, the former jettisoning from 15,500 feet at 02.00 after being unable to establish a position, and the latter taking similar action from 19,000 feet at 02.18, which happened to be their e.t.a., after being hit by flak. The remainder battled through the conditions to reach the target area, which was concealed beneath seven to ten-tenths cloud. While some crews caught a glimpse of the Elbe and isolated yellow and green Path Finder flares, the majority bombed on e.t.a., and on the glow of fires beneath the cloud and the smoke rising through it. Those from Woodhall Spa bombed what they believed to be Hamburg from 15,000 to 19,000 feet between 01.50 and 02.49, before returning to unanimously report an unsuccessful operation, described by some from other units as "pure hell". Little fresh damage occurred in Hamburg as bombs were sprayed over an area of a hundred miles, but that was of little consequence in view of what had gone before. The Command suffered the relatively heavy loss of thirty aircraft, and some of these had fallen victim to the weather conditions. During the course of the four raids of Operation Gomorrah, the squadron despatched fifty-six sorties, of which fifty-four claimed to have bombed in the target area and there had been no losses. (*The Battle of Hamburg*. Martin Middlebrook).

Italy was now teetering on the brink of capitulation, and Bomber Command was invited to help nudge it over the edge with a short offensive against its major cities. It began with elements of 1, 5 and 8 Groups making ready to attack Genoa, Milan and Turin on the 7th, and, with preparations already in hand for, perhaps, the most important operation of the war to date to be launched in ten days' time, the Turin raid was to be used to test the merits of employing a controller, or Master of Ceremonies, in the manner of W/C Gibson during Operation Chastise. The man selected for the job was Group Captain John Searby, currently serving as commanding officer of 83 Squadron of the Path Finder Force, and, before that, Gibson's successor as commanding officer of 106 Squadron. 5 Group detailed seventy-eight Lancasters divided between Genoa and Milan, and it was for the latter, that 619 Squadron made ready ten of its own and sent them on their way from Woodhall Spa between 21.01 and 21.12 with S/L Churcher the senior pilot on duty. The city was home to many war-industry factories, including the Isotta Fraschini luxury car works, which had been converted to military vehicle and aero engine manufacture, the Pirelli rubber works, Alfa Romeo, the Caproni aircraft plant, the Breda locomotive, armaments and aircraft works and the Innocenti machinery and vehicle factory. It is believed that all 197 aircraft reached their respective targets after flying out in excellent weather conditions, and, at Milan, the visibility was good enough for the crews to pick out ground features, before bombing mostly on a cluster of green TIs from 15,000 to 20,000 feet between 01.16 and 01.27. Fires were just beginning to take hold as they turned for home, and the glow of fires from the other targets was also visible and remained so for a hundred miles into the return flight. F/L Jones and crew enjoyed a challenging sortie after a bird strike soon after take-off caused damage to the nose, and then the wireless needed running repairs to keep them in touch with group, after which, the starboard-inner engine oil pressure dropped to zero, but kept running, and the port-inner caught fire as they crossed the east coast homebound. All three operations appeared to be effective, and, although the Master Bomber experiment at Turin was not entirely successful, experience was gained which would prove useful for the forthcoming Operation Hydra.

The rest of the heavy brigade remained inactive until the 9th, when a force of 457 Lancasters and Halifaxes was made ready for an operation that night against Mannheim. 619 Squadron prepared fourteen Lancasters as part of a 5 Group contribution of 143, and they departed Woodhall Spa between 22.50 and 23.24 with S/L Churcher the senior pilot on duty. After climbing out, they headed for the rendezvous point over Reading, before exiting England via Beachy Head on course for the French coast at Boulogne. There were no early returns as they made their way across Belgium on a direct track to the target, where they were greeted by a five-tenths layer of broken cloud at 4,000 feet and eight-tenths at 10,000 feet. Despite this, the visibility was fair, and the yellow skymarkers and green TIs were sufficient to provide a reference for the bomb-aimers. The 619 Squadron participants carried out their attacks from 17,000 to 21,000 feet between 01.34 and 02.03, and returned home to report a number of very large fires but a generally scattered raid. In fact, according to local reports, 1,316 buildings had been destroyed, forty-two industrial concerns had lost production, and more than fifteen hundred fires of varying sizes had required attention. Six Halifaxes and three Lancasters failed to return, two of the latter belonging to 5 Group.

Nuremberg was posted as the target on the 10th, for which a force of 653 aircraft was assembled, 128 of the Lancasters provided by 5 Group. 619 Squadron briefed fourteen crews while their Lancasters were being loaded with a cookie and up to twelve SBCs of incendiaries and sufficient fuel and reserves for the 1,300-mile round trip. Take-off was safely accomplished between 21.55 and 22.32 with F/Ls Aytoun and Dampier-Crossley the senior pilots on duty, and, after climbing out and forming up, they set course for Beachy Head on the Sussex coast to follow a route similar to that of the previous night. Sgt Hughes and crew lost the use of their Gee after about an hour, and decided to abandon their sortie, leaving the others to press on and arrive in the target area in conditions that also reflected those of twenty-four hours earlier with eight to ten-tenths cloud at 12,000 feet. The Path Finders had prepared a ground-marking plan, and there were no release-point flares to draw the head of the main force on, but the green TIs on the ground were visible to most, as were the fires for those arriving later. The Woodhall Spa crews delivered their bombs from 16,500 to 20,400 feet between 01.04 and 01.40, and all but one returned safely to report a good concentration of fires, the glow from which remained visible for 150 miles into the return journey. Among sixteen missing aircraft was 619 Squadron's EE112, which came down in southern Germany with no survivors from the crew of New Zealander, F/L Dampier-Crossley DFC RAAF, whose experience would be sorely missed by the squadron. W/C John Bell, who at the time was a lowly Sgt Bell, bomb-aimer in the crew of Bob Knights, recalled Dampier-Crossley taking Knights under his wing and imparting advice which would help the Knights crew to survive their time at both 619 and 617 Squadrons. Post-raid reconnaissance and local reports confirmed that the city had sustained much housing and industrial damage in mostly central and southern districts, and a death toll of 577 people was evidence of the intensity of the bombing.

During the course of the 12th, two forces were prepared for a return to Italy that night, one of 504 Lancasters and Halifaxes to attack Milan, and the other of 152 Stirlings, Halifaxes and Lancasters to target Turin. 5 Group contributed 130 Lancasters to the former, of which a dozen represented 619 Squadron, and they departed Woodhall Spa between 21.21 and 21.42 with F/L Jones the senior pilot on duty and a round trip of some 1,600 miles ahead of them. The route would take the bomber stream via Selsey Bill to Cabourg on the Normandy coast, and then south-east in a straight leg across central France to the northern tip of Lake Bourget, to cross the Alps and skirt southern Switzerland for the final run-in on the target. They arrived at the target to find three to five-tenths cloud with tops at 10,000 feet with a little ground mist to spoil the view, and bombed visually or on yellow flares and green TIs from 18,000 to 20,500 feet between 01.16 and 01.31. They observed large fires surrounding the aiming point in the city centre, and a thick column of black smoke rising through 20,000 feet as they turned away, and, with the glow in the sky remaining visible for 150 miles into the return flight, crews were confident of success. On return, F/O Arden and crew crossed the English coast at Selsey Bill descending through 6,000 feet, and were only a mile inland at 05.50 when a Lancaster, which turned out to belong to 207 Squadron, burst out of the cloud to pass in front and slightly below from starboard to port. Its port rudder made contact with F/O Arden's port wing, causing about four feet of the trailing edge to curl up and sending the aircraft into a diving turn to port, during which, both starboard engines caught fire. The pilot regaining control at 1,000 feet, while the flight engineer activated the extinguishers, quelled the fires and feathered the engines. They planned to land at the nearest airfield, which was Shoreham, but got no response as they lined up on the runway and fired their distress flare. This brought to their notice an aircraft halfway down the runway blocking their landing, and, with the Lancaster sinking, F/O Arden took the decision to circle back out to sea to carry out a ditching. He ran parallel to the shore, but at the last second, the port wing dropped, and, although he levelled the wings just in time, it all happened too quickly to implement the correct ditching procedure. JA844 hit the sea some five hundred yards off Littlehampton, and all but one of the occupants managed to vacate it and board the dinghy. However, the navigator, Sgt Jones, drifted away in the darkness and, sadly, was not found when the ASR launch picked them up forty-five minutes later. The rear gunner, Sgt Maddaford, was taken to Littlehampton hospital, where he died shortly afterwards. The 207 Squadron crew took to their parachutes and all but the rear gunner survived. Local reports from

Milan, though short on detail, confirmed that four important war-industry factories had sustained serious damage during August, and most of it probably occurred on this night, as did the majority of the 1,174 fatalities in the city in 1943.

Friday the 13th brought a stand-down, and many stations held dances and other entertainments, which were an important part of daily life on Bomber stations. ENSA (Entertainments National Service Association) put on regular shows to help maintain morale and create a distraction from the war.

Milan would face two further attacks before the Command's interest in Italy ceased for good, and the first of these was posted on the 14th, for which 1, 5 and 8 Groups put together a force of 140 Lancasters. Fifty-nine of them represented 5 Group, with 619 Squadron providing just six, which departed Woodhall Spa between 21.14 and 21.20 with F/Ls Aytoun and Pullen the senior pilots on duty. They all reached the target under clear skies and in good visibility aided by a brilliant moon and Path Finder route markers, and found the marking with green TIs to be accurate and concentrated. This was exploited by the main force crews, those from 619 Squadron delivering their loads of either a cookie and incendiaries or four 1,000 pounders and incendiaries from 14,800 to 17,000 feet between 01.18 and 01.26. Many fires were seen to take hold as the force turned away, leaving a glow that remained visible for a considerable distance into the return flight, and, at debriefing, F/Sgt Metcalfe and crew reported a large explosion at the Breda works.

There was to be no respite for Milan as a force of 199 Lancasters was made ready later on the 15th for a return that night for what would be the last time over Italy for main force Lancasters. 619 Squadron provided eight of the eighty-five of the type belonging to 5 Group, and they took off from Woodhall Spa between 20.23 and 20.38 with S/L Churcher the senior pilot on duty. There were no early returns, and as they entered northern France with the rest of the bomber stream, night-fighters were waiting to pounce, and succeeded in bringing down five 5 Group Lancasters, three from 61 Squadron and two belonging to 467 Squadron. The others reached the target to find clear skies, and to be guided to the aiming point by green Path Finder flares over Lake Bourget. Haze and smoke hung over the city from the previous night to spoil to an extent the vertical visibility, but the Path Finders marked the city-centre aiming point with green TIs, and these were bombed to good effect by the 619 Squadron crews from 14,500 to 16,000 feet between 00.05 and 00.25. Returning crews were confident not only that they had been part of an effective raid, but also that they had played their part in knocking Italy out of the war.

The 16th was a stand-down for all but 3 and 8 Groups, and many stations organised sporting events and other distractions as, behind the scenes, the final details were being incorporated into the plan for Operation Hydra. The final raid of the war on an Italian city was carried out by 154 aircraft of 3 and 8 Groups against Turin that night, and was concluded successfully for the modest cost of four aircraft. However, many of the participating Stirlings were diverted on return, and did not reach their home stations in time on the 17th to be made ready for the night's highly important operation, for which a maximum effort had been planned. This would deplete the available number of Stirlings by sixty, and heap an even greater responsibility upon the rest of the force to complete the job at the first attempt.

Since the very beginning of the war, intelligence had suggested that Germany was researching into and developing rocket technology, and, although scant regard was given to the reports by most, photographic reconnaissance had confirmed the existence of an establishment at Peenemünde at the northern tip of the island of Usedom on the Baltic coast. The activities there were monitored through Ultra intercepts and surreptitious reconnaissance flights, and the V-1, known to the photographic interpreters at Medmenham because of its wingspan as the "Peenemünde 20", was captured on a photograph. The brilliant scientist, Dr R V Jones, had been able to gain vital information concerning the V-1's range, which would ultimately be used to feed disinformation to the enemy, largely through the double agent, Eddie Chapman, otherwise known as "Zigzag". Unfortunately, Churchill's chief scientific adviser, Professor Lindemann, or Lord Cherwell as he became, steadfastly refused to give credence to the existence and feasibility of rocket weapons, and held stubbornly to his viewpoint even when confronted with a photograph of a V-2 on a trailer, taken by a PRU Mosquito in June 1943. It required the combined urgings of Duncan Sandys and Dr Jones to persuade Churchill of the urgency to act, and Operation Hydra was planned for the first available opportunity, which occurred on the night of the 17/18th. It was vital that the Peenemünde installation be destroyed, ideally, at the first attempt, and a force of 596 aircraft and crews answered the call. 5 Group contributed 117 of the 324 Lancasters, with Woodhall Spa making ready twelve, and the rest of the force preparing to take off in the late evening was comprised of 218 Halifaxes and fifty-four Stirlings. Earlier in the day, the USAAF 8th Air Force had carried out its first deep-penetration raids into Germany to attack ball-bearing production at Schweinfurt and the Messerschmidt aircraft plant at Regensburg, and, to the shock of its leaders, had learned a harsh lesson. They had been warned by the RAF since beginning shallow penetration operations in 1942, that unescorted daylight raids deep into Germany were not viable, but had been confident that the tactics employed would result in acceptable losses, and brushed aside the RAF's concerns. The folks at home would not be told that sixty B17s had failed to return, or, later, that a similar reversal in October had brought the future of US bomber operations from England onto question.

Operation Hydra had been meticulously planned to account for the three vital components of Peenemünde, the housing estate, where the scientific and technical staff lived, the factory buildings and the experimental site. Each was assigned to a specific wave of aircraft, which would attack from medium level, with the Path Finders bearing the huge responsibility of shifting the point of aim accordingly. After last minute alterations, 3 and 4 Groups were given the first mentioned, 1 Group the second, and 5 and 6 Groups the third. The whole operation was to be overseen by a Master of Ceremonies (referred to hereafter as Master Bomber), and the officer selected for this hazardous and demanding role was G/C Searby of 83 Squadron, who, as already mentioned, had stepped into Gibson's shoes at 106 Squadron after Gibson was posted out to form 617 Squadron. Searby's role was to direct the marking and bombing by VHF, and to encourage the crews to press on to the aiming point, a task requiring him to remain in the target area and within range of the defences throughout the attack. In an attempt to protect the bombers from the attentions of enemy night-fighters for as long as possible, eight Mosquitos of 139 Squadron were to carry out a spoof raid on Berlin, led by the previously mentioned highly experienced G/C Len Slee. In the expectation of encountering drifting smoke as the last wave on target, the 5 Group crews were instructed to employ their time-and-distance approach to the aiming point, and had practised this over a stretch of coast near the Wainfleet bombing range at the mouth of the Wash in Lincolnshire, progressively cutting the margin of error from one thousand to three hundred yards.

The 619 Squadron element took off between 21.44 and 21.58 with W/C McGhie the senior pilot on a night when many squadron commanders elected to fly, in some cases, with fatal consequences. There were no early returns to Woodhall Spa, and the overall early-return rate was lower than normal, suggesting that crews had taken to heart the importance of the operation. The various groups made their way individually to a rendezvous point some ninety minutes flying time or three hundred miles from the English coast and sixty miles from Denmark's western coast, where they formed into a stream. Darkness had fallen as they crossed the North Sea, and, twenty miles short of landfall over the southern tip of Fanø island, south of Esbjerg, windowing began, in order to simulate a standard raid on a northern or north-eastern city. Southern Denmark was traversed by the Lancaster brigade at 18,000 feet, twice the altitude required for the attack, but, worryingly, in a band of cloudless sky under a bright moon. They adopted an east-south-easterly course and began to shed altitude gradually during the 240-mile run to the target a little over an hour away, and, at the rear of the stream, the 5 Group crews focussed on the island of Rügen, the ideal starting point for their time-and-distance run to Peenemünde, which lay some fifteen miles beyond to the south-east.

The initial marking of the housing estate went awry, and some target indicators fell onto the forced workers' camp at Trassenheide, more than a mile south of the intended aiming point. Many of the 3 and 4 Group bombs fell here, inflicting grievous casualties on friendly foreign nationals, who were trapped inside their wooden barracks. Once rectified, however, the attack proceeded according to plan, and a number of important members of the technical staff were killed. The 1 Group second-wave crews encountered strong crosswinds over the narrow section of the island where the construction sheds were located, but this phase of the operation largely achieved its aims, and they were on their way home before the night-fighters arrived from Berlin, having been attracted by the glow of fires well to the north. On arrival at Rügen, the 5 Group crews began their timed runs to the experimental site, where they encountered the expected smoke, before delivering their mix of high explosive bombs onto green TIs. The 619 Squadron element mostly heard the Master Bomber instructing them to bomb the green TIs on the right, as those to the left were in the water, and carried out their attacks from within two hundred feet of each other at a uniform 6,000 feet between 00.42 and 00.58, F/Sgt Metcalfe and crew carrying out two passes seven minutes apart. They and the 6 Group Halifaxes and Lancasters then ran into the night-fighters, which proceeded to take a heavy toll of bombers, both in the skies over the target, and on the route home towards Denmark. Twenty-nine of the forty missing aircraft came from this third wave, seventeen of them belonging to 5 Group and twelve to 6 Group, which represented a loss rate for the Canadians of 19.7%. Three crews failed to return to Woodhall Spa, among them that of the commanding officer, W/C McGhie. EE117 came down somewhere near Aabenraa on Jutland's south-eastern coast, killing all eight occupants, while EE147 crashed south of the target at Anklam, now in Poland, possibly having been chased there by a night-fighter. P/O O'Leary RCAF and his crew perished, and none survived either from the crew of Sgt Pearce in ED982, which met its end in the Baltic. Many of the returning crews brought home aiming point photographs, despite the fact that the time-and-distance method was found to have been not entirely effective. Returning crews praised the work of the Path Finders and the Master Bomber, and F/L Jones and crew claimed a FW190 as probably destroyed. Post-raid reconnaissance revealed the raid to have been sufficiently effective to delay the V-2 development programme by a number of weeks, and, ultimately, to force the manufacture of secret weapons underground. The flight testing of the V-2 was eventually withdrawn eastwards into Poland, beyond the range of Harris's bombers, and thus, the attempt to nullify Peenemünde as a threat had been achieved.

Before the next campaign began, the new commanding officer, the balding Scotsman, W/C Abercromby, was posted in from his flight commander post at 50 Squadron on the 20th. The Ruhr city of Leverkusen was posted on the 22nd as the target for a heavy force of 449 Lancasters and Halifaxes with 8 Group Oboe-Mosquito to provide the initial marking. The aiming point was to be a factory belonging to the infamous I.G. Farben chemicals company, which was engaged in the development and production of synthetic oil and employed slave labour at all of its factories across Germany, including 30,000 from the Auschwitz concentration camp, where it had built a plant. One of the company's subsidiaries manufactured the Zyklon B gas used during the Holocaust to murder millions of Jewish victims. 619 Squadron made ready nine Lancasters in a 5 Group contribution of 108, and they departed Woodhall Spa between 21.10 and 21.40 with W/C Abercromby displaying excellent leadership qualities by putting himself on the Order of Battle immediately. After climbing out, they headed for the Belgian coast at Knokke, to follow a well-worn route to the southern Ruhr, which would require them to pass through the searchlight and flak belt near Cologne that was guaranteed to provide a hot reception. All made it safely through the narrow searchlight and flak corridor to reach the target, situated on the eastern bank of the Rhine between Düsseldorf to the north and Cologne to the south, where ten-tenths cloud with tops as high as 18,000 feet blanketed the area. Oboe-equipment failures forced most crews to bomb on e.t.a in the absence of markers, until the glow of fires came to their aid as the raid developed, although a small number of crews spotted green TIs on the ground and aimed for them. Bombing was carried out by the 619 Squadron crews in the face of intense flak from 17,000 to 22,000 feet between 00.05 and 00.29, and the glow of fires and the flash of explosions was initially the only confirmation of something happening under the cloud, until a column of smoke was observed to be rising through 12,000 feet. Local reports would reveal that up to a dozen neighbouring towns had been hit, Düsseldorf suffering the destruction of 132 buildings.

Harris had long believed that the key to ultimate victory lay in the destruction of Berlin, the seat of the Nazi government and the symbol of its power. On the 23rd, orders were received on stations across the Command to prepare for a maximum effort that night against Germany's capital city, which had not been visited by the heavy brigade since the end of March. The crews, of course, could not know that this was to be the first of an eventual nineteen raids on the "Big City", in a campaign which, with an autumn break, would drag on until the following spring. It was a campaign that would test the resolve of the crews to the absolute limit, whilst also sealing the fate of the Stirlings and the Mk II and V Halifaxes as front-line bombers. There are varying opinions concerning the true start date of what became known as the Berlin offensive or the Battle of Berlin, some commentators believing these first three operations in August and September to be the start, while others point to the sixteen raids from mid-November. However, there was little doubt in Bomber Command circles that this was it, a fact demonstrated by the comments in numerous squadron ORBs, which spoke of the "long-awaiting Berlin campaign" and similar sentiments. There would be a Master Bomber on hand for this operation, and the officer chosen was Canadian W/C "Johnny" Fauquier, the tough, grizzled and popular onetime bush pilot and frequent brawler, who was enjoying his second spell as the commanding officer of 405 (Vancouver) Squadron, now of the Path Finders, and formerly of 4 Group. The route had been planned to take the bomber stream to a rendezvous point over the North Sea, before crossing the Dutch coast near Haarlem and heading on a course to pass between Bremen and Hannover to skirt the southern rim of Berlin. The intention was then to turn back to approach the city from the south-east, and, after bombing, to pass out over the Baltic coast and make for the Schleswig-Holstein peninsula. Finally, seventeen Mosquitos were to precede the Path Finder and main force elements to drop route markers at key points in an attempt to keep the bomber stream on track.

A force of 727 aircraft was assembled, of which 124 Lancasters represented 5 Group, ten of them belonging to 619 Squadron, which departed Woodhall Spa between 20.03 and 20.34 with S/L Churcher the senior pilot on duty. After climbing out, they joined the bomber stream, crossed northern Holland and entered Germany between Meppen to the north and Osnabrück to the south. An error by F/O Joss's navigator led to them arriving at point "A" so late, that there was no point in continuing, and they returned home. After passing to the south of Hannover, the others headed to a turning point south-east of Berlin, where they were to turn sharply to port to adopt a north-westerly course across the city centre. Those of the main force that reached the target area found clear skies and moonlight, but the Path Finders had been unable to identify the aiming point in the centre of the city, a result of the inherent difficulties of interpreting the H2S images over such a massive urban sprawl. They released their TIs over the southern outskirts instead, prompting many main force crews to cut the corner and approach the city from the south-west rather than south-east, which would result in the wastage of many bomb loads in open country and on outlying communities. The 619 Squadron crews each delivered their cookie and incendiaries visually and on red and green TIs from 18,500 to 20,000 feet between 23.47 and 00.21 in the face of intense searchlight activity with moderate flak. Returning crews reported large explosions and many fires, the glow from which remained visible for at least 140 miles, and a pall of smoke had already risen to meet them as they turned towards the north-west. Curiously, only a few crews commented on hearing the Master Bomber and finding his instructions helpful. A new record of fifty-six aircraft failed to return, twenty-three Halifaxes, seventeen Lancasters and sixteen Stirlings, representing a percentage loss rate respectively of 9.1, 5.1 and 12.9, which perfectly reflected the food chain when all three types operated together. 619 Squadron's ED981 crashed in Eckernförde Bay just off the shore at Surendorf, a Baltic coastal community to the north-west of Kiel, and only Sgt Coomber and his flight engineer survived to be taken into captivity. Sgt Coomber's commission would come through while he was a PoW. Berlin experienced a scattered raid, but, because of the numbers attacking, extensive damage was caused, a little in or near the centre, but mostly in south-western residential districts and industrialised areas a little further east. 2,611 buildings were reported to have been destroyed or seriously damaged, and the death toll of 854 people was surprisingly high, caused largely, perhaps, by a failure to heed the alarms and go to the assigned shelters.

Orders were received on the 27th to prepare for an operation that night against Nuremberg, for which a force of 674 aircraft ultimately lined up for take-off in mid-evening. 5 Group contributed 140 Lancasters, the twelve at Woodhall Spa taking to the air between 20.52 and 21.15 with W/C Abercromby the senior pilot on duty. After climbing out, they headed for the French coast, but P/O Vickerstaffe and crew turned back early after their oxygen system failed. From the French coast, the bomber stream followed the line of the frontier with Belgium until crossing into Germany south of Luxembourg on course for the target, where clear skies and intense darkness prevailed. The Path Finders had been briefed to check their H2S equipment by dropping a 1,000 pounder on Heilbronn, and some crews complied, while others, it seems, experienced technical difficulties. The initial marking was accurate, but a creep-back developed, which the backers-up and the Master Bomber could not correct, and this resulted in many bomb loads falling into open country, while others hit Nuremberg's south-eastern and eastern districts. The 619 Squadron crews aimed at red and green TIs from 19,000 to 21,400 feet between 00.32 and 01.05, and gained an impression of a fairly concentrated and accurate attack, which produced many fires. At debriefing, they described searchlights and night-fighters as numerous, and this was confirmed by the failure to return of thirty-three aircraft, eleven of each type, which again confirmed the vulnerability of the Stirlings and Halifaxes when operating alongside Lancasters. The loss rate on this night was 3.1% for the Lancaster, 5% for the Halifax and 10.6% for the Stirlings.

The twin towns of Mönchengladbach and Rheydt were posted as the targets for a two-phase operation on the 30th, and it would be the first major attack for both of them. Situated some ten miles west of the centre of Düsseldorf in the south-western Ruhr, they would face an initial force of 660 aircraft of four types, in what, for the crews, was a short-penetration trip across the Dutch frontier, which would be a welcome change from the recent long slogs to eastern and southern Germany. The plan called for the first wave to hit Mönchengladbach, before a two-minute pause in the bombing allowed the Path Finders to head south to mark Rheydt. 619 Squadron made ready fourteen Lancasters as part of a 5 Group contribution of 138, and divided them between the two waves, the first five departing Woodhall Spa between 23.29 and 23.35 and the remainder between 23.47 and 00.04, with S/L Scorer the senior pilot on duty. Engine issues, including a port-outer on fire, persuaded Sgt Ward and crew to turn back, leaving the others to press on to the target, where they encountered good visibility above the seven to ten-tenths cloud at 8,000 feet. A near-perfect display of target-marking by Oboe Mosquitos delivered red and green flares, which the main force crews focused on to bomb with scarcely any creep-back. The 619 Squadron element carried out their bombing runs from 18,000 to 20,000 feet between 02.02 and 02.46, and on return, reported many fires, the glow from which could be seen from the Dutch coast homebound. Photo-reconnaissance confirmed a highly accurate and concentrated attack, which destroyed more than 2,300 buildings in the two towns, 171 of them of an industrial nature, along with 869 residential properties. Twenty-five aircraft failed to return, and Halifaxes narrowly sustained the highest numerical casualties.

The month ended with preparations for the second of the Berlin operations on the night of the 31st, for which 622 aircraft were made ready, more than half of them Lancasters, 129 of them provided by 5 Group. 619 Squadron loaded thirteen of its own with a cookie and nine SBCs of incendiaries each, and dispatched them between 19.38 and 20.22 with S/L Churcher the senior pilot on duty. The route on this night took the bomber stream on an east-south-easterly heading across Texel to a position between Hannover and Leipzig, before turning to pass to the south-east of Berlin and approach the city-centre aiming point on a north-westerly track. The return leg would involve a south-westerly course to a position south of Cologne for an exit over the French coast, but, despite the attempts to outwit the enemy night-fighter controller, he would be able to predict to some extent where to concentrate his forces. F/O Macdonald and crew were struggling to gain height as they crossed the North Sea, and, still five thousand feet below where they wanted to be as they reached the northern tip of Texel, they decided to turn back. The others pressed on towards north-eastern Germany, and, for the first time, crews reported the use by the Germans of "fighter flares" to mark out the path of the bombers to and from the target. As the spearhead, the Path Finders encountered five to six-tenths cloud in the target area, and this combined with H2S equipment failure and a spirited night-fighter response to cause the markers to be dropped well to the south of the planned aiming point. The main force crews became involved in an extensive creep-back, which would stretch some thirty miles into open country and outlying communities. The 619 Squadron crews reported up to eight-tenths thin cloud, and bombed on red and green TIs from 17,500 to 20,200 feet between 23.35 and 00.03, observing many fires over a wide area. It was noted by some that two groups of green TIs were ten miles apart, and both attracted attention from the main force. The outcome of the raid was a major disappointment, brought about by woefully short marking and a pronounced creep-back, and resulted in the destruction of just eighty-five houses, a figure in no way commensurate with the effort expended and the loss of forty-seven heavy bombers. There were two empty dispersals at Woodhall Spa, which should have been occupied by EE115 and JA848, the former having crashed outbound near Höxter, some forty miles south-west of Hannover, killing F/Sgt Metcalfe DFM and all but his mid-upper gunner, who fell into enemy hands. The latter was shot down by a night-fighter and crashed near Jüterbog, twenty-five miles south-west of Berlin while homebound, and F/Sgt Bower RCAF perished with five others, leaving the navigator to join his squadron colleague in captivity. The percentage loss rates made alarming reading at Bomber Command HQ, the Lancasters with an acceptable and sustainable 3%, the Halifaxes with 11.3% and the Stirlings with 16%.

While the above operation was taking place, ENSA presented a concert at Bottesford starring Gracie Fields, the Rochdale "lass" who was one of the most popular singers and actresses in Britain. The performance was held in a hangar and was attended by guests from neighbouring stations, including many senior officers, among which was the 5 Group Air-Officer-Commanding, AVM Cochrane. Despite the absence of so many on operational duties, an estimated 1,500 people attended and enjoyed a wonderful evening with excellent catering, which continued for the more distinguished guests in the mess. During the course of the month, the squadron participated in thirteen operations and dispatched 148 sorties for the loss of eight Lancasters, seven complete crews and two crew members.

September 1943

The new month began with a sizeable mining effort on the night of the 2/3rd involving eighty-nine aircraft, which were assigned to gardens from the Frisians in the north to the Biscay ports in the south. 619 Squadron made ready five Lancasters for the Nectarine I garden and dispatched them from Woodhall Spa between 20.17 and 20.20 with crews on board of limited operational experience. All reached the target area off Texel having established their positions by Gee until it became jammed, and then DR (dead reckoning), and found three-tenths cloud at 6,000 to 7,000 feet but good visibility, in which each delivered five vegetables into the briefed locations from 6,000 feet between 21.29 and 21.48.

Probably as a result of the heavy losses recently incurred by the Halifaxes and Stirlings, an all-Lancaster force would conclude the current series of operations against the "Big City". 316 aircraft were made ready on the 3rd, of which 121 were provided by 5 Group, including thirteen by 619 Squadron, and they departed Woodhall Spa between 19.31 and 19.49 with W/C Abercromby and S/L Scorer the senior pilots on duty and watched by two British and eight Latin American journalists. A fuel feed problem to the starboard-outer engine from both starboard tanks forced

F/Sgt Mason and crew to abandon their sortie early on, while starboard-inner engine failure caused the crew of P/O Tomlin also to turn back, both before even crossing the English coast. To complete a bad night for the squadron, a hydraulics issue deprived F/O Bell and crew of a serviceable rear turret to end their interest in proceedings, and this left ten 619 Squadron crews to rendezvous with the bomber stream over the North Sea, before crossing the Dutch coast over the Den Helder peninsula, and adopting a direct course of 350 miles, which took them north of Hannover to Brandenburg, some thirty-five miles short of the target. Long, straight legs were rarely employed because of the risk of interception by the Luftwaffe, but the forecast heavy cloud with tops at up to 22,000 feet accompanied the stream all the way from the Dutch coast to the target area, and helped to keep the enemy at bay. The Path Finders had been briefed to use H2S to navigate their way via the region's lakes to the city centre aiming point, but the cloud miraculously dispersed in time to leave clear skies and allow the Path Finders to drop ground-marking TIs rather than the less reliable skymarkers. The first TIs fell right over the aiming point, before others crept back for between two and five miles along the line of approach from the west. Fortunately, the backers up maintained the marking as the main force Lancasters came in in a single wave, and, although much of the bombing fell short of the city centre, most of it landed within the city boundaries, principally into the largely residential districts of Tiergarten, Wedding, Moabit and Charlottenburg, and the industrial Siemensstadt, where much useful damage occurred to cause a loss of war production. The 619 Squadron crews carried out a time-and-distance run from yellow track markers and bombed on red and green TIs from 16,000 to 20,000 feet between 23.27 and 23.34. Many fires were observed, which appeared to be merging as the bombers turned towards the north for a return route that would intentionally violate Swedish airspace. Four Mosquitos laid spoof route marker flares well away from the actual track to mislead the night-fighters, but, in the absence of the poorer performing Halifaxes and Stirlings, twenty-two Lancasters failed to return, almost 7% of those dispatched.

Whether by design, or as a result of the losses sustained, Berlin was now shelved for the next ten weeks, while Harris sought other suitable targets, of which there were many. He would shortly begin a four-raid series against Hannover stretching over a four-week period, but, first, he focused on southern Germany, beginning on the 5th with the twin cities of Mannheim and Ludwigshafen, which face each other from the east and west banks respectively of the Rhine. The plan was to exploit the creep-back phenomenon that attended most large operations, by approaching the target from the west, and marking the eastern half of Mannheim, with the expectation that the bombing would spread back along the line of approach across central and western Mannheim and into Ludwigshafen. A force of 605 aircraft was assembled, which included 108 Lancasters of 5 Group, ten of them at Woodhall Spa loaded with a cookie each and a mix of 4lb and 30lb incendiaries. They took off between 19.30 and 20.01 with no senior pilots on duty, and, after climbing out, set course for Beachy Head on the Sussex coast to begin the Channel crossing. There were no early returns among the 619 Squadron element, and the bomber stream progressed across France and into Germany in favourable weather conditions to find clear skies over the target, where the Path Finders performed at their absolute best. After first observing red and yellow markers, the 619 Squadron crews had green TIs in their bomb sights as they let their loads go from 18,800 to 20,700 feet between 23.02 and 23.23, and all reported hitting them. Those arriving towards the later stages of the raid were drawn on by the burgeoning fires fifty miles ahead, and a number of large, red explosions were observed at 23.12, 23.23 and 23.27, the last of which was followed by a purplish-red mushroom of fire. Searchlights were numerous, but the flak negligible, and it was the abundance of night-fighters that posed the greatest risk to life and limb, although most of the Woodhall Spa crews appeared to avoid any contact. Black smoke was rising through 15,000 feet as the bombers withdrew to the west, and the glow from the burning cities was visible for 150 miles into the return journey, which thirty-four aircraft would fail to complete. F/Sgt Goddard and crew were flying straight and level at cruising altitude when JB133 burst suddenly into flames and broke up before anyone could respond to the bale-out order. Navigator, Sgt Jostling, was ejected into space and landed safely in the same area as the wreckage to the north of Pirmasens on the edge of the Palatinate Forest, and fell into enemy hands. The destruction bore all the hallmarks of a night-fighter attack employing upward firing cannons, known as Schräge Musik, literally slanting music, the German term for jazz, a weapon unknown at the time to the RAF. It would maintain its secrecy by not using tracer rounds, and it would be some months before its existence came to light. The device enabled night-fighters to adopt a new, and for them, less hazardous tactic of approaching a bomber from below to one side, to aim the fire at the fuel tanks between the engines. Once on fire, the bomber was doomed and the night-fighter could stand off at a safe distance to watch its end. Thirteen Lancasters, an equal number of Halifaxes and eight Stirlings were missing, and the percentage loss rates continued to tell the same story. Local reports confirmed that both Mannheim and Ludwigshafen had suffered catastrophic destruction, with almost two thousand fires in the latter alone, 986 of them classed as large. Mannheim's reporting system broke down completely, and little detail emerged of this raid, although it would recover in time for the next assault in less than three weeks' time.

Munich was posted as the target on the 6th, for which the squadron made ready ten Lancasters as part of the ninety-two-strong 5 Group element in an overall force of 257 Lancasters and 147 Halifaxes, the Stirling brigade made conspicuous by its absence. The Woodhall Spa crews were airborne between 19.46 and 19.56 with F/L Jones the senior pilot on duty, each carrying a similar bomb load and adopting the same route as for the previous night, and all reached the Bavarian capital under conditions that were not ideal. The cloud varied between three and nine-tenths with tops at 16,000 feet, although some ground features, like the River Isar, could be identified and the red, yellow and green TIs observed. The 619 Squadron crews were among those carrying out a timed run from the Ammersee, located twenty-one miles away to the south-west, and bombed mostly from 19,500 to 20,000 feet between 23.36 and 23.46, while Sgt Hughes and crew went in at 15,000 feet. A large number of fires was observed to be grouped around the markers, but an accurate assessment was not possible, and local reports would suggest that the attack had been scattered across southern and western districts. The searchlights were ineffective because of the cloud, but large numbers of night-fighters were again evident, and sixteen aircraft failed to return, thirteen of them Halifaxes, a percentage loss rate of 8.8, compared with 1.2 for the Lancasters.

5 Group largely left the war to the other groups for the ensuing two weeks, during which period, Italy's unconditional surrender was announced on the 8th, while, that night, attacks were carried out against coastal batteries at Le Portel near Boulogne under Operation Starkey, a kind of rehearsal for the invasion. On the 11th, W/C Abercromby, who had a reputation as a disciplinarian and seemed to enjoy ruffling feathers, implemented an intense programme of ground activities during periods of stand-down that included drill, lectures, physical training and sport. On the 13th, six crews took part in low-level training and followed it up with night cross-country exercises on the next two nights. The reason became clear on the 16th, when briefing revealed that they and six crews from 617 Squadron were to attack the Antheor Viaduct, situated on the main line between

France and Italy on the Cote-d-Azur, south-west of Cannes. 617 Squadron was reeling from the tragic loss on the previous night of five crews while attacking the Dortmund-Ems Canal to the south of Ladbergen. That was on top of the tragic deaths twenty-four hours earlier of Dambuster F/L David Maltby and his crew as the operation was aborted over the North Sea following an adverse weather report by a Meteorological Flight Mosquito crew monitoring the route. As the Lancasters turned for home, Maltby's was seen to cartwheel into the sea, and post-war research suggests that it had collided with a 139 Squadron Mosquito returning from Berlin. After the failure of the raid to breach the canal banks, 617 Squadron's stand-in commanding officer, S/L Martin, had wanted to return to the heavily defended canal immediately, but it was considered prudent to get the squadron back on the horse with a less demanding operation, which W/C Abercromby would lead. The other members of the 619 Squadron element were the crews of S/Ls Churcher and Scorer, F/Ls Aytoun and Jones and F/O Bell, and they departed Woodhall Spa between 19.54 and 20.06, only to lose the services of F/L Aytoun and crew to severe icing over France, which locked the controls and almost induced a stall. P/O Clayton of 617 Squadron had a similar experience and also turned back, leaving the others to press on to reach the target after on outward flight of more than five hours. Visibility was good as they carried out their attacks from 300 feet between 01.18 and 01.28, but no results were observed, and four extremely tired crews landed at Predannack in Cornwall between 06.05 and 07.08. W/C Abercromby and crew were the last to touch down after more than eleven hours aloft, and this left F/L Jones and crew unaccounted for. An SOS signal had been picked up at 05.50, which was plotted to be off Oporto on the Portuguese coast, and it transpired that EE106 had been damaged by flak over the target and F/L Jones had made for neutral territory. The crew was brought ashore by Portuguese fisherman, and would spend a brief period in internment before returning home. It would be left to photo-reconnaissance to confirm that no direct hits had been scored on the viaduct, and that the rim of one of three large craters was a mere fifteen yards from one of the piers. A near-miss was not enough at this kind of target, and 617 Squadron would return for another crack in the New Year.

What had been known as RAF Base Scampton since the "Base" system had been adopted in May, was redesignated 52 Base on the 16th, and still included the stations at Fiskerton and Dunholme Lodge. However, Scampton had been closed on the 1st to allow the construction of concrete runways, and, when declared operational again in the autumn of 1944, this most famous of stations would have been transferred to 1 Group.

It was not until the commencement of the series of raids on Hannover that 5 Group, as a whole, was roused from its slumber. The irony of such long layoffs was, that despite occupying the most dangerous jobs in the fighting services, aircrew personnel grew listless and bored when left to kick their heels, and much preferred the dangers of operations to the enforced lectures and PT. There was, no doubt, a uniform cheer when the tannoys called them to briefing on the 22nd, to learn that they were to be part of a force of 711 aircraft to attack the ancient city of Hannover, situated in northern Germany midway between the Dutch frontier and Berlin. The city was a major centre of war production, the home among others to the Accumulatoren-Fabrik A.G, manufacturers of lead acid batteries for U-Boots and torpedos, the Continental tyre and rubber factory at Limmer, the Deurag-Nerag synthetic oil refinery at Misburg, the VLW (Volkswagen) metalworks, and the Maschinenfabrik Niedersachsen Hannover and Hanomag factories, which were producing guns and tracked vehicles. The region was also the location of seven Nazi concentration camps, although this was not known at the time among the Allies. According to Martin Middlebrook and Chris

Everitt in Bomber Command War Diaries, the first two operations produced concentrated bombing, but mostly outside of the target, while only the third one succeeded in causing extensive damage, which, if the figures are to be believed, seem to be massively out of proportion. The author contends that the reports of the crews after the first two operations suggest strongly that the damage to Hannover was accumulative over the first three raids and did not result from just one, as will be explained in the following narrative. The telling feature is, perhaps, that no reports came out of Hannover to corroborate the testimony of the crews on the first two raids, although post-raid reconnaissance by the RAF after the second one did show that some of the bombing had fallen into open country, and the Path Finders did admit to at least one poor performance.

619 Squadron prepared thirteen Lancasters, which took off between 18.44 and 19.07 with S/L Scorer the senior pilot on duty, before climbing out and joining up with the other 135 participants from 5 Group for the 430-mile outward leg. There were no early returns to Woodhall Spa, and all reached the target area, where good visibility prevailed, but stronger-than-forecast winds would play their part in pushing the marking and bombing towards the south-east. The 619 Squadron crews carried out their bombing runs from 18,000 to 20,500 feet between 21.32 and 21.50, aiming at red and green TIs and dodging the intense searchlights and heavy flak, which was bursting at around 18,000 feet. Some returning crews reported a line of fires developing from west to east, with smoke rising through 14,000 feet, while others claimed that fires ran from the aiming point in a north-north-westerly direction across the city, but all were unanimous, that the raid had been highly successful, and that the glow of fires was still visible from the Dutch coast, a distance of two hundred miles. Twenty-six aircraft failed to return, twelve of them Halifaxes, which, again, sustained the highest numerical losses, and, this time, at 5.3%, even exceeded the loss rate of the Stirling.

Let us now examine the claim that the main weight of bombs fell two to five miles south-south-east from the city centre, and that the operation largely failed. Firstly, two to five miles in any city means that the bombing fell within the boundaries, and, therefore, within the built-up area. Secondly, the majority of crews, if not all, reported a highly successful raid with fires right across the city, smoke rising to 14,000 feet as they left the scene and the glow visible from the Dutch coast. It is true that crews were very frequently mistaken in their belief that an attack had been successful, but the evidence on this occasion would seem to confirm their testimony. Decoy fire-sites do not produce a glow visible from a distance of two hundred miles, or sufficient volumes of smoke to reach bombing height during the short duration of a raid, and remain dense enough to be visible at night.

On the 23rd, and for the second time in the month, Mannheim was posted as the target for that night, and would face a force, which, at take-off, numbered 628 aircraft, 139 of them 5 Group Lancasters. Eleven of these were made ready at Woodhall Spa, and took off between 18.24 and 19.06 with F/Ls Aytoun, O'Shaughnessy and Sandison the senior pilots on duty. There were no early returns among the 619 Squadron element as the bomber stream pushed on across France and into southern Germany, where they encountered predominantly clear skies and good visibility. At the head of the stream, the Path Finders had marked out the northern districts, which had not been hit so severely during the previous operation. The marking was accurate and concentrated, allowing the main force crews to attack on red, green and yellow TIs, those from Woodhall Spa from 16,500 to 21,000 feet between 21.45 and 22.12. Later bombing spilled over into the northern fringe of

Ludwigshafen and out into the nearby towns of Oppau and Frankenthal, where much damage resulted. Returning crews reported that smoke had reached around 6,000 feet as they turned away, and that the glow of fires remained visible for 150 miles into the return journey. Thirty-two crews were absent from debriefing, and, this time, eighteen of them were in Lancasters, compared with seven each for the Halifaxes and Stirlings. This provided a somewhat topsy-turvy and unusual loss-rate of 5.7%, 3.6% and 6% respectively. Post-raid reconnaissance and local reports revealed that 927 houses and twenty industrial premises had been destroyed in Mannheim, and that the I.G. Farben factory in Ludwigshafen had sustained serious damage.

A force of 678 aircraft was assembled for a return to Hannover on the 27th, 5 Group contributing 141 Lancasters, of which a dozen were made ready by 619 Squadron and departed Woodhall Spa between 19.11 and 19.36 with no pilots above flying officer rank and "Nick" Knilans now wearing the insignia of a pilot officer. They climbed out over the station before setting course through ice-bearing cloud for the North Sea, where continuing challenging weather conditions began to deplete the bomber stream. Among those dropping out before even reaching the Norfolk coast was the 619 Squadron crew of P/O Mearis, who were south of King's Lynn when they headed for the jettison area. The remainder pressed on in the wake of the Path Finders, who were unaware that the weather forecasts, on which their performance would be based, were incorrect. The result of that would be to push the marking some five miles from the city centre towards the north, but, at least, the weather improved markedly over Germany to present the crews with clear skies on their arrival. The 619 Squadron crews delivered their cookie and 4lb and 30lb incendiaries mostly on green TIs from 19,500 to 22,500 feet between 22.03 and 22.20, and observed many fires with smoke rising to 15,000 feet. Returning crews again reported the glow of fires visible from the Dutch coast, and confidence in the success of the operation was unanimous across the Command, giving lie to the claim that little damage resulted. Post-raid photos did reveal many bomb craters in open country, but the fire and smoke evidence did not support decoy fire-sites, and no local report was forthcoming to shed further light. The loss of thirty-eight aircraft was probably something of a shock, but, at least, common sense returned to the statistics to re-establish the status quo after the topsy-turvy outcome of the Mannheim raid. Seventeen Halifaxes, ten Lancasters, ten Stirlings and one Wellington failed to return, giving loss-rates for the four-engine types of 9% for the Stirling, 7.3% for the Halifax and 3.2% for the Lancaster.

The month ended with an operation to Bochum in the central Ruhr on the 29th, for which 619 Squadron made ready ten Lancasters in a 5 Group effort of 111, and they were part of an overall heavy force of 343 aircraft. They departed Woodhall Spa between 18.08 and 18.37 with S/L Scorer the senior pilot on duty, and arrived at the Dutch coast guided by two route-marker flares at 20,000 feet. After a two-and-a-half-hour outward flight, they established their positions visually in good visibility, before focussing on the aiming point, which had been marked by the Path Finders with green TIs. The bombing was carried out by the 619 Squadron crews from 18,500 to 21,000 feet between 20.47 and 21.08 in the face of a strong searchlight and moderate flak defence. P/O Mearis and crew crossed the Lincolnshire coast at Mablethorpe in low cloud, and, at 00.05, ED983 smacked into high ground at Cadwell Hill some five miles to the west of the town, killing four of the occupants outright, and a fifth succumbed shortly afterwards in hospital. The flight engineer and wireless operator sustained severe injuries, but would survive. Some returning crews described the target as a mass of flames, with smoke rising rapidly to meet them, while local reports confirmed the destruction of 527 houses, with 742 others seriously damaged.

F/L Tom O'Shaughnessy and crew were posted to 617 Squadron at Coningsby on the 30th, and had taken part in four operations, when, on the 20th of January, while practising low-level bombing, they bounced off the sea and crashed onto the beach at Snettisham, killing O'Shaughnessy and his navigator, F/O Holding, and severely injuring two others. During the course of the month, the squadron carried out nine operations and dispatched ninety sorties for the loss of three Lancasters and two crews and the temporary loss of another in internment.

October 1943

The start of October was a busy time for the Lancaster squadrons, which would be called upon to participate in six major operations in the first eight nights. The month's account was opened at Hagen, a town at the eastern end of the Ruhr on the 1st, for which a moderately-sized heavy force of 243 Lancasters was drawn from 1, 5 and 8 Groups. 5 Group contributed 125 aircraft, a dozen of them representing 619 Squadron, and they were loaded with a cookie and up to sixteen SBCs of incendiaries each, before departing Woodhall Spa between 18.13 and 18.44 with S/L Churcher the senior pilot on duty. They flew out over Skegness aiming for Egmond on the Dutch coast, to then skirt the northern edge of the Ruhr as far as Werl, to the north of the now famous Möhne reservoir, from where they would turn sharply to the south-west to run in on the target. They arrived to find ten-tenths cloud with tops at 12,000 feet in places and red and green Oboe-laid skymarkers to aim at, and carried out their attacks from 18,000 to 20,500 feet between 20.55 and 21.11. On return EE110 crashed into the Bristol Channel some twelve miles south-west of Cardiff, and there were no survivors from the crew of F/O Joss, whose remains were all recovered for burial. Returning crews reported a column of black smoke rising through the clouds and described a large bluish-green explosion at 21.03 and the glow of fires beneath the cloud. There was also praise for an effective Path Finder performance. Only two Lancasters failed to return in exchange for the usual housing damage, and, according to local sources, the destruction of forty-six industrial firms, among them a manufacturer of accumulator batteries for U-Boots, and this would have an impact on U-Boot production.

On the following afternoon, 294 crews from 1, 5 and 8 Groups were called to briefings to learn that Munich was to be their target for that night. 5 Group detailed 113 Lancasters, whose crews were to adopt the time-and-distance method of bombing, and the seven at Woodhall Spa were loaded with a cookie and ten SBCs each before taking off between 18.17 and 18.47 with F/Ls Bell and Sandison the senior pilots on duty. They climbed out and set course for the south coast to begin the Channel crossing, planning to make landfall in the Dunkerque region, before traversing France to enter Germany south of Strasbourg. There were no early returns among the 619 Squadron participants, who reached the target area after an outward flight of some three-and-a-half hours to encounter cloud over the Wörthsee, situated some fifteen miles west-south-west of the centre of Munich, and the starting point for the time-and-distance run. The skies over the city were clear of cloud, but the marking was scattered and this led to most of the early bombing falling into southern and south-eastern districts. The 5 Group crews were unable to establish a firm fix on the Wörthsee, and this would create a creep-back of up to fifteen miles along the line of approach. The 619

Squadron crews bombed on red and green TIs from 18,000 to 20,500 feet between 22.35 and 22.44, and all returned safely to make their reports. At debriefing, crews suggested that the raid had appeared to be concentrated on the eastern side of the city, and local authorities reported that 339 buildings had been destroyed in return for bringing down eight bombers.

Kassel, the industrial city located some eighty miles to the east of the Ruhr, had been an occasional target since the summer of 1940, and would receive two visits from the Command during the month. It was home to the Henschel Company, the presence of whose numerous manufacturing sites dominated the city, and employed eight thousand workers in addition to a large number of slaves. Aside from building the Dornier Do17Z bomber under licence, Henschel was the main producer of the Panzer III tank and the Tiger I and II, as well as narrow-gauge locomotives. The Fieseler aircraft company also had a manufacturing plant in the city, where it built BF109s and FW190s under licence, but was also responsible for the design of what would become the V-1 flying bomb. The first Bomber Command raid was posted on the 3rd, for which a force of 547 aircraft was assembled consisting of 223 Halifaxes, 204 Lancasters and 113 Stirlings. 5 Group supported the operation with ninety-two Lancasters, of which just five were made ready at Woodhall Spa and sent on their way between 18.17 and 18.44 with no pilots on duty above the rank of flying officer. There were no early returns, and all reached the target area to find largely clear skies but thick ground haze. The Path Finder H2S "blind" marker crews overshot the planned aiming point, and, because of the haze and, possibly, decoy markers, the backers-up, whose job was to confirm their accuracy by visual means, were unable to correct the error. The 619 Squadron crews identified the target visually and by green TIs, and bombed from 18,500 to 20,000 feet between 21.08 and 21.35, reporting on their return what appeared to be a good concentration of fires and a pall of smoke rising to meet them. In fact, the main weight of the attack had fallen onto the western suburbs, where the Henschel aircraft and tank factories and the Fieseler aircraft plant were hit, but a stray bomb load had also detonated an ammunition dump at Ihringshausen, situated close to the north-eastern suburb of Wolfsanger, which was left devastated by the blast. P/O Knilans and crew arrived back with a badly damaged rear turret following an engagement with a night-fighter, and Knilans himself assisted in the removal of Sgt Jackson's remains. Twenty-four aircraft failed to return, fourteen Halifaxes, six Stirlings and four Lancasters, which gave a loss-rate of 6.3%, 3.2% and 2.9% respectively.

The busy schedule of operations was to continue at Frankfurt on the 4th, for which a force of 406 aircraft was made ready. The American confidence in the ability of its forces to deliver daylight attacks on military and war production targets in Germany had been shaken by the high loss rates, which were not sustainable. Since the first Hannover raid, a small number of 8th Air Force B17s had been flirting with night raids alongside their RAF colleagues, and this night would bring their final involvement. 5 Group detailed ninety-five Lancasters, of which seven would represent 619 Squadron, and they departed Woodhall Spa between 18.06 and 18.26 with F/L Aytoun the senior pilot on duty. They had to follow a somewhat circuitous route, which departed England over the Sussex coast and tracked across Belgium as if heading for southern Germany, before swinging to the north-east and passing to the west of Frankfurt for the final run-in of around eighty miles. This added significantly to the mileage, but avoided the flak hotspots from the Dutch coast and north of the Ruhr. There were no early returns among the 619 Squadron element, which reached the target after a four-hour outward flight, although an hour of that was generally accounted for in climbing-out and gaining height before setting course. Frankfurt was found to be clear of cloud, and the Path

Finders produced a masterful marking performance to leave the city at the mercy of the main force element. The Woodhall Spa crews bombed on red and green TIs from 17,000 to 20,500 feet between 21.35 and 21.51, and witnessed a highly concentrated attack taking place that left the eastern half of the city and the docks area a sea of flames. A large, red explosion was observed at 21.37, which threw flames up to 3,000 feet, and smoke was rising through 8,000 feet as the bombers turned away, some crews reporting the glow from the burning city to be visible for 120 miles into the homeward leg. The success was gained at the modest cost of ten aircraft, half of which were Halifaxes.

The hectic first week of the month concluded with an operation against Stuttgart, for which a force of 343 Lancasters was drawn from 1, 3, 5, 6 and 8 Groups on the 7th. A new weapon in the Command's armoury was introduced for the first time in numbers on this night with the participation of a night-fighter-communications-jamming device called "Jostle". It required a specialist operator in addition to the standard crew of seven, who, though not necessarily a German speaker, could recognise the language, and, on hearing it, jam the signals on up to three frequencies by broadcasting engine noise over them. At 1 Group's 101 Squadron, where the device was being pioneered, it was referred to as ABC or Airborne Cigar, and, once proved to be effective, ABC Lancasters would be spread throughout the bomber stream on all major operations, whether or not 1 Group was otherwise involved. The Lancaster would also carry a full bomb load reduced by 1,000 pounds to compensate for the weight of the equipment and its operator. 5 Group put up 128 Lancasters, of which nine were made ready at Woodhall Spa, and they took off between 20.35 and 20.47 with F/L Tomlin the senior pilot on duty. About an hour after taking off, F/O Heffernan and crew were on their way home with a valve and air-pressure issue. The others flew out over France and reached the target area to find ten-tenths cloud at 10,000 feet, which concealed the ground from view and led to the Path Finders employing H2S and establishing two areas of marking. This resulted in bombs falling in many parts of the city from the centre to the south-west, those from the 619 Squadron element falling from 18,800 to 20,700 feet between 00.09 and 00.20. The Woodhall Spa crews returned safely to report their impressions of a scattered attack, which cost a remarkably modest four aircraft, and, according to local sources, destroyed 344 buildings and damaged more than four thousand others. Whether or not the presence of the radio-countermeasures Lancasters was responsible for the low loss could not be certain, but it was a promising start, and would lead, ultimately, to the formation of a dedicated RCM group, 100 Group, in November.

Many crews had been forced to divert on return from Stuttgart, and their tardy return to their home stations resulted in a reduced force of 504 aircraft being made available for the third raid of the series on Hannover posted for that night. 619 Squadron had only one aircraft land away, and was able to provide nine of the Lancasters in the 5 Group force of eighty-four, and eight of them departed Woodhall Spa between 22.41 and 22.55 with S/L Churcher the senior pilot on duty. Last to begin their take-off run was the crew of F/O Thompson RCAF in ED839 at 22.58, which swung as it gathered speed and slid to a halt on the grass with its undercarriage wrecked. The crew scrambled clear before fire took hold and the Lancaster was consumed. The others probably observed some of the excitement as they climbed out over the airfield, before setting course to rendezvous with the bomber stream en route for the northern tip of Texel, from where they would cross northern Holland and pass south of Bremen on their way to the target area. On arrival, they found largely clear skies and red and green TIs marking out the city-centre aiming point, and bombed from 19,000 to 21,000 feet between 01.35 and 01.54. Those towards the front of the bomber stream observed fires just beginning to take hold, while it became clear to the later arrivals that the fires were developing into a serious conflagration, but, curiously, despite the claim by some commentators that this was the one successful raid of the series, there was no mention of the glow being visible from a considerable distance, as had been the case with the first two operations. This time a local report did emerge, which described heavy damage in all districts except for those in the west, and a large area of fire engulfing the central districts. A total of 3,932 buildings was destroyed, and thirty thousand others damaged to some extent, while a death toll of 1,200 people was reported. These statistics seem somewhat excessive for a single operation by fewer than five hundred aircraft, particularly in the absence of the kind of crew reports common to the first two raids, and this adds weight to the author's contention, that the damage was accumulative over the three operations. Twenty-seven aircraft failed to return, but there were no unaccounted-for empty dispersals at Woodhall Spa.

The Path Finder and main force squadrons would effectively stand down now for a period of ten days, while 8 Group Mosquitos took the war to Germany. Lectures, training and sporting activities filled the time, and dances and ENSA productions entertained the station communities in the afternoon and evenings, but the crews were, no doubt, relieved, when the lull in operations came to an end on the 18th with a call on Lancaster stations to attend briefings. The wall map revealed Hannover as the target for the fourth and last time in this series, and the crews learned that this was to be an all-Lancaster affair involving 360 aircraft. 5 Group provided 143 of them, a dozen made ready by 619 Squadron, and they departed Woodhall Spa between 17.02 and 17.50 with W/C Abercromby the senior pilot on duty. P/O Firth and crew were twenty miles out from Skegness when overheating engines persuaded them to turn back, while P/O Knights and crew had made it to the mid-point of the North Sea crossing before their entire oxygen supply had leaked away. This left the others to make landfall over Texel, and continue on an easterly track across Holland aiming for Cloppenburg, and thence Nienburg and Celle, before turning to the south-west to run in on the target close to the Misburg oil refinery. They remained unmolested by the defences until encountering a nest of night-fighters on crossing the frontier into Germany, and at least thirteen aircraft were brought down during the ensuing forty-five minutes encompassing the approach and withdrawal phases. A layer of eight to ten-tenths cloud hung over Hannover with tops at 12,000 to 15,000 feet, and these conditions made it difficult for the Path Finders to establish the aiming point. It resulted in them dropping both sky and ground markers, which lacked concentration, and led to a scattering of the effort. The 619 Squadron crews bombed mostly on red and green TIs or on release-point flares from 19,500 to 21,300 feet between 20.18 and 20.28, and a colossal explosion was observed at around 20.19. The strong night-fighter presence dissuaded crews from hanging around to assess the outcome further, and the impression of those returning was of a scattered attack. It was established later that most of the bombs had fallen into open country, a disappointment compounded by the loss of eighteen Lancasters. Among these was 619 Squadron's EE109, which crashed into the centre of Hannover at 20.21 and took with it the eight-man crew of P/O Fuller DFC. The four raids on Hannover had cost the Command 110 aircraft from 2,253 sorties, a loss rate of 4.9%, but much of the city now lay in ruins, and would receive no further attention for a year, when the oil offensive and the close proximity of the Misburg synthetic oil plant to the east would keep the region in the firing line.

The first major attack of the war on the eastern city of Leipzig was planned for the 20th, and an all-Lancaster force of 358 aircraft representing 1, 5, 6 and 8 Groups assembled. 5 Group was responsible for 140 Lancasters, and 619 Squadron thirteen, which took off from Woodhall Spa between 17.14 and 17.39 with F/L Bell the senior pilot on duty. Sgt Olsen and crew were some fifty miles out from Skegness when the failure of the artificial horizon and gyro equipment ended their interest in proceedings, leaving the others to run into the most atrocious weather conditions in a towering front of ice-bearing cumulonimbus cloud east of Hannover that extended beyond 20,000 feet. This persuaded many crews to turn back as engines began to fail and ice-accretion destroyed lift, and among them was the crew of P/O Knights who had reached a position some ten miles north of Braunschweig when both inboard engines faltered, and the rear turret became unserviceable. F/L Bell and crew progressed perhaps twenty miles further before icing shut down both inboard engines and forced them to jettison their load, despite which, they decided to remain within the bomber stream and the port-inner eventually picked up. All of those pressing on experienced a torrid time before reaching the target after a three-and-a-half-hour outward flight, and then encountered seven to ten-tenths cloud with tops at between 14,000 and 20,000 feet, which prevented the Path Finders from establishing and marking the aiming point. This condemned the crews to bombing on e.t.a., on fires glimpsed through the cloud or on scattered skymarkers. F/O Macdonald and crew climbed to 27,000 feet in an attempt to reach clear air, and bombed the centre of searchlights and fires at 21.12, assuming that they were over the target. The others from 619 Squadron carried out their attacks from 19,500 to 20,800 feet between 21.05 and 21.14, and all but one made it home, relieved to have come through such a demanding and frightening experience. Sixteen Lancasters failed to return, four of them belonging to 5 Group, and among them was 619 Squadron's EE114, which crashed outbound between Celle and Salzwedel with fatal consequences for P/O Firth and his crew. Debriefing provided the Intelligence Sections with little information of use, and Leipzig would be put on the backburner for a few weeks.

The final major operation of the month was the second one against Kassel, for which preparations were put in hand on the 22nd. A force of 569 aircraft stood ready to take off in the early evening, 133 of them 5 Group Lancasters, thirteen of which were provided by 619 Squadron. They became airborne from Woodhall Spa between 17.31 and 17.52 with S/L Churcher the senior pilot on duty, but lost the services of F/O Morrison and crew to port-inner engine failure at the mid-point between the Suffolk and Dutch coasts. The others pressed on across Belgium in continuing unfavourable weather conditions, which miraculously improved in the target area to leave clear skies between the bombers and the target, but ten-tenths cloud above them at 24,000 feet. At the opening of the raid, the H2S "blind" markers overshot the city-centre aiming point, leaving the success of the operation reliant upon the visual marker crews backing up, and they did not disappoint. The red and green TIs were concentrated right on the aiming point, and the main force followed up with accurate and concentrated bombing with scarcely any creep-back. The 619 Squadron crews carried out their attacks from 19,200 to 21,000 feet between 21.02 and 21.10, and observed the fires just beginning to take hold as they turned away. It was after the sound of their engines had receded that the fires joined together to engulf the city in what, in some areas, developed into a firestorm, though not one as fierce as that experienced in Hamburg. The shell-shocked inhabitants emerged from their shelters to find their city devastated and unrecognisable, and, after 3,600 fires had been dealt with, it would be established eventually that more than 4,300 apartment blocks containing 53,000 dwelling units had been destroyed or damaged, leaving up to 120,000 people without homes, and in excess of six thousand others killed. 155 industrial buildings had also been destroyed or severely damaged, along with numerous schools, hospitals, churches and public buildings. This massively successful operation was achieved at a high cost of forty-three bombers, twenty-five of them Halifaxes, but 619 Squadron came through unscathed and F/Sgt Smith and crew claimed a FW190 as destroyed.

During the course of the month, the squadron participated in nine operations and dispatched eighty-seven sorties for the loss of four Lancasters, three crews and a rear gunner.

November 1943

November brought with it the long, dark, cloudy nights, which enabled Harris to return to his main theme, the destruction of Germany's capital city. The next four months would bring the bloodiest, hardest-fought air battles between Bomber Command and the Luftwaffe Nachtjagd, and test the crews to the limit of their endurance. In a minute to Churchill on the 3rd, Harris stated, that with the participation of the American 8th Air Force, he could "wreck Berlin from end to end". He estimated that the campaign would cost the two forces between four and five hundred aircraft, but that it would cost Germany the war. This would remove the need for the kind of bloody, expensive and protracted land campaign, which he had personally witnessed during the Great War, and had prompted him to "get into the air" at the earliest opportunity. It should be remembered that this was the first time in the history of air warfare, that the means had existed to prove the theory, that an enemy could be defeated by bombing alone. It is only in the light of more recent experiences, that we have learned of the need, in a conventional conflict at least, to occupy the enemy's territory to secure submission. The Americans, however, were committed to victory on land, where film cameras could capture the glory, and would not accompany Harris to Berlin.

Düsseldorf was selected to open the month's operational account that very night, and, no doubt, while the Prime Minister was digesting Harris's epistle, a force of 589 Lancasters and Halifaxes was being prepared for action. 5 Group's contribution amounted to 147 Lancasters, of which fifteen represented 619 Squadron, and they were each loaded with a cookie and up to eighteen SBCs of various incendiaries before taking off between 16.48 and 17.25 with W/C Abercromby and S/L Churcher the senior pilots on duty. After climbing out, they joined the bomber stream over the North Sea, and approached the south-western Ruhr after flying out over Belgium and on through the concentration of fifty to sixty searchlights in the Mönchengladbach-Cologne corridor, some fifteen miles from the target. They encountered small patches of cloud and smoke from the early fires drifting across the target at 12,000 feet, despite which, the visibility remained generally good, and the Path Finders employed both sky and ground markers to good effect to identify the aiming point in the city centre. Bombing took place by the 619 Squadron crews on red and green TIs and skymarkers from 20,000 to 22,000 feet between 19.43 and 19.59, and fires were observed to be developing on both sides of the Rhine with black smoke rising through 6,000 feet as they turned away. Eighteen aircraft failed to return, and, unusually, eleven were Lancasters and only seven Halifaxes. It was on this night, that 61 Squadron's F/L Bill Reid earned the award of a Victoria Cross for pressing on to bomb the target after his Lancaster was severely damaged, and a number of his crew either killed or wounded. Post-raid reconnaissance revealed that central and southern districts had sustained widespread damage to industry and housing, but no report came out of Düsseldorf to provide detail.

The only serious activity for 619 Squadron thereafter, until the resumption of the Berlin campaign, was as part of a 5 and 8 Group force of 313 Lancasters, which was sent to destroy railway yards at Modane, situated in the foothills of the Alps in south-eastern France on the night of the 10/11th. 5 Group supported the operation with 136 Lancasters, of which the thirteen representing 619 Squadron departed Woodhall Spa between 20.50 and 21.20 with F/Ls Bell, Sandison and Tomlin the senior pilots on duty and "Nick" Knilans going to war for the final time as an RAF pilot officer. Ahead of them lay an outward flight of more than 650 miles, but F/O Morrison and crew were still over Cambridgeshire when a port-inner engine issue persuaded them to turn back, while F/L Bell and crew had managed to reach a position some fifteen miles south-east of Caen before their port-inner engine let them down also. The others completed the outward leg in around four-and-a-quarter hours to be rewarded by the presence of a full moon shining brightly from a cloudless sky. They pinpointed on Lake Bissorte, from where they carried out a time-and-distance run to the target, which they identified visually and by red and green TIs, before bombing from 15,000 to 15,500 feet between 01.00 and 01.13. The attack seemed to be concentrated around the markers, and fires appeared to be taking hold, while a large explosion was observed at 01.13. Returning crews were fairly confident in the quality of their night's efforts, and two hundred bombing photos revealed extensive damage to track and installations within one mile of the aiming point, and not a single aircraft had been lost.

Undaunted by the American response to his invitation to join the Berlin party, Harris would return there alone, and the rocky road to the capital was re-joined by an all-Lancaster heavy force on the night of the 18/19th, while a predominantly Halifax and Stirling contingent of 395 aircraft acted as a diversion by raiding Mannheim and Ludwigshafen three hundred miles to the south-west. The Berlin-bound crews would benefit from four Mosquitos dropping dummy fighter flares, while other Mosquitos carried out a spoof raid on Frankfurt to protect the Mannheim force. The two forces would cross the enemy coast simultaneously some 250 miles apart to confuse the enemy night-fighter controllers, and the route chosen for the Berlin brigade was via the Frisian island of Texel to a point north of Hannover, and thence to the target to pass over its centre on an east-north-easterly heading. After bombing they would return south of Berlin and Cologne, before crossing central Belgium to gain the English Channel via the French coast. An innovation for this operation was a shortening of the bomber stream to reduce the time over the target to sixteen minutes. When the first Thousand Bomber raid had taken place in May 1942, with an unprecedented twelve aircraft per minute crossing the aiming point, there had been considered to be a high risk of collisions. The number had since been increased to sixteen per minute, with large raids lasting up to forty-five minutes, but, on this night, twenty-seven aircraft per minute were to pass over the aiming point.

619 Squadron made ready a record nineteen Lancasters as part of a 5 Group force of 182, and dispatched them from Woodhall Spa between 16.58 and 17.29 with W/C Abercromby, S/L Churcher and the newly promoted S/L Aytoun the senior pilots on duty. After climbing out, they set course for the North Sea via the East Anglian coast, but F/O McGilvray and crew were still over Cambridgeshire when the rear turret became unserviceable and brought their sortie to an end. The others continued the outward leg to Germany's capital over a blanket of cloud covering the whole of northern Germany, and were grateful for the red spotfire route marker dropped by the

Path Finders north-east of Hannover, which confirmed that they were on track. The horizontal visibility was described as good, despite the absence of a moon, and the cloud persisted all the way to the target with tops at 6,000 feet. The underside was illuminated by searchlights as the Path Finder red and green skymarkers were delivered by H2S to drift down over the aiming point. The 619 Squadron participants mostly delivered their loads from 20,000 to 24,000 feet between 21.00 and 21.18, but F/O Mears and crew let their load go over the defences at Stendal from 17,000 feet at 20.47, after their starboard-outer engine had been damaged by flak. F/Sgt Olsen and crew lost their port-outer engine to flak and bombed on e.t.a at 21.08 from 16,000 feet, which was the best they could achieve on three engines. It was not possible to accurately assess the conduct of the raid, and those returning home had nothing useful to pass on to the Intelligence Section at debriefing, most considering the bombing to have been scattered and probably ineffective. Local sources confirmed that there had been no concentration and reported the destruction of 169 houses and a number of industrial units, with many more damaged to some extent. The diversion at Mannheim was deemed to have been successful in its purpose, and caused some useful industrial damage, most seriously to the Daimler-Benz motor factory, which suffered a 90% loss of production for an unknown period. In addition to this, more than three hundred buildings were destroyed at a cost of twenty-three aircraft, while the losses from Berlin were encouragingly low at just nine.

The Lancasters stayed at home on the 19th, while 3, 4, 6 and 8 Groups combined to put 170 Halifaxes, eighty-six Stirlings and 10 Mosquitos into the air for a raid on the Ruhr city of Leverkusen. They were greeted in the target area by ten-tenths cloud and an absence of marking, which was caused by equipment failure among the Oboe Mosquitos. A few green TIs were spotted some five to ten miles to the north-west of the target during the approach, but the crews were left to establish their positions on the basis of their own H2S, which, over a region as densely built-up as the Ruhr, was a challenge. As a result, the operation was a complete failure, which sprayed bombs over twenty-seven towns in the region, mostly to the north of Leverkusen.

Harris called for a maximum effort on Berlin on the 22nd, and 764 aircraft were made available, of which sixteen of 5 Group's 166 Lancasters were provided by 619 Squadron. They departed Woodhall Spa between 16.43 and 17.18 with S/L Aytoun the senior pilot on duty, and, after climbing out, they rendezvoused with the rest of the bomber stream to adopt an outward route similar to that employed by the all-Lancaster force four nights earlier. This took them from Texel to a point north-west of Hannover, where a slight dogleg to port put them on a due-easterly heading directly to the target. Unlike the previous raid, however, rather than the circuitous return south of Cologne and out over the French coast, they would come home via a reciprocal route. This was based on a forecast of low cloud and fog over Germany, which would inhibit the night-fighter effort, while broken, medium-level cloud over Berlin would facilitate ground marking. An additional bonus was the availability to the Path Finders of five new H2S Mk III sets, while a new record of thirty-four aircraft per minute passing over the aiming point would be achieved by abandoning the long-standing practice of allocating aircraft types to specific waves. On this night, aircraft of all types would be spread through the bomber stream, and this was bad news for the Stirlings, which, by the very nature of their design, would be below the Lancaster and Halifax elements, and in danger of being hit by friendly bombs.

On arrival at the target, the Path Finders discovered that the meteorological forecast had been inaccurate, and that the city was hidden under a blanket of ten-tenths cloud with tops at around 12,000 feet. This meant that ground marking would be largely ineffective, and that the least reliable Wanganui (skymarking) method would have to be employed. Crews ran into intense predicted flak and a mass of searchlights as they began their bombing runs, and those from 619 Squadron aimed at red and green TIs and release-point flares from 18,500 to 21,700 feet between 20.07 and 20.25. The glow of fires was observed beneath the clouds, and a very large explosion lit up the sky at 20.10. The impression was of a successful operation, but an assessment through the clouds was impossible. Post-raid reconnaissance and local reports confirmed that this attack on Berlin had been the most effective of the war to date, and had caused a swathe of destruction from the city centre through the western residential districts of Tiergarten and Charlottenburg as far as the suburb town of Spandau. A number of firestorm areas were reported, and the catalogue of destruction included three thousand houses and twenty-three industrial premises. Many thousands more sustained varying degrees of damage, costing 175,000 people their homes and an estimated two thousand their lives, and, by daylight on the 23rd, the smoke had risen to almost 19,000 feet.

Twenty-six aircraft failed to return, eleven Lancasters, ten Halifaxes, and five Stirlings, which amounted to a loss-rate among the types respectively of 2.3%, 4.2% and 10.0%. This proved to be the final straw for Harris as far as the Stirling was concerned, which, because of its short wing design, was restricted to a low service ceiling, and by the configuration of its bomb bay to small calibre bombs. Unlike the Lancaster and Halifax, it lacked development potential, and was immediately withdrawn from future operations over Germany. It would still have an important role to play on secondary duties, however, such as bombing over occupied territory, mining, and, in 1944, it would replace the Halifax to become the aircraft of choice for the two SOE squadrons, 138 and 161, at Tempsford. Many of those released from Bomber Command service would find their way also to 38 Group, where they would give valuable service as transports and glider-tugs for airborne landings.

A heavy force of 365 Lancasters and ten Halifaxes was made ready with some difficulty on the 23rd for a return to Berlin. Back-to-back long-range operations put a strain on those charged with the responsibility of getting the aircraft off the ground, and the Ludford Magna armourers were unable to load all nineteen 101 Squadron Lancasters with the intended weight of bombs, sending them off 2,000lb short. 5 Group detailed 141 Lancasters, of which the sixteen belonging to 619 Squadron were each loaded with a cookie and SBCs of incendiaries and departed Woodhall Spa between 16.52 and 17.27 with S/L Churcher the senior pilot on duty. The effects of back-to-back long-range operations soon began to manifest themselves, and the crews of P/Os Vickerstaffe and Rumble turned back with engine issues after reaching the mid-point of the North Sea crossing. These were among eighteen "boomerangs" from 5 Group and forty-six from the force as a whole, many of whom might have pressed on in other circumstances. Another sign of malcontent was the dumping of bombs over the North Sea by crews intending to push on to the target, but wanting to gain more height. It involved largely those from 1 Group, who were shedding their cookies in protest at their A-O-C's policy of loading each Lancaster to its maximum all-up weight at the expense of altitude. The slogan "H-E-I-G-H-T spells safety" could be found on the walls of most bomber station briefing rooms at the time.

The target was reached by way of the same route adopted on the previous night, and was found to be covered by ten-tenths cloud with tops at between 10,000 and 15,000 feet. Guided by the glow of fires still burning beneath the clouds from the night before, and the presence of red and green TIs, the 619 Squadron crews bombed from 18,500 to 21,000 feet between 20.02 and 20.15 to contribute to another stunning blow. Returning crews described a column of smoke reaching 20,000 feet, and the glow of fires visible again from the Hannover area some 150 miles from the target. It was on this night that fake broadcasts from England caused annoyance to the night-fighter crews by ordering them to land because of fog over their bases, despite which, they still had a major hand in the bringing-down of twenty Lancasters, five of them from 5 Group. Post-raid reconnaissance and local reports confirmed that this operation had destroyed a further two thousand buildings and killed around fifteen hundred people.

A new Australian squadron was formed on the 25th at Waddington, when 467 Squadron's C Flight became the nucleus of 463 Squadron. After a three-night rest for most of the Lancaster crews, 443 of them were briefed on the 26th for a return to the "Big City" for the fourth attack on it since the resumption of the campaign. 5 Group detailed 161 Lancasters, sixteen of them made ready by 619 Squadron, and they departed Woodhall Spa between 17.08 and 17.32 with F/Ls Bell, Rayment and Tomlin the senior pilots on duty. A diversionary raid on Stuttgart by a predominantly Halifax force followed the same route as those bound for Berlin, which involved an outward leg across the French coast and Belgium to a point north of Frankfurt, where they separated. An indication of the beneficial effects of the three-day lay-off was a 44% reduction in early returns by 5 Group crews compared with the previous Berlin raid, but P/O Thompson was notified of an overheating starboard-inner engine as he approached the south coast, and, with Beachy Head lighthouse below, headed for the jettison area. The rest of the 619 Squadron element pressed on to find Berlin under clear skies, "Nick" Knilans now wearing the uniform of a USAAF lieutenant. He had been invited to transfer out of the RAF, but expressed a desire to complete his tour, and would just have to put up with the large increase in pay and benefits. It had not been an uneventful outward flight for this crew, after they were attacked by two night-fighters when some twenty miles north-east of Frankfurt, one of which, a Ju88, paid for its affrontery by being shot down, while the other, a Me110, sustained damage. The Lancaster lost an engine, but Lt Knilans was determined to reach the target even if it had to be at a much-reduced altitude. Despite the favourable conditions, the Path Finders overshot the city centre aiming point by six or seven miles, and marked an area well to the north-west, which happened to contain many war-industry factories. Lt Knilans apart, the 619 Squadron crews bombed on red and green TIs from 19,500 and 21,500 feet between 21.17 and 21.27, and returning crews spoke of a mass of fires and thick smoke rising to 15,000 feet. Lt Knilans and crew came home on three engines to land at Spilsby and report bombing from 13,000 feet at 21.23. P/O Mears had been attempting to land at the 4 Group station at Elvington in south Yorkshire, but DV336 crashed just to the south at 02.00, and all on board were killed. Thirty-two minutes later, EE111 was abandoned by F/L Bell and crew over the Humber estuary, and they all arrived safely on the ground. Within minutes, EE168 had crashed and caught fire at Common Fal, just to the east of Hutton Cranswick airfield, also in Yorkshire, but, again, the occupants, F/L Tomlin and crew, emerged more or less unscathed. DV381 did not return with the crew of F/L Rayment, and it was assumed that they had gone down over the sea. The bodies of the pilot and flight engineer were recovered for burial at Becklingen War Cemetery in north-western Germany, which suggested that they had remained with the aircraft while the rest of the crew baled out, and that all five had come down in the sea. At debriefing, a number of crews commented on a chaotic situation over Beachy Head on the way out, where some sections of the bomber stream were orbiting to shed time, while others were arriving to begin the next leg, all at the same altitude. It was learned later that thirty-eight war-industry factories had been destroyed in Berlin and many others damaged, in return for the loss of twenty-eight Lancasters, many of which had fallen victim to night-fighters on the return flight.

These last three operations against Berlin undoubtedly represented the best phase of the entire campaign, and, according to local reports, the total death toll on the ground resulting from them amounted to 4,330 people, while the destruction of 8,700 apartment buildings containing more than 104,500 flats, and damage to several times that number, robbed 450,000 residents of their homes for varying lengths of time. However, Berlin was not Hamburg, where narrow streets had aided the spread of fire. Berlin was a modern city of concrete and steel with wide thoroughfares and open spaces to create natural firebreaks, and each building destroyed added to these, so that the campaign would become a bitter struggle of ever decreasing returns. During the course of the month the squadron took part in six operations and dispatched ninety-five sorties for the loss of four Lancasters and two crews.

December 1943

Berlin would continue to be the dominant theme during December, and, as November had ended, so December would begin. A heavy force of 443 aircraft stood ready to take off in the late afternoon of the 2nd, all but fifteen of them Lancasters, after the main force Halifax element had been withdrawn because of fog over their Yorkshire stations. 5 Group contributed 145 Lancasters, of which ten represented 619 Squadron, and they departed Woodhall Spa between 16.39 and 16.49 with W/C Abercromby the senior pilot on duty. Accompanying the commanding officer and crew to Berlin was the American war correspondent, Ed Morrow, whose nightly radio reports home, particularly during the London Blitz of 1940, had become legendary. After climbing out, they headed for the Lincolnshire coast to rendezvous over the North Sea with the rest of the force for a straight-out-straight-in route across Holland and northern Germany with no feints or diversions. First, however, the crews had to negotiate a towering front of ice-bearing cloud over the North Sea, which would contribute to a 10% rate of early returns. The remainder made it through the challenging conditions to reach the target area, although mostly south of track after variable winds had thrown them off course and dispersed the bomber stream. They also had to contend with large numbers of enemy night-fighters that would harass the bomber stream all the way to the target, after the controller had been able correctly to predict it. The Path Finders were using H2S to establish their position at Stendal, but had strayed some fifteen miles south of track and mistakenly used the town of Genthin as their reference for the run-in. The 619 Squadron crews found good visibility, and were drawn by release-point flares to the aiming point, where they encountered a thin layer of two to three-tenths cloud at around 5,000 feet, but up to nine-tenths between 10,000 and 12,000 feet, which the searchlights were able to pierce. They bombed on skymarkers and red and green TIs, and, where possible, ground detail like burning streets, from 20,000 to 20,500 feet between 20.21 and 20.35. They reported scattered fires and a number of large explosions, and some claimed the glow to be visible from 120 miles into the homeward leg. It was a bad night for the bomber force, which lost forty aircraft, mostly in the target area and on the way home, and among them were two from 619 Squadron. EE170 was hit by flak when north of Magdeburg, and erupted in flames, and, before the crew of P/O Ward had time to save themselves, it exploded, flinging the flight engineer into space. He landed safely, albeit with a number of broken ribs, and was taken into captivity. JA847 crashed into the Tegel, a lake to the north-west of the capital, killing F/O Bowyer RCAF and his two gunners, and delivering the four survivors into enemy hands. The remaining 619 Squadron crews landed at Coningsby, where the debriefing was attended by AVM Cochrane, G/Cs Patch and Evans-Evans and W/C Jeudwine, who was about to be appointed successor to W/C Abercromby as commanding officer of 619 Squadron. The bombing photographs suggested that the raid had been only partially successful, causing useful damage in industrial districts in the west and east, but scattering the main weight of bombs over the southern districts and outlying communities to the south.

Having been spared by the weather from experiencing an effective visitation from the Command in October, and exploiting the enemy expectation that Berlin would be the target again, Leipzig found itself at the end of the red tape on briefing-room wall-maps from County Durham to Cambridgeshire on the 3rd. A force of 527 aircraft was made ready, which included 103 Lancasters of 5 Group, seven of them belonging to 619 Squadron, which had flown over to Coningsby for the briefing. It was then that they learned of the imminent departure to 83 Squadron of W/C Abercromby to succeed G/C Searby as commanding officer, after the latter had stepped in as a stop-gap following the loss of W/C Ray Hilton over Berlin on the 23rd. The 619 Squadron element departed Coningsby between 00.14 and 00.23 with S/L Aytoun the senior pilot on duty and W/C Jeudwine accompanying him as second pilot. Lt Knilans and crew turned back when ten miles out from Great Yarmouth after the artificial horizon failed, while F/O Vickerstaffe and crew had crossed the Dutch coast and were east of Amsterdam when the port-inner engine caught fire. The others remained with the bomber stream as it headed for Berlin as a feint, passing north of Hannover and Braunschweig with ten-tenths cloud beneath them and an hour's journey to Leipzig still ahead of them. Then, as they turned towards the south-east, the Mosquito element continued on to carry out a diversion at the capital. Night-fighters had already infiltrated the stream at the Dutch coast, but the feint had the desired effect, and few night-fighters were encountered in the target area, where two layers of ten-tenths cloud prevailed with tops at around 7,000 and 15,000 feet. The Path Finders marked by H2S with green skymarkers, and the 619 Squadron crews bombed on these within a few hundred feet of each other from 20,400 to 20,700 feet between 04.08 and 04.15, observing explosions and a strong glow beneath the clouds. The emergence through the cloud tops of black smoke suggested that an accurate and concentrated attack had taken place, and the smoke and glow remained visible for 150 miles into the return journey south-east towards the French frontier. Had many aircraft not then strayed into the Frankfurt defence zone, the losses may have been fewer, but twenty-four aircraft failed to return, fifteen of them Halifaxes. Some 5 Group crews reported that they had observed many bombs splashing into the North Sea on the way out. Local reports confirmed this as a highly successful operation, which had hit residential and industrial areas, and was the most destructive raid visited upon this eastern city during the war. Sadly, for the Command, it would take its revenge in time.

W/C John Jeudwine was appointed commanding officer on the 4th and brought with him a wealth of operational experience and a record of great determination. Born in 1913, he attended Cranwell, where he excelled as an athlete and graduated as a pilot officer in July 1934. He joined 12 Squadron and spent a year flying Hawker Hart biplanes, before transferring to the Fleet Air Arm in 1935 for a tour on Fairey Seals and Swordfish on board the carrier HMS *Glorious*. By June 1939, he had attained the rank of squadron leader, and served for two years in a signals intelligence unit in Egypt until his promotion to wing commander rank and appointment to command 84 Squadron, a Blenheim unit at the end of 1941. He took the squadron from Egypt to the Far East in January 1942, but the base was captured by the Japanese in March and it became necessary to evacuate the region. In the absence of transport, Jeudwine and eleven other British and Australian airmen found a lifeboat on a derelict ship, and sailed in it from Java towards Australia, before being rescued by US Navy flying boats after forty-seven days at sea. For his leadership he was made an OBE, and returned to Egypt in July 1942 to command 55 Squadron, completing twenty-five sorties on Baltimore aircraft before being ordered to rest in a staff job. Typical of men of his ilk, he became restless and wangled his way into ferry and transport flying, until arriving back in the UK and learning the ways of the Lancaster at 1654 Conversion Unit, where he acquired a crew to accompany him on the next stage of his operational career.

Fog settled over Lincolnshire for much of the remainder of the month and restricted the crews to ground activities for long periods, during which, lectures and sporting events occupied their time and kept them out of trouble. On the 8th, Lt Knilans was awarded an immediate DSO, which would be a source of great pride to him. Meanwhile, over at Wyton in Cambridgeshire, W/C Abercromby did not arrive physically until the 10th, following a Path Finder induction course at Upwood. The 83 Squadron ORB extolled his virtues as an officer held in high esteem in 5 Group, and added, "we consider ourselves very lucky to have a man of his vast flying experience under all sorts of operational conditions, and also gained through many hours of practical aviation, to lead us." During the afternoon of the 10th, the crews gathered in the briefing room for a discussion on tactics with their new commanding officer, whose views reflected those of 5 Group's A-O-C, AVM Cochrane, in being aggressive with regard to aircraft defence. 5 Group crews had been ordered to fly straight and level to provide a stable platform for the gunners to open fire as soon as a night-fighter came into range. AVM Bennett of 8 Group took a different approach, and ordered his pilots to weave, to allow the gunners to search blind spots below the Lancasters, where night-fighters might hide. He also believed that it was prudent not to draw attention to oneself by opening fire, if not under attack. The squadron's lower-than-average loss rate during the second half of the year would seem to support Bennett's contention, and the discussion between W/C Abercromby and the crews centred upon these matters. The author of the ORB went out of his way to report the outcome in as diplomatic a fashion as possible. "Some excellent points were brought up in favour of both. As the policy of the squadron up to the present has been in favour of corkscrewing, the instinctive feeling among the crews was for its continuance. Unfortunately, we were unable to bring the discussion to a satisfactory conclusion owing to a) the very excellent points, of which both were about equal, and b) our old enemy, TIME." What the author might like to have recorded was, that Abercromby banned weaving, and, thereby, ruffled a few feathers, most notably and appropriately those of F/L Chick, whose flying he apparently described as cowardly. Chick refused to abandon a policy that had seen him through more than forty operations, and predicted that Abercromby would survive no more than three weeks if he continued to fly straight and level. It is highly likely, although unrecorded, that the other crews shared Chick's opinion, and Chick would complete his tour on forty-eight operations shortly afterwards, having seen his prophecy fulfilled.

Fog and frost continued to impact on the flying programme, but the news of an operation on the 16th was greeted enthusiastically at Woodhall Spa, particularly when Berlin was posted as the target. Fifteen 619 Squadron crews attended to learn that it was to be an all-Lancaster affair, involving 483 of the type and ten Mosquitos, for what would be the sixth attack on the city since the resumption of the campaign. 5 Group put up 165 aircraft, the 619 Squadron element departing Woodhall Spa between 16.19 and 16.44 with F/L Sandison and Tomlin the senior pilots on duty. They were to cross the Dutch coast in the region of Castricum-aan-Zee, and then head due east all the way to the target with no deviations. A three-quarter moon would rise during the long return leg over the Baltic and Denmark, but it was hoped that the very early take-off and the expectation of fog to keep the enemy night-fighters on the ground would reduce the risk of interception. There were no early returns to Woodhall Spa, and, it seems that the 619 Squadron contingent avoided contact with the night-fighters sent to meet the bomber stream at the Dutch coast. However, when approaching Berlin, EE150 was badly shot-up and lost the power from its port-outer engine, despite which, F/L Tomlin pressed on to find the target area obscured by ten-tenths cloud with tops at around 5,000 feet. Berlin could be identified by red and green skymarkers, which he and his crew aimed at from 14,500 feet at 20.09, while the rest of the squadron bombed from 15,000 to 22,000 feet between 20.01 and 20.10. The return over Denmark passed largely without major incident, but the greatest difficulties awaited the 1, 6 and 8 Group crews as they arrived home to find their airfields covered by a blanket of dense fog. With little reserves of fuel, the tired crews began a frantic search to find somewhere to land, stumbling blindly through the murk to catch a glimpse of the ground. For many, this proved fatal, while others gave up any hope of landing, and abandoned their aircraft. Twenty-nine Lancasters and a mine-laying Stirling were thus lost, and more than 150 airmen killed in these most tragic of circumstances. On return to the Woodhall Spa circuit, EE150's port-outer engine caught fire and could not be feathered because of the loss of electrical connections. F/L Tomlin carried out a controlled crash-landing near the outer marker, and there were no crew casualties. Twenty-five Lancasters failed to return from the raid, many of which were accounted for by night-fighters over Holland and Germany while outbound, but the loss of JA867 occurred to the north-east of Berlin at Finow near Eberswalde, and there were no survivors from the crew of P/O Loney RCAF. At debriefing, crews reported the glow of fires, while others saw nothing through the cloud, and it was a local report that confirmed a moderately effective raid, which had fallen predominantly onto central and eastern districts, where housing had suffered most.

This was not the only operation to take place during the evening, and one of those of a more minor nature was to have great significance for the future of the Command, 5 Group and the Path Finders. Two flying bomb sites in the Pas-de-Calais, at Tilley-le-Haut and Flixecourt, were attacked by small forces, the former by 3 Group Stirlings, and the latter by nine Lancasters of 617 Squadron under W/C Leonard Cheshire. The marking was carried out by Oboe Mosquitos at both locations, although it was by just a single aircraft at the latter. Neither operation was a success, after the markers missed the aiming points by a few hundred yards, and this demonstrated the shortcomings of the Oboe system. Whilst it was ideal for marking an urban target, where there was a large margin for error, it was too imprecise for use against a small target like a flying bomb site or an individual building. This was precisely the kind of target to which 617 Squadron was to be assigned for the remainder of the war, and it was frustrating for Cheshire and his crews to have plastered the markers, only for the target to escape damage. A similar disappointment would take place at the end of the month at the same flying bomb site, and this set minds working at 617 Squadron.

A three-day stand-down allowed the crews to recover from the Berlin operation, before all stations were notified on the 20th of an operation that night to Frankfurt, for which a force of 390 Lancasters and 257 Halifaxes was assembled. 5 Group made ready 168 Lancasters, and, at Woodhall Spa, thirteen 619 Squadron Lancasters were loaded with the requisite amount of fuel and a cookie and sixteen SBCs of incendiaries each, and dispatched between 16.58 and 17.14 with W/C Jeudwine the senior pilot on duty for the first time. F/O Thompson's port-outer engine burst into flames immediately after take-off, and he headed directly for the jettison area to dump his incendiaries and a proportion of the fuel load. He could not gain sufficient height to jettison the cookie, but landed safely with it still aboard. After climbing out, the others set course for Southwold and the North Sea-crossing to the Scheldt estuary, before passing north of Antwerp and flying the length of Belgium to the German frontier north of Luxembourg. While the main operation was in progress, forty-four Lancasters and ten Mosquitos of 1 and 8 Groups were to carry out a diversion at Mannheim, some forty miles to the south of the primary target. The German night-fighter controller had picked up transmissions from the bomber stream as soon as it left the English coast, and was able to track it all the way to the target and vector his fighters into position. Many combats took place during the outward flight, and the diversion failed to draw fighters away from the main action. The problems continued at the primary target, where the forecast clear skies failed to materialize, and the crews were greeted by four to nine-tenths cloud at between 5,000 and 10,000 feet. This allowed some of them to pick out ground features, while others fixed their positions by H2S, if so equipped, and the main force Lancaster crews simply waited for TIs on e.t.a. The Path Finders had prepared a ground-marking plan in expectation of good vertical visibility, and dropped red, green and yellow TIs, while the Germans lit a decoy fire-site five miles to the south-east of the city. Some crews described the marking as late and erratic, and those from 619 Squadron bombed on red and green TIs from 19,400 to 21,500 feet between 19.42 and 19.49. Most thought the attack to be scattered in the early stages, becoming more concentrated as it progressed, and many commented on the new cookies detonating with a brighter flash than the old ones. All of the 619 Squadron Lancasters returned to Woodhall Spa, having contributed to a moderately successful raid, and at least one crew reported the glow of fires remaining visible for 150 miles into the return journey. Any success was achieved largely as the result of the creep-back from the decoy site falling across the suburbs of Offenbach and Sachsenhausen, situated on the southern bank of the River Main. 466 houses were destroyed and more than nineteen hundred seriously damaged, despite which, the operation fell well short of its aims, and the loss of forty-one aircraft was a high price to pay. The Halifaxes suffered heavily, losing twenty-seven of their number, a loss-rate of 10.5%, compared with the Lancasters' 3.6%.

Just two more operations remained before the year ended, and both were to be directed at Germany's capital city. The first was posted on the 23rd, and would involve an all-Lancaster heavy force with seven 35 (Madras Presidency) Squadron Halifaxes among the Path Finder element, and eight Mosquitos to provide a diversion. 619 Squadron had been briefed to take part and had carried out night flying tests (NFTs), but the take-off time was pushed back, and during the wait, hoarfrost built up on the aircraft, and the squadron's participation was scrubbed. This left 130 Lancasters of 5 Group to launch themselves into the cold night air after midnight, before adopting a somewhat circuitous route that took the bomber stream in a south-easterly direction to the Scheldt estuary, before hugging the Belgian/Dutch frontier to cross into Germany south of Aachen, as if threatening Frankfurt. When a point was reached south of Leipzig, the route turned sharply towards the north and Berlin, while the Mosquito feint threatened Leipzig as the target. The vanguard of the bomber stream reached the target to find it enveloped in up to eight-tenths cloud at between 5,000 and 10,000 feet, which might not have been critical had the Path Finders not suffered an unusually high failure rate of their H2S equipment, which resulted in scattered and sparse sky-marking. Well-concentrated fires and at least four large explosions were reported, one described as being orange and red and lasting for thirty seconds. A relatively modest sixteen Lancasters failed to return, six of them from 5 Group, and a local report named the south-eastern suburbs of Köpenick and Treptow as sustaining the most damage, with 287 houses and other buildings suffering complete destruction.

The fifth wartime Christmas was observed like all of the others according to RAF tradition, and the station returned to normal on the 27th. The "Big City" was posted as the target again on the 29th, for what, for the Lancaster operators, would be the first of three raids on it in five nights spanning the turn of the year. A force of 712 aircraft included 163 Lancasters of 5 Group, of which fourteen represented 619 Squadron, and they departed Woodhall Spa between 16.39 and 17.04 with W/C Jeudwine and S/L Aytoun the senior pilots on duty. It was from this juncture that the intolerable strain on the crews of successive long-range flights in difficult weather conditions would begin to become manifest in some squadrons through the rate of early returns, which, on this night, reached forty-five or 6.3%. The bomber stream was routed out over the Dutch Frisian islands pointing directly for Leipzig, and, having reached a point just to the north of that city, was to turn to the north towards Berlin, while Mosquitos carried out spoof raids on Leipzig and Magdeburg. 619 Squadron was exempt from early returns, and its crews reached the target area to find ten-tenths cloud with tops at anywhere between 7,000 and 18,000 feet. Red and green Path Finder release-point flares could be seen hanging over the city, upon which they aimed their bombs from 18,500 to 24,000 feet between 20.09 and 20.32. At debriefing, crews reported a considerable red glow beneath the clouds, which remained visible for a hundred miles, and gave the impression of a concentrated and successful assault. This was not entirely borne out by local reports, which revealed that the main weight of the raid had fallen onto southern and south-eastern districts, and, also, into outlying communities to the east. 388 buildings were destroyed, although none of significance, and ten thousand people were bombed out of their homes. Eleven Lancasters and nine Halifaxes failed to return, a loss-rate of 2.4% for the former and 3.5% for the latter.

During the course of the month the squadron participated in five operations and dispatched fifty-nine sorties for the loss of four Lancasters and three crews. It had been a testing end to a year which had brought major successes and advances in tactics, but it had also been a year of high losses, particularly among the Stirling and Halifax squadrons. While Window had been an instant success, it had also caused the Luftwaffe to rethink and reorganise, and the night-fighter force which emerged from the ruins of the old system, was a leaner, more efficient and altogether more lethal beast than that of before. As far as the crews of Bomber Command were concerned, the New Year offered the same fare as the old one, and few would view that with relish.

ACM Sir Arthur Harris, Commander in Chief of Royal Air Force Bomber Command, seated at his desk at Bomber Command HQ, High Wycombe.

Anthéor Viaduct targeted by 619 Squadron in company with 617 Squadron in September 1943.

Present day Anthéor Viaduct

F/Sgt T P Murphy crew killed on Cologne raid on 29th of June 1943

P/O Robert 'Bob' Knights

F/Sgt Robert Edward Tofts
from P/O McCulloch crew.
Killed 1943 while raiding Oberhausen.

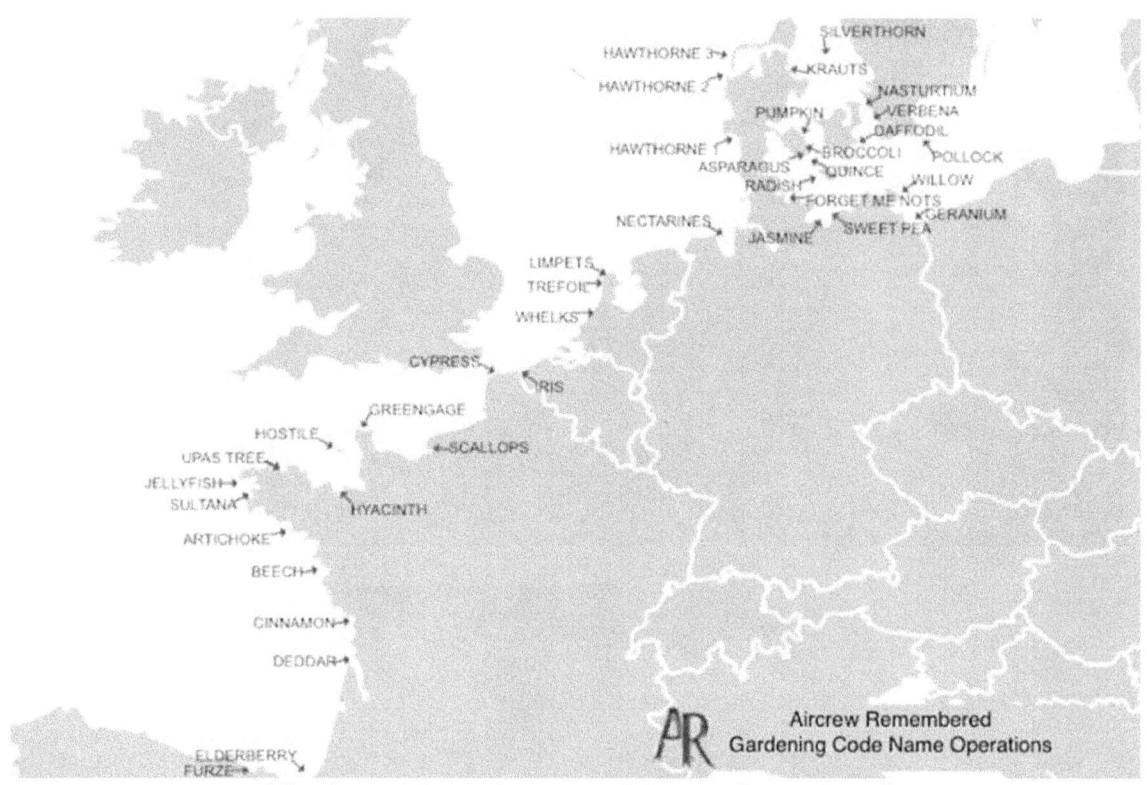

'Gardening' Areas (courtesy of Aircrew Remembered)

        Sgt G Dillnutt   *Possibly the Firth Crew*

Sgt George Dillnutt was serving as W/Op/AG on Lancaster EE114 PG-B on an operation to Leipzig. on the 20/21st of October 1943. It crashed at Langwedel killing all seven crew members. Crew: Sgt Douglas Demaine, Sgt George Walter Dillnutt, P/O Christopher Firth, Sgt Myrddin Jones, Sgt Alfred George Osborne, Sgt George Myron Weighell, W/OII Charles Notley Dawson Wright.

Penrhos North Wales, 15th of June 1943. Canadian Bomb Aimers in training.
Front: L-R: G Allen, W Baxter, J S Baldwin, R J Thompson.
Rear: G E Hexter, N A F MacKenzie, R W Baldwin, W C Thompson, D C McNie
G E Hexter DFM completed 1 tour with 619 Squadron and was wounded.

P/O Bob Knights and Crew

F/L E Dampier-Crossley
KIA 11th of August 1943.
(Crown copyright)

619 Squadron, Woodhall Spa, July 1943.
Lancaster ED981 PG-V. Missing from raid on Berlin, 23rd of August 1943. The crew pictured may be those lost with the aircraft. P/O D Coomber (PoW), Sgt G A Stamper (PoW), Sgt W H Cade (KIA) Sgt H R Snell (KIA) Sgt K R Wallace (KIA), Sgt A Castle (KIA) Sgt L Gardner (KIA)

P/O N A Gampe RAAF

Lt Hubert 'Nick' Knilans

17/18th of August 1943 Peenemünde Raid

Ruins of Peenemünde Research Facility

Ruins of Peenemünde Research Facility

F/Sgt L F English RNZAF.
KIA 18th of August 1943 on the
Peenemünde Raid

Gilbert Charles King
619 Squadron Rear Gunner

Hamburg ruins after the Firestorm raid.

619 Squadron. November 1943.
L-R: F/Sgt Ron Thompson (W/Op), F/L Antony Tomlin DFC & Bar (Pilot), Thomas Peatfield (Nav). J Simpkin.

Wartime Petwood Hotel, Woodhall Spa.

Present day Petwood Hotel

Crew of 619 Lancaster JB131. 20th of December 1943. Prior to Frankfurt raid.
L-R: F/Sgt Peter Derham (RG), Sgt Bill Hobbs (MUG), F/O Bob Knights (Pilot), Major Cotterell (War Correspondent), Sgt Ernie Twells (FE) Sgt Jock Rowan (W/Op), F/Sgt John Bell (BA), F/Sgt Bryant (Nav). Major Cotterell also flew on a daylight operation with the USAAF. He was killed at Arnhem while serving with the 1st Parachute Brigade Headquarters.

619 Squadron Lancaster LM418. December 1943. Piloted by Lt 'Nick' Knilans.

Lancaster named "Dumbo" PG-D of 619 Squadron RAF at Strubby, Winter 1943/44 with possibly the Gampe crew.

Lt Knilans and Crew

F/O Francis Victor Anderson of F/O D M Joss' Crew. KIA 2nd of October 1943.

P/O G B Loney   F/Sgt J Gray   F/O Max Gennis   Sgt Corbitt
All killed on the 16th of December 1943 together with F/O H A De Vries, Sgt L Banks and Sgt R F Dearden in Lancaster JA867 PG-X while raiding Berlin.

Buildings destroyed in Milan after the August 1943 bombings.

January 1944

The change of year was not destined to effect a change in the emphasis of operations, and this was, no doubt, a disappointment, not only to the hard-pressed crews of Bomber Command, but also to the beleaguered residents of Germany's capital city. Proud of their status as Berliners first and Germans second, they were a hardy breed, and just like their counterparts in London during the Blitz of 1940, they would bear their trials with fortitude and humour, and would not buckle under the constant assault from above. "You may break our walls," proclaimed banners in the streets, "but not out hearts", and the most popular song of the day, 'Nach jedem Dezember kommt immer ein Mai' (After every December comes always a May), was played endlessly over the airwaves, its sentiments hinting at a change in fortunes with the onset of spring. This was, to an extent, prophetic, as both camps would, indeed, have to endure throughout the remainder of the winter, before Berlin ceased to be the main focus of attention. Harris allowed the Berliners little time to enjoy New Year, and, as New Year's Day dawned, plans were already in hand to continue the onslaught. Before it ended, the first of 421 Lancasters, 161 representing 5 Group, would be taking off and heading eastwards to arrive over the city as the clock showed 03.00 hours on the 2nd.

Take-off had actually been delayed because of doubts over the weather, and this meant that insufficient hours of daylight remained to allow the planned outward route over Denmark and the Baltic. Instead, the bomber stream would adopt the previously used almost direct route across Holland and northern Germany, but return, as originally planned, more circuitously, passing east of Leipzig, before racing across Germany between the Ruhr and Frankfurt and traversing Belgium to reach the Channel near the French port of Boulogne. 619 Squadron's fourteen participants took off between 23.49 and 00.09 with S/L Churcher the senior pilot on duty and each Lancaster carrying a cookie and mix of 4lb and 30lb incendiaries. They climbed away to rendezvous with the rest of the force, which was gradually depleted by twenty-nine early returns, among them P/O Langford and crew, who turned back from a position over the North Sea some thirty miles east of Skegness after contending with three malfunctioning engines since take-off. 83 Squadron Lancaster, ND354, had crossed into Germany, and was passing the northern rim of Vechta, a town about thirty-five miles south-west of Bremen, at 03.00, when it was torn asunder by an explosion and fell in pieces about three miles further on. The flight engineer, Sgt Lewis, was thrown clear and survived as a PoW, but W/C Abercromby and the other occupants lost their lives. Were they, perhaps, the victims of his policy of flying straight and level? The rest of the bomber stream covered the four-hundred-mile leg from the Dutch coast to Berlin in under two hours without once catching a glimpse of the ground through the dense cloud, and it was no different at the target, which was completely obscured by a layer of ten-tenths cloud with tops in places as high as 19,000 feet. The Path Finders had to employ skymarking (Wanganui), which was somewhat scattered, and the 619 Squadron crews aimed for these parachute flares from 18,500 to 21,500 feet between 03.04 and 03.17. They observed the glow of fires and smoke rising through the cloud tops, and some crews witnessed a huge explosion at 03.07, which lit up the clouds for three seconds, but it was impossible to assess what was happening on the ground. It was established, ultimately, that the operation had been a failure, which had scattered bombs across the southern fringes of the city, causing only minor damage, while the main weight of the attack had fallen beyond the city boundaries into wooded and open country. The disappointment was compounded by the loss of twenty-eight Lancasters, although all from Woodhall Spa returned safely to offer their impressions.

During the course of the 2nd, a heavy force of 362 Lancasters and nine of the new Mk III Hercules-powered Halifaxes was made ready for a return to Berlin that night. There was snow on the ground, and many of the crews called to briefing were still tired from being late to bed following the almost-eight-hour round trip the night before. Some of these were in a mutinous frame of mind at being on the Order of Battle again so soon. 5 Group cancelled twenty-five of its intended contribution, leaving 119 to take part, ten of which belonged to 619 Squadron. The outward route crossed the Dutch coast near Castricum and took the bomber stream to a point south-east of Bremen, followed by a dogleg to the north-east and, finally, a ninety degree change of course to the south-east in the Parchim area to leave a ninety-mile run to the target. The 619 Squadron element departed Woodhall Spa between 23.25 and 23.51 with W/C Jeudwine the senior pilot on duty, and headed for the rendezvous, having to battle with the severe icing conditions that defeated many crews, while others abandoned their sorties because of minor problems that might have seen them carry on had they been fully rested. F/L McGilvray reached the Suffolk coast at Orfordness before turning back with an unserviceable rear turret. The route changes worked well to throw off the night-fighters, but they would congregate in the target area after the controller correctly identified the capital as the target forty minutes before zero-hour. Ten-tenths cloud with tops at 16,000 feet forced the bombing to take place on the red skymarkers with green stars or on the glow of fires, the 619 Squadron crews carrying out their attacks from 19,200 to 21,000 feet between 02.46 and 02.55. They reported smoke rising to 20,000 feet as they turned away, but it was not possible to make an accurate assessment of the outcome, and the impression was of an effective attack, when, in fact, it had been another failure. Bombs had been scattered across the city and destroyed just eighty-two houses for the loss of twenty-seven Lancasters, most of which had fallen victim to night-fighters in the target area. Two empty dispersals at Woodhall Spa should have been occupied by JB123 and LM423, the former crashing homebound near Wendeburg to the north-west of Braunschweig, with no survivors from the crew of F/O Heffernan RCAF. The latter was attacked by a night-fighter, also on the way home near Cleves (Kleve), and was partially abandoned from 21,000 feet, the three survivors from the crew of F/O Cox, the flight engineer, navigator and bomb-aimer, falling into enemy hands. As soon as it became clear that a crew was missing, a team from the Committee of Adjustment would descend upon their billet and remove all trace of their existence, leaving the bed and storage units ready for the next occupant.

After three trips there in five nights, Berlin would now be left to the Mosquitos of 8 Group until the final third of the month, allowing Harris to turn his attention on the 5th upon the Baltic port-city of Stettin, which had not been attacked in numbers since the previous April. It was to be another predominantly Lancaster affair, involving 348 of the type accompanied by ten Halifaxes, with a 5 Group contribution of 120 aircraft, a dozen of them provided by 619 Squadron. They took off from Woodhall Spa for the final time between 23.48 and 00.14 with F/L Sandison the senior pilot on duty, and, in contrast to the seventeen early returns by 5 Group crews during the last Berlin operation, only one came home early on this night, and those continuing on found themselves in thick cloud at cruising altitude, some struggling to find a clear lane even when as high as 23,000 feet. On the plus side, they all benefitted from a Mosquito diversion at Berlin, which kept the night-fighters off the scent. Stettin was found to be partially visible through five-tenths thin cloud with tops at around 10,000 feet, and crews were able to identify some ground features before focusing on H2S-laid flares and green TIs, which the 619 Squadron crews bombed from 19,500 to 21,000 feet between 03.45 and 04.00. At debriefing, the Intelligence Section was provided with accounts of a highly accurate and concentrated attack, which seemed to leave the entire city on fire. Fourteen Lancasters and two Halifaxes failed to return, and among them was ED977, 619 Squadron's oldest Lancaster with forty-seven sorties to its credit. It was now a smouldering wreck in the target area, from which the remains of the crew of F/O Day had been removed for burial. Post-raid reconnaissance and local reports confirmed heavy damage in central and western districts, where 504 houses and twenty industrial buildings had been destroyed, a further 1,148 houses and twenty-nine industrial buildings seriously damaged, and eight ships sunk in the harbour.

The tour of Lt Knilans and his crew with 619 Squadron came to an end on the 6th when they were posted to 617 Squadron. This did not require of them a physical move either from Woodhall Spa aerodrome or, in the case of the officers among them, their comfortable billets in the Petwood Hotel, as 617 Squadron was effectively posted to them. The two squadrons were to exchange residences, and 619 Squadron spent the 8th packing up its goods and chattels, before moving to its new home at Coningsby on the 9th. The move happened, conveniently, during a break in operations, which allowed the squadron time to settle in and familiarise itself with the station and the circuit.

When briefings finally took place on the 14th, there was, doubtless, some relief to see the red tape on the wall maps terminate some way short of Berlin. It led, in fact, to Braunschweig (Brunswick), the historic and culturally significant city situated some thirty-five miles to the east of Hannover. It had not been attacked by the Command in numbers before, and was a garrison city, home to a number of Nazi organisations, along with concentration camps containing thousands of forced workers, particularly women from the east. On this night, it would face a force, which, at take-off, numbered 496 Lancasters and two Halifaxes, 5 Group supporting the operation with 153 Lancasters. The eleven 619 Squadron participants departed Coningsby for the first time between 15.54 and 16.45 with F/L McGilvray the senior pilot on duty. After climbing out, they headed towards Germany's north-western coast, where they were met by part of the enemy night-fighter response, which would harass the bomber stream all the way to the target and back. Complete cloud cover at the target, in places, at around 15,000 feet, dictated the use of red skymarkers with green stars, at which the 619 Squadron crews aimed their cookies and incendiaries from 20,000 and 21,500 feet between 19.16 and 19.23. The enemy night-fighters scored consistently and accounted for the majority of the thirty-eight missing Lancasters, many of which came down around Hannover. The attack almost entirely missed the city, falling mostly onto outlying communities to the south, and was reported locally as a light raid. This would be a continuing theme in future attacks up to the autumn, as Braunschweig enjoyed something of a charmed life, leading to a belief among the populace that the surrounding villages were being targeted intentionally, in an attempt to drive the residents into the city, before a major operation destroyed it with them in it! One concern to emerge was the number of aircraft being hit by incendiaries from above and near-misses by cookies, and some 5 Group aircraft returned on this night with damage sustained in this way.

The Path Finders, in particular, had been taking a beating since the turn of the year, with 156 Squadron alone losing fourteen Lancasters and crews in just three operations, four and five on Berlin, and five again on Braunschweig. This was creating something of a crisis in Path Finder manpower, particularly with regard to experienced crews, and a number of sideways postings took place between the squadrons to ensure a leavening of experience in each one. One of the solutions was to take the cream from among the crews emerging from the training units, rather than wait for them to gain experience at a main force squadron. P/O Knights and crew were posted to 617 Squadron on the 19th, and would take part in many of the memorable operations undertaken by the squadron, including all three against the *Tirpitz*, until being declared tour-expired at the end of November 1944.

Another lull in operations kept the crews on the ground until the 20th, when orders were received to assemble a maximum effort force for the next round of the Berlin offensive. The Halifax squadrons, which had appeared to be in hibernation since late December, were roused from their slumber, and 264 of them joined 495 Lancasters to constitute the Path Finder and main force elements, while two small Mosquito sections carried out spoof raids on Kiel and Hannover. 5 Group weighed in with 155 Lancasters, of which thirteen were made ready by 619 Squadron, and they took off between 16.21 and 16.48 with F/Ls McGilvray and Sandison the senior pilots on duty. It was a rare pleasure for them to be taking off in some degree of daylight, and they circled as they climbed out above Coningsby before setting course, while observing the dozens of Lancasters rising up into the dusk to join them from the neighbouring stations. They turned their snouts towards the west coast of the Schleswig-Holstein peninsula at a point opposite Kiel, rendezvousing with the other groups over the North Sea and all the time shedding individual aircraft as a hefty seventy-five crews abandoned their sorties and turned back. Among these was that of P/O Vickerstaffe, whose starboard-inner engine caught fire thirteen minutes after take-off and the port-outer forty minutes later. The spearhead of the bomber stream made landfall over the Nordfriesland coast, before turning to the south-east on a more-or-less direct course for Berlin, and soon found themselves being hounded by night-fighters. The enemy controller had fed a proportion of his resources into the bomber stream east of Hamburg, and they would remain in contact until reaching a point between Leipzig and Hannover on the way home, although, curiously, the 5 Group brigade saw nothing of this and would lose just a single 57 Squadron Lancaster. The two Mosquito diversions had been completely ignored by the Luftwaffe controller, who knew well in advance that Berlin was to be the target. The Path Finders arrived over the Müritzsee to the north of Berlin with a sixty-mile run-in to the aiming point, and they found this to be concealed beneath the same ten-tenths cloud that had accompanied them for the entire outward leg. The tops of the cloud lay beneath the bombers at up to 15,000 feet as the main force crews carried out their attacks on red skymarkers with green stars, those from 619 Squadron running in at 19,500 to 22,000 feet between 19.35 and 19.49. On return, the crews commented on the lack of flak activity over Berlin, and reported the glow of large fires under the cloud and smoke rising through the tops. Thirty-five aircraft failed to return, twenty-two of them Halifaxes, which represented an 8.3% casualty rate compared with 2.6% for the Lancasters. It took a little time for an assessment of the operation to be made because of continuing cloud over north-eastern Germany, by which time four further raids had been carried out. It seems from local reports that the eastern districts had received the heaviest weight of bombs in an eight-mile stretch from Weissesee in the north to Neukölln in the south, although no details of destruction emerged.

On the following day, the city of Magdeburg was posted to host its first major attack of the war. Situated some fifty miles from Braunschweig and slightly to the south of east, it was on an increasingly familiar route as far as the enemy night-fighter controllers were concerned, and within easy striking distance of the night-fighter assembly beacons. As the home of a ship lift at the eastern end of the Mittelland Canal at its junction with the Elbe, and a Bergius-process synthetic oil refinery (hydrogenation plant), both located in the same Rothensee district to the north of

Magdeburg city centre, it had been a target for small-scale Bomber Command attacks from time to time since the summer of 1940. Also, on the target list at that time had been a second ship lift at Hohenwarthe, close by to the north-east, which, in reality, had not been built, and, as a result of the war, would not be. In an attempt to deceive the enemy, a small-scale diversion was planned at Berlin involving twenty-two Lancasters of 5 Group and twelve Mosquitos of 8 Group. 5 Group contributed 122 Lancasters to the main event, seven of them made ready by 619 Squadron, which were loaded with a cookie and SBCs of incendiaries each, while the crews of F/L Bell and F/O Rumble would take part in the diversion. They departed Coningsby together between 19.49 and 20.18, and flew out over the North Sea to a point some one hundred miles off the west coast of the Schleswig-Holstein peninsula, before turning to the south-east to pass between Hamburg and Hannover. Enemy radar was able to detect H2S transmissions during night-flying tests and equipment checks, and the night-fighter controller was, thereby, always aware of an imminent heavy raid. On this night, the night-fighters were able to infiltrate the bomber stream even before the German coast was crossed, and the recently introduced "Tame Boar" night-fighter system provided a running commentary on the bomber stream's progress, enabling the fighters to latch onto it and remain in contact. The final turning-point was twenty-five miles north-east of the target, and this was identified by Path Finder route markers, while, ahead, the target was brought into focus by the bombs from twenty-seven main force aircraft. These had been driven by stronger-than-forecast winds to arrive ahead of schedule and contained crews anxious to get the job done and get out of the target area as soon as possible. They bombed using their own H2S without waiting for the TIs to go down, and, together with dummy fires, were blamed by the Path Finders as the reason for their failure to produce concentrated marking.

The conditions over Magdeburg varied according to the time of arrival, the early birds encountering seven to nine-tenths thin cloud at around 6,000 feet, while those turning up towards the end of the raid found the northern half of the city completely clear with cloud over the southern half only. The 619 Squadron crews encountered between zero and seven-tenths thin and broken cloud with tops at up to 8,000 feet, and, in the face of fairly modest opposition, bombed on green TIs from 20,000 to 22,000 feet between 23.02 and 23.25, all gaining the impression that the attack was concentrated around the markers. Returning crews reported explosions and fires or their glow, and smoke beginning to rise as they turned away. A number reported a flash some twelve minutes after bombing, that lit up the clouds for seven seconds, and two large explosions at 23.15. Fires that initially seemed to be scattered, became more concentrated as the crews headed for home, and the impression was of a successful operation. However, some crews were of the opinion that they had attacked a dummy target between Magdeburg and Berlin, while a few overshot the aiming point and let their bombs go randomly rather than go round again. While all of this was in progress, the diversionary force arrived at Berlin, some eighty miles away to the north-east, where they found a layer of eight to ten-tenths cloud at 10,000 feet. They had been told at briefing that there would be no Path Finder presence, and the 619 Squadron pair bombed on e.t.a from 20,300 and 22,200 feet at 22.49 and 22.53, observing the activity over Magdeburg as they turned for home. The 5 Group ORB expressed the opinion that the diversion had succeeded in the early stages in reducing the impact of the Nachtjagd, although this was not borne out by the figures. In the absence of post-raid reconnaissance and a local report, the outcome at Magdeburg was not confirmed, and it is generally believed now that most of the bombing fell outside of the city boundaries. A record fifty-seven aircraft failed to return, thirty-five of them Halifaxes, and this provided another alarming statistic of a 15.6% loss-rate compared with 5.2% for the Lancasters.

The final concerted effort to destroy Berlin would come in three operations in the space of an unprecedented four nights. This hectic round began on the 27th, after five nights of rest since the bruising experience of Magdeburg, and involved an all-Lancaster heavy force of 515 aircraft. 5 Group put up a record 172 aircraft, fourteen of them belonging to 619 Squadron, which departed Coningsby between 17.07 and 17.43 with S/L Churcher the senior pilot on duty. After climbing out and rendezvousing with the rest of the group, they set course on a complex route that would take the bomber stream towards the north German coast, before swinging to the south-east to enter enemy territory over the Frisians and northern Holland. Having then feinted towards central Germany, suggesting Leipzig as the target, the force was to turn north-east to a point west of Berlin, from where the final run-in would commence. The long return route passed to the west of Leipzig before turning due west to miss Frankfurt on its northern side and traverse Belgium to gain the Channel south of Boulogne. F/L Bell and crew turned back shortly after crossing the Lincolnshire coast because of instrument failure, leaving the others to press on towards the target, while a mining diversion off Heligoland, and the dispensing of dummy fighter flares and route-markers, partially succeeded in reducing the numbers of enemy night-fighters making contact. It was, therefore, a relatively intact bomber force that approached the target over ten-tenths cloud with tops at 15,000 feet. This required the Path Finders to use sky-marking, and it was the red Wanganui flares with green stars that led the 619 Squadron crews to the aiming point, where all bombed from 19,500 to 23,000 feet between 20.31 and 20.59. At debriefings, crews reported the glow of fires and the appearance of a successful raid, but no detailed assessment was forthcoming. Of course, not all would make it back to tell their stories at debriefing, and thirty-three Lancaster dispersals stood empty in dawn's early light. Reports from Berlin described bombs falling over a wide area, more so in the south than the north, and damage to fifty industrial premises, a number of them engaged in important war work, while twenty thousand people were bombed out of their homes. A feature of the campaign was the number of outlying communities suffering collateral damage, and, on this night, sixty-one such hamlets recorded bombs falling.

The early time-on-target had allowed crews to get a full night in bed, and they were, hopefully, fully rested, when news came through on the 28th that many of them would be returning to the "Big City" that night. A heavy force of 673 aircraft was assembled, of which 432 were Lancasters and 241 Halifaxes, 155 of the former provided by 5 Group. 619 Squadron made ready fourteen Lancasters, which departed Coningsby between 23.58 and 00.37 with W/C Jeudwine the senior pilot on duty. They were routed out over southern Denmark before turning south-east on a direct course for the target, with an almost reciprocal return and various diversionary measures to distract the night-fighter controller. Sixty-six crews turned back early, suggesting some adverse reaction to the back-to-back operations, but none of these was from 619 Squadron. However, P/O Roberts and crew ran into severe icing conditions, and jettisoned their cookie over the North Sea in order to maintain height, but continued on to the target with their incendiaries. Those reaching the target area encountered ten-tenths cloud, and a mixture of sky and ground-marking to aim at, and the 619 Squadron crews delivered their bombs on red and green release-point flares from 19,000 to 22,000 feet between 03.16 and 03.36. Some crews reported two huge explosions at 03.18 and 03.25, the earlier one described by a 10 Squadron crew as lighting up the sky over a radius of fifty miles. Forty-six aircraft failed to return, twenty-six of them Halifaxes, as the defenders fought back to exact another heavy toll of bombers, but 619 Squadron again welcomed all of its crews home. The impression expressed by returning crews at debriefing was of a concentrated and effective attack, and this was partly borne-out by local reports of heavy damage in western and southern districts, where 180,000 people were bombed out of their homes. However, as had been the pattern throughout the campaign against Berlin, seventy-seven outlying communities had also been afflicted.

After a night's rest, a force of 534 aircraft was made ready on the 30th for the final operation of this concerted effort against Berlin. 5 Group offered 156 Lancasters, of which eleven were made ready by 619 Squadron, and they took off between 16.48 and 17.35 with F/Ls Fuller, McGilvray and Sandison the senior pilots on duty. After climbing out, they joined with the rest of the group to follow a route similar to that adopted two nights earlier, and the bomber stream remained relatively free of harassment until approaching the target, where it was greeted by ten-tenths cloud at around 8,000 feet and the sight of Path Finder skymarking in progress. Above the cloud the bomber stream basked in bright moonlight under a canopy of stars, and the 619 Squadron crews bombed on the red-with-green-stars skymarkers from 19,500 to 22,500 feet between 20.19 and 20.31. On return, all commented on the smoke rising through 12,000 feet and the glow of fires beneath the cloud, which, according to some, was still visible from a hundred miles into the return flight. Thirty-two Lancasters and a single Halifax failed to make it home, but 619 Squadron's excellent loss-free run since moving to Coningsby continued. In return for these significant losses, and according to local reports, central and south-western districts of Berlin suffered heavy damage and serious areas of fire. Other parts of the city were also hit, while many bomb loads were again scattered liberally onto outlying communities, and at least a thousand people lost their lives. 112 heavy bombers and their crews had been lost to the Command as a result of these three operations, and, with the introduction of the enemy's highly efficient Tame Boar night-fighter system based on running commentaries, the advantage had swung back in the defenders' favour.

Two further heavy raids would be directed at Berlin before the end of the winter offensive, one in February and the other in March, but they would be almost in isolation. There is no question that Germany's capital had been sorely afflicted by the three latest operations, but it remained a functioning city, and showed no signs of imminent collapse. During the course of the month the squadron participated in ten operations and dispatched 108 sorties for the loss of three Lancasters and their crews.

February 1944

Bad weather during the first two weeks of February allowed the crews to draw breath and the squadrons to replenish. Harris had intended to maintain the pressure on Berlin, and would have launched a further attack, had he not been thwarted by the conditions, and as a result, the time was filled with training, lectures and mining operations. The squadron welcomed the highly experienced S/L Whamond on posting from 1654 Conversion Unit on the 8th to assume flight commander duties. He had served with distinction under Guy Gibson at 106 Squadron throughout 1942. When the Path Finder and main force squadrons next took to the air, it would be for a record-breaking effort to Berlin on the 15th, and would also be the penultimate operation of the campaign, and, indeed, of the war by Bomber Command's heavy brigade, against Germany's capital city. The force of 891 aircraft represented the largest non-1,000 force to date, and, therefore, the greatest-ever to be sent against the capital, and it would be the first time that more than five hundred Lancasters and three hundred Halifaxes had operated together. 5 Group would surpass its previous best effort by fifty Lancasters when putting 226 of them into the air, and twenty of them would be representing 619 Squadron, in addition to which, P/O Roberts and crew operated out of East Kirkby in a 630 Squadron aircraft. The bomb bays of this huge armada would convey to Berlin the greatest-ever tonnage of bombs to any target to date. 619 Squadron's contribution would be twenty cookies and 960 x 30lb and 21,900 x 4lb incendiaries. F/O "Mac" Hamilton and crew missed this operation having been posted to 617 Squadron earlier in the day, and they would survive their tour and, indeed, the war.

The 619 Squadron element departed Coningsby between 16.50 and 17.26 with W/C Jeudwine and S/L Aytoun the senior pilots on duty, while over at East Kirkby, P/O Roberts and crew took off in a 630 Squadron aircraft at 17.23. After joining up with the rest of the 5 Group squadrons, they set course for the western coast of Denmark, before crossing Jutland and entering Germany via the Baltic coast between Rostock and Stralsund, with a direct heading, thereafter, for the target. The return route would require the bombers to pass south of Hannover and Bremen, and cross Holland to the North Sea via Castricum. Extensive diversionary measures included a mining operation in Kiel Bay ahead of the arrival of the bombers, a raid on Frankfurt-an-Oder to the east of Berlin by a small force of 8 Group Lancasters, and Oboe Mosquitos attacking five night-fighter airfields in Holland. The force had been depleted by seventy-five early returns by the time that the remainder homed in on the target, and among these was the crew of F/L Morrison, who had been making their way across the North Sea when the starboard-inner engine and the electrical system failed. Those reaching the target found it concealed beneath ten-tenths cloud at around 10,000 feet, which was not a problem for the H2S-equipped aircraft, while the others relied on the Path Finders' red release-point flares with green stars and red and green TIs on the ground. The 619 Squadron crews bombed on these from 19,500 to 24,000 feet between 21.15 and 21.38, and, on return, reported the markers to be highly effective and well-concentrated, while the burgeoning glow beneath the clouds convinced them that they had taken part in a successful operation. This was borne out by local reports, which confirmed that the 2,642 tons of bombs had caused extensive damage in central and south-western districts, but had also spilled out into surrounding communities. A thousand houses and more than five hundred temporary wooden barracks were destroyed, and important war-industry factories in the Siemensstadt district were damaged in return for the loss to the Command of forty-three aircraft, twenty-six Lancasters, (4.6%) and seventeen Halifaxes, (5.4%). Perhaps slightly disturbing was the fact that eight of the missing Halifaxes were Mk IIIs, only one fewer than the nine Mk II/Vs. DV330 crashed into the Baltic and took with it to their deaths the crew of F/O Rumble RCAF. Probably much to the annoyance of 630 Squadron, P/O Roberts crash-landed their Lancaster three miles west of Spilsby and wrote it off, fortunately, without casualty to the crew.

Despite the recent heavy losses, when orders were received on the 19th to prepare for another major assault that night, this time on Leipzig, the heavy squadrons were able offer 816 aircraft in the form of 561 Lancasters and 255 Halifaxes. 5 Group managed 209 Lancasters, of which nineteen represented 619 Squadron, and they departed Coningsby between 23.41 and 00.21 with S/Ls Aytoun and Whamond the senior pilots on duty and the crew of Sgt Wadsworth in a 61 Squadron aircraft. After climbing out over the station, they joined up with the others heading for the Dutch coast, where a proportion of the Luftwaffe Nachtjagd was waiting for them, while others had been drawn away by a mining diversion off Kiel. As they continued on their way, many became embroiled in a running battle with night-fighters all the way into eastern Germany, where inaccurately forecast winds caused some aircraft to arrive at the target early. They were forced to orbit, while they waited for the Path Finders to arrive to mark the target, and the local flak batteries accounted for around twenty of these, while four others were lost through collisions. The 619 Squadron crews encountered ten-tenths cloud with tops at around 10,000 feet, and bombed on green Wanganui flares and red and green TIs from 21,000 to 23,500 feet between 03.55 and 04.20. It seems that there was a brief period during the attack when skymarking stopped and led to some scattering of bombs, but the marker-flares were soon replenished with the arrival of more backers-up, and a considerable glow beneath the cloud remained visible for some fifty minutes into the return journey, giving the impression of a successful assault. When all of those aircraft returning home had been accounted for, there was a massive shortfall of seventy-eight, a record loss by a clear twenty-one aircraft. Forty-four Lancasters and thirty-four Halifaxes had failed to return, a loss-rate of 7.8% and 13.3% respectively, and a dozen of the former were from the ranks of 5 Group. Somehow, 619 Squadron avoided the carnage and welcomed all of its crews home. The Halifax casualty figure prompted Harris to immediately withdraw the Mk II and V variants from further operations over Germany, which, at a stroke, removed a proportion of 4 and 6 Groups' fire-power from the front line until they could re-equip with the Mk III Halifax. In the meantime, the Mk II and V operators would focus their energies for the remainder of the month on gardening duties.

This depletion on top of the huge loss at Leipzig reduced the number available for the next operation, which would be the first of three against Stuttgart over a three-week period. A force of 598 aircraft was made ready on the 20th, of which 176 Lancasters were contributed by 5 Group, fifteen of them belonging to 619 Squadron. Each was loaded with a cookie and eleven SBCs of incendiaries, before being dispatched from Coningsby between 23.51 and 00.14 with W/C Jeudwine the senior pilot on duty. The bomber stream made its way across the Channel to the French coast, from where the cloud remained at ten-tenths with tops at 8,000 feet all the way into southern Germany. A North Sea sweep and a diversionary raid on Munich two hours ahead of the main activity had caused the Luftwaffe to deploy its forces early, and this allowed the bomber stream to push on unmolested to the target. By the time it hove into view, the cloud had thinned to five to eight-tenths at around 12,000 feet, and the excellent visibility enabled the crews to draw a bead on the Path Finder red and green sky-markers and similar-coloured TIs on the ground. The 619 Squadron crews bombed from 21,000 to 24,000 feet between 04.00 and 04.12, observing many large fires, and, on return, there were reports that the glow from the burning city was still visible from 250 miles into the return flight. Despite some scattering of bombs, local reports described central districts and those in a quadrant from north-west to north-east, suffering extensive damage, and a Bosch factory was one of the important war industry concerns to be hard-hit. In contrast to twenty-four hours earlier, a modest nine aircraft failed to return.

In an attempt to reduce the prohibitive losses of recent weeks, a new tactic was introduced for the next two operations. A force of 734 aircraft was assembled on the 24th for an operation to the centre of Germany's ball-bearing production, Schweinfurt, situated some sixty miles to the east of Frankfurt in south-central Germany. The plan called for 392 aircraft to depart their stations between 18.00 and 19.00, and to be followed into the air two hours later by 342 others in the hope of catching the night-fighters on the ground refuelling and re-arming as the second wave passed through. While this operation was in progress, extensive diversionary measures would be put in hand that involved more than three hundred other aircraft, including 179 from the training units conducting a North Sea sweep, and 110 Halifaxes and Stirlings mining in northern waters. 5 Group contributed 204 Lancasters, of which eighteen were made ready by 619 Squadron, five assigned to the first phase and taking-off from Coningsby between 18.26 and 18.57, and thirteen to the second phase departing between 19.56 and 20.30 with W/C Jeudwine the senior pilot on duty and in the second element. The 619 Squadron early birds reached the target area to find three-tenths cloud at 3,000 to 4,000 feet and haze, which spoiled the vertical visibility to an extent, while other crews over the target at this time saw no cloud, and described the visibility as excellent, enabling them to pick out the River Main as they ran in to bomb. The aiming point was identified by red and green TIs and already established fires towards the south-western edge of the town, which the 619 Squadron participants bombed from 19,500 to 24,000 feet between 23.09 and 23.17. Two columns of black smoke were observed to be rising through 5,000 feet as they turned away, and the consensus was of an effective, if, somewhat scattered attack.

Meanwhile, the second phase crews were well on their way, and picked up the glow of fires from the earlier raid at a distance of two hundred miles. The visibility in the target area remained good, despite the rising smoke, and bombing by the 619 Squadron element took place out of almost cloudless skies onto red and green TIs from 20,400 to 23,000 feet between 01.04 and 01.18. All indications suggested an effective raid, but, unfortunately, both phases of the operation had suffered from undershooting after some Path Finder backers-up had failed to press on to the aiming point. In that regard, it was a disappointing night, but an interesting feature was the loss of 50% fewer aircraft from the second wave in comparison with the first, in an overall casualty figure of thirty-three, and this suggested some merit in the tactic. 619 Squadron posted missing the crew of F/O Williams RCAF in LM419, which had been shot down by a night-fighter in the general target area, killing the pilot and both gunners and delivering the four survivors into enemy hands. Since the turn of the year a wind-finder system had been in use, in which selected crews monitored wind speed and direction, and passed their findings back to HQ, where the figures were collated, and any changes from the briefed conditions re-broadcast to the bomber stream. This had been found to be extremely useful, but, as would be discovered in the ensuing weeks, the system had its limitations.

The main operation on the following night was directed at the beautiful and culturally significant Bavarian city of Augsburg, situated around thirty miles north-west of Munich. It was home to a major Maschinenfabrik Augsburg Nuremberg (M.A.N) diesel engine factory, which had been the target for the epic low-level daylight raid by 44 and 97 Squadron in April 1942. On this night, 594 aircraft were divided into two waves, and among them were 164 Lancasters of 5 Group, including thirteen representing 619 Squadron. Nine of these were assigned to the first phase, taking-off between 18.17 and 18.53 with F/L Morrison the senior pilot on duty, and four to the second, departing Coningsby between 21.20 and 21.41 led by S/L Whamond. The first wave flew out over Belgium with ten-tenths cloud beneath them, and Sgt Wadsworth and crew were almost three hours out when hydraulics failure ended their interest in proceedings. The cloud had dissipated by the time the other approached the target, and, on arrival, it was possible for crews to gain a visual reference. The Path Finders' red and green TIs were in the bomb sights as the 619 Squadron crews carried out their attacks from 20,500 to 23,000 feet between 22.41 and 23.07, and fires were beginning to take hold as they turned away. The second wave crews were drawn on by the glow in the sky from a hundred miles away, and arrived to find visibility still good despite copious amounts of smoke rising through 10,000 feet, and they bombed on existing fires and red and green Wanganui flares and TIs from 20,000 to 23,000 feet between 01.15 and 01.21. The loss of twenty-one aircraft seemed to confirm the benefits of splitting the forces, and this tactic would remain an important part of Bomber Command planning for the remainder of the war. It had been a devastatingly destructive operation, in which all facets of the plan had come together in near perfect harmony, spelling disaster for this lightly defended treasure trove of culture. Its heart was torn out by blast and fire that destroyed almost three thousand houses along with buildings of outstanding historical significance, and centuries of irreplaceable culture was lost forever. There was also some industrial damage, and around ninety-thousand people were bombed out of their homes.

The Secretary of State for Air, Sir Archibald Sinclair, visited Coningsby on the 26th. During the course of the month the squadron carried out five operations and dispatched eighty-six sorties for the loss of two Lancasters and their crews.

March 1944

March would bring an end to the winter campaign, but a long and bitter month would have to be endured first before any respite came from long-range forays into Germany. The crews had benefitted from a few nights off when the second raid of the series on Stuttgart was posted on the 1st, for which a force of 557 aircraft was made ready. This number included 178 Lancasters representing 5 Group, sixteen of which were provided by 619 Squadron and loaded with a cookie and mix of 4lb and 30lb incendiaries, before setting off from Coningsby between 22.37 and 23.35 with W/C Jeudwine and S/L Whamond senior pilots on duty. As they headed south to rendezvous with the rest of the force, F/L Morrison's starboard-inner engine caught fire over Hertfordshire, and he headed straight for the jettison area. The others set course for the enemy coast and the passage across France, where they flew over ten-tenths cloud with tops at between 12,000 and 17,000 feet, before encountering similar conditions in the target area. The Path Finders employed a combination of sky and ground-marking techniques, which became scattered, and the bombing was directed between two main concentrations, the 619 Squadron crews carrying out their attacks on green TIs and red Wanganui skymarkers with green stars from 19,800 to 23,000 feet between 03.00 and 03.14. It was not possible to assess the accuracy of the attack, although a column of smoke had reached 25,000 feet by the end of the raid, and large fires were evident from the glow in the sky visible from up to 150 miles away. The presence of thick cloud all the way there and back made conditions difficult for enemy night-fighters, and a remarkably modest four aircraft failed to return. It was eventually established that the raid had been an outstanding success, which had caused extensive damage in central, western and northern districts, where a number of important war-industry factories, including those belonging to Bosch and Daimler-Benz, had sustained damage.

At the end of the first week, the Halifax brigade, particularly those withdrawn from operations over Germany, fired the opening salvoes of the pre-invasion campaign, the purpose of which was to dismantle by bombing thirty-seven railway centres in France, Belgium and western Germany. It began on the night of the 6/7th at Trappes marshalling yards, situated some ten miles west-south-west of Paris, and continued at Le Mans in north-western France on the following night. For most of the heavy crews, however, there was no employment following Stuttgart, until a return there in mid-month, but, in the meantime, matters were afoot at 5 Group, and had been ever since the frustrating series of operations against flying bomb launching sites by 617 Squadron since December had produced disappointing results. The problem had been an inability to achieve pinpoint accuracy, which was vital to destroy small, precision targets, and Oboe was just not precise enough. Accurate though Oboe undoubtedly was at an urban target, where a margin of error of 400 to 600 yards was considered pinpoint, precision targets required more. W/C Cheshire and S/L Martin experimented with a dive-bombing technique, which had proved to be successful, but impracticable in a Lancaster, and Cheshire had borrowed a Mosquito for further trials. These were so promising, that the 5 Group A-O-C, AVM Cochrane, authorised a number of operations by the squadron against factory targets in France, before taking the idea to Harris.

The first of these was to be carried out by the squadrons on the 53 Base stations of Bardney, Skellingthorpe and Waddington on the 9th, and each prepared eleven Lancasters for the operation against the Lioré et Olivier aircraft factory at Marignane, situated a few miles to the north of Marseilles in southern France. The area had been the main pre-war hub for commercial flying boat operations, particularly for the Pan American Clipper Class flights, and the factory had been engaged in the manufacture of the LeO 45 twin-engine medium bomber for the French Air Force. It was a round trip of some 1,350 miles if they flew direct, and they were aided in the target area by clear skies and bright moonlight, which facilitated an easy identification of the factory buildings and an accurate attack, in which high-explosive bombs were seen to fall from medium level among the buildings.

5 Group's 54 and 55 Bases received orders on the 10th to prepare 102 Lancasters to form four small forces, each to attack a specific factory in France that night. The targets were the Michelin tyre factory at Clermont-Ferrand, the Bloch aircraft factory at Châteauroux, which was the first to be set up by the famed designer, Marcel Dassault in 1935, the Morane Saulnier aircraft plant at Ossun, just north of the Pyrenese and the Ricamerie needle-bearing works at St-Etienne, the last-mentioned the objective for sixteen Lancasters from 617 Squadron. 619 Squadron was assigned to the Bloch factory in central France and made ready ten Lancasters, which departed Coningsby between 19.35 and 20.17 with W/C Jeudwine and S/L Whamond the senior pilots on duty and the base commander, A/C Sharp, flying with the former. They all arrived in their respective target areas to find bright moonlight, and a Master Bomber on hand to direct the bombing at each target, and, in the absence of opposition, all four operations were concluded successfully for the loss of a single Lancaster. At Châteauroux, the 619 Squadron crews carried out their attacks on three red spotfires from 8,000 to 9,500 feet between 22.40 and 22.58, and observed the factory buildings to be burning fiercely as they turned away.

Now that the Mk III Halifax was becoming available in larger numbers, the Command was quickly returning to full strength, and it was a force of 863 aircraft that set out for Stuttgart in the early-evening of the 15th. This number included 206 Lancasters provided by 5 Group, sixteen of them containing 619 Squadron crews, which departed Coningsby between 18.39 and 19.15 with S/L Whamond the senior pilot on duty, and rendezvoused with the rest of the force as they passed over Reading on their way to the south coast. It was an elongated bomber stream that crossed the French coast at 20,000 feet over broken cloud with clear conditions above, maintaining a course parallel with the frontiers of Belgium, Luxembourg and Germany as if heading for Switzerland, before turning towards the north-east for the run-in to the target. It was during this final leg that the night-fighters managed to infiltrate a section of the stream and score heavily, although this was not apparent to most of the 619 Squadron element. The exception was the crew of F/Sgt Schofield, who were attacked repeatedly and lost their hydraulics, electrical and oxygen systems and their mid-upper turret, while sustaining damage to control surfaces. The bomb-aimer was wounded, but remained at his post, and, on attempting to release the bombs over the aiming point, he found the bomb doors would not deploy, and the load had to be brought all the way home to a landing at Ford on the south coast, where the incendiaries caught fire and caused further damage. Adverse winds were responsible for the Path Finders arriving up to six minutes late to open the attack, when they employed both sky and ground-markers in the face of seven to ten-tenths cloud at between 8,000 and 15,000 feet. The Wanganui flares drifted in the wind, marking an area to the north-east of the River Neckar, while the TIs landed far apart in the north and south of the city. The 619 Squadron crews bombed on whatever markers presented themselves, mostly red TIs, from 19,000 to 23,000 feet between 23.12 and 23.33, observing a spread of fires, including two large ones ten miles apart, and smoke rising to bombing altitude. It would be established later that some of the early bombing had been accurate, but, that most of it had undershot and fallen into open country, a disappointment compounded by the loss, mostly to night-fighters, of thirty-seven aircraft. 619 Squadron escaped the carnage, but P/O Roberts and crew were another to experience a narrow escape after being attacked by a Ju88 as they were leaving the target. All six guns in the rear and mid-upper turrets jammed, while the night-fighter stood off at close range firing short bursts of cannon fire, knocking off the port fin and rudder. The rear gunner managed to clear a single gun, and fired at the assailant from point-blank range, driving it off with its port engine in flames and claiming it as destroyed. The claim was confirmed later, presumably, after the encounter had been witnessed by another crew, which observed the enemy aircraft to crash.

Many operations had been mounted against Frankfurt during the preceding two years, only a small number of which had been really effective. This state of affairs was about to be rectified, however, and the first of two raids against this south-central powerhouse of industry was posted on the 18th, and a force of 846 aircraft made ready. 5 Group supported the operation with 212 Lancasters, fifteen of which were made ready by 619 Squadron. They were loaded at Coningsby with a cookie each and a mix of 4lb and 30lb incendiaries, before taking off between 18.45 and 19.14 with F/Ls Fuller and Moore the senior pilots on duty. F/Sgt Schofield had reached Suffolk when his artificial horizon failed, and P/O Buttar and crew turned back at Orfordness ten minutes later because of an engine issue, leaving the others to adopt the familiar route to south-central Germany via France, and enjoy good weather conditions as they crossed the frontier. They encountered a layer of haze 20,000 feet thick over the target, and, according to most, no more than three-tenths cloud, which allowed the Path Finders to employ the Newhaven ground marking technique (blind marking by H2S, followed by visual backing-up). The 619 Squadron crews exploited the conditions to carry out their attacks on red and green TIs from 20,000 to 23,000 feet between 21.59 and 22.12, and witnessed a large explosion at 22.05, which sent them on their way home confident that their efforts had been worthwhile. They had, indeed, contributed to an outstandingly successful raid, during which, 5 Group alone dropped more than one thousand tons of bombs for the first time at a single target. Local reports calculated that six thousand buildings had been destroyed or seriously damaged in predominantly eastern, central and western districts, and this was in return for the loss of twenty-two aircraft, five of which were from 5 Group.

Frankfurt was named again on the 22nd as the target for that night, and 217 crews of 5 Group learned that they were to be part of another huge force of 816 aircraft. The eighteen participants from 619 Squadron took off from Coningsby between 18.30 to 19.13 with the newly promoted S/L McGilvray the senior pilot on duty. After climbing out above their stations and forming up, they adopted an unusual route for a target south of the Ruhr, crossing the enemy coast over Vlieland and Teschelling, before passing to the east of Osnabrück on a direct course due south for the target. They arrived at their destination to find five to six-tenths thin, low cloud at around 4,000 feet, and Paramatta marking (blind marking by H2S) in progress. They focussed their attention on the release-point flares and red and green TIs marking out the aiming point, before bombing from 20,500 to 23,000 feet between 21.51 and 22.05. A massive rectangular area of unbroken fire was observed across the centre of the city, the glow from which could be seen for at least a hundred miles into the return flight. Returning crews reported numerous searchlights lighting up the cloud, and moderate to intense flak that reached up to the bombers' flight level. Local reports confirmed the enormity of the devastation, which was particularly severe in western districts and left this half of the city without electricity, gas and water for an extended period. More than nine hundred people lost their lives and a further 120,000 were bombed out of their homes, at a cost to the Command of twenty-six Lancasters and seven Halifaxes, a loss-rate of 4.2% and 3.8% respectively. It was a bad night for senior officers, however, 207 and 7 Squadrons losing their commanding officers, while Bardney's station commander, G/C Norman Pleasance, failed to return in a 9 Squadron Lancaster. What was about to happen over the next week and a half, though, would overshadow anything that had gone before, and would certainly not fall within what might be considered acceptable.

It was more than five weeks since the main force had last visited the capital, and 811 aircraft were made ready on the 24th for what would be the final raid of the war by RAF heavy bombers on the "Big City". 5 Group put up 193 Lancasters, of which eighteen were made ready by 619 Squadron, and they departed Coningsby between 18.13 and 19.14 with W/C Jeudwine and S/L Whamond the senior pilots on duty. They had a long flight ahead of them, which would take them across the North Sea to the Danish coast near Ringkøbing and then to a point on the German Baltic coast near Rostock. When north-east of Berlin they were to adopt a south-westerly course for the bombing run, and, once clear of the defence zone homebound, dogleg to the west and then north-west to pass around Hannover on its southern and western sides, before heading for Holland and an exit via the Castricum coast. The extended outward leg provided a time-on-target of around 22.30, but an unexpected difficulty would be encountered, which would render void all of the meticulous planning. The existence of what we now call "Jetstream" winds was unknown at the time, and the one blowing from the north with unprecedented strength on this night pushed the bomber stream south of its intended track. Navigators, who were expecting to see the northern tip of Sylt on their H2S screens, were horrified to find the southern end, which meant that they were thirty miles south of track, and about to fly over Germany rather than Denmark. The previously mentioned "windfinder" system had been set up for precisely this eventuality, but the problem on this night was that the windfinders refused to believe what their instruments were telling them. Winds in excess of one hundred m.p.h had never been encountered before, and, fearing that they would be disbelieved, many modified the figures downward. The same thing happened at raid control, where the figures were modified again, so that the information rebroadcast to the bomber stream bore no resemblance to the reality of the situation.

This was all academic to the crew of F/L Moore, who had turned back shortly after beginning the North Sea crossing after losing power in the port-inner engine. The others pressed on, and by the time that they had reached Westerhever on the west coast of the Schleswig-Holstein peninsula, most realised that they were some distance south of track, and set course for the north to try to regain the planned route and avoid the defences that would be met if they turned east over Germany. Many commented on the inaccurate wind information received during the outward journey, and, having arrived in the target area, some were convinced that the Path Finders were up to ten minutes late in opening the raid. This was confirmed to some by the voice of the Master Bomber exhorting them to hurry up. Crews reported a variety of cloud conditions, from three to ten-tenths at between 6,000 and 15,000 feet, but most were able to pick out the red and green TIs on the ground, and, if not, found red Wanganui flares with green stars to guide them to the aiming point. The 619 Squadron crews confirmed their positions by H2S before bombing from 20,000 to 23,000 feet between 22.18 and 23.13, and observed what appeared to be a scattered attack in the early stages, until fires began to become more concentrated in three distinct areas, and large explosions were witnessed at 22.42 and 22.54. The defences were very active with moderate flak bursting at up to 24,000 feet, and light flak attempting to shoot out the skymarkers, but night-fighter activity was described by the 5 Group ORB as unusually quiet. There was a shock awaiting the Command as the returning aircraft landed to leave a shortfall of seventy-two, and it would be established later that two-thirds of them had fallen victim to the Ruhr flak batteries after being driven into that region's defence zone by the wind on the way home. 619 Squadron posted missing the crew of P/O Thompson RNZAF, who all perished when DV328 crashed at Teltow, some nine miles south-west of Berlin city centre. A post-raid analysis revealed that the wind had also played havoc with the marking and bombing and had pushed the attack towards the south-western districts of the capital, where most of the damage occurred, while 126 outlying communities also received bombs. 619 Squadron had been present on each of the nineteen main raids to the capital, and the diversion there on the night of the Magdeburg debacle in January and had dispatched 258 sorties for the loss of ten of its Lancasters and a further five in crashes, with seventy-two men killed and twelve surviving as PoWs. (*The Berlin Raids*. Martin Middlebrook).

Twenty 5 Group Lancasters were invited to take part in an attack on the extensive railway yards at Aulnoye in north-eastern France to be carried out on the evening of the 25th, while twenty-two 617 Squadron Lancasters returned to the Sigma aero-engine factory at Lyons. W/C Humphreys had become attached to 619 Squadron to gain experience before being appointed to command 57 Squadron in mid-April, and he and his crew were the sole representatives to be involved at Aulnoye, departing Coningsby at 19.19 and returning after midnight to report a successful sortie.

Although Berlin had now been consigned to the past, the winter campaign still had a week to run, and two more major operations for the crews to negotiate. The first of these was posted on the 26th, and would bring a return to the old enemy of Essen that night, for which a force of 705 aircraft was made ready. 5 Group contributed 172 of the 476 Lancasters, thirteen of them provided by 619 Squadron, which took off from Coningsby between 19.37 and 20.02 with F/Ls Fuller and Thompson the senior pilots on duty. They climbed out over Lincolnshire and set course for the Dutch coast to pass north of Haarlem and Amsterdam, before swinging to the south-east on a direct run to the target. F/Sgt Paterson and crew turned back shortly before reaching the Dutch coast on suspecting that a fire had broken out in the bomb bay, leaving the others to reach the target area to find it under eight to ten-tenths cloud with tops in places as high as 14,000 feet. Oboe performed well and enabled the Path Finders to mark the city with red and green TIs and Wanganui flares, which the 619 Squadron crews bombed from 18,800 and 22,500 feet between 22.00 and 22.14, before returning safely, having been unable to assess the results of their efforts. The impression was of a successful raid, and this was based on a considerable glow beneath the clouds as they withdrew. Post-raid reconnaissance soon confirmed another outstandingly destructive operation against this once elusive target, thus continuing the remarkable run of successes here since the introduction of Oboe to main force operations a year earlier. Over seventeen hundred houses were destroyed in the attack, with dozens of war industry factories sustaining serious damage, and, on a night when the night-fighter controllers were caught off guard by the switch to the Ruhr, the success was gained for the modest loss of nine aircraft.

The period known as the Battle of Berlin, but which was more accurately referred to as the winter campaign, was to be brought to an end on the night of the 30/31st, with a standard maximum-effort raid on Nuremberg. The plan of operation departed from normal practice in only one important respect, and this was to prove critical. It had become standard routine over the winter for 8 Group to plan operations and to employ diversions and feints to confuse the enemy night-fighter controllers. Sometimes they were successful and sometimes not, but with the night-fighter force having clearly gained the upper hand with its "Tame Boar" running commentary system, all possible means had to be adopted to protect the bomber stream. During a conference held early on the 30th, the Lancaster Group A-O-Cs expressed a preference for a 5 Group-inspired route, which would require the bomber stream to fly a long straight leg across Belgium and Germany, to a point about fifty miles north of Nuremberg, from where the final run-in would commence. The Halifax A-O-Cs were less convinced of the benefits, and AVM Bennett, the Path Finder chief, was positively overcome by the potential dangers and predicted a disaster, only to be overruled. A force of 795 aircraft was made ready, of which 201 Lancasters were to be provided by 5 Group, sixteen of them representing 619 Squadron, and the crews attended briefings to be told of the route, wind conditions and the belief that a layer of cloud would conceal them from enemy night-fighters. Before take-off, a 1409 Meteorological Flight Mosquito crew radioed in to cast doubts upon the weather conditions, which they could see differed markedly from those that had been forecast. This also went unheeded, and, from around 21.45 for the next hour or so, the crews took off for the rendezvous area, and headed into a conspiracy of circumstances, which would inflict upon Bomber Command its heaviest defeat of the war.

At Coningsby, take-off took place between 21.54 and 22.44 with S/Ls McGilvray and Whamond the senior pilots on duty, and it was not long into the flight before they and the other crews began to notice some unusual features in the conditions, which included uncommonly bright moonlight, and a crystal clarity of visibility that allowed them the rare sight of other aircraft in the stream. On most nights, crews would feel themselves to be completely alone in the sky all the way to the target, until, bang on schedule, TIs would be seen to fall and other aircraft would make their presence known by the turbulence of their slipstreams as they funnelled towards the aiming point. Once at cruising altitude on this night, however, they were alarmed to note that the forecast cloud was conspicuous by its absence, and, instead, lay beneath them as a white tablecloth, against which they were silhouetted like flies. P/O Whiteley and crew were twenty miles from the Belgian coast when intercom failure persuaded them to turn back, and this may have saved their lives. Condensation trails began to form in the cold, clear air to further advertise their presence to the enemy, and the Jetstream winds, which had so adversely affected the Berlin raid a week earlier, were also present, only this time blowing from the south. As then, the windfinder system would be unable to cope, and this would have a serious impact on the outcome of the operation. The final insult on this sad night was, that the route into Germany passed close to two night-fighter beacons, which the enemy aircraft were orbiting while they awaited their instructions, unaware initially that they were about to have the cream of Bomber Command handed to them on a plate.

The carnage began over Charleroi in Belgium, and from there to the target, the route was signposted by the burning wreckage on the ground of eighty Bomber Command aircraft. The windfinder system broke down again, and those crews who either failed to detect the strength of the wind, or simply refused to believe the evidence, were driven up to fifty miles north of their intended track, and, consequently, turned towards Nuremberg from a false position. This led to more than a hundred aircraft bombing at Schweinfurt in error, which combined with the massive losses sustained before the target was reached to reduce considerably the numbers arriving at the primary target. The 619 Squadron crews arrived over Nuremberg to encounter eight to nine-tenths cloud with tops as high as 16,000 feet, and bombed from 19,000 to 23,000 feet between 01.14 and 01.27, aiming at red and green TIs and sky-markers. Many fires were observed, the glow from which, according to some reports, remained visible for 120 miles into the return journey. Ninety-five aircraft failed to return home, twenty-one of them from 5 Group, and many others were written off in landing crashes or with battle damage too severe to repair. Among the latter was 619 Squadron's only casualty, LM418, which was hit by flak immediately after bombing and lost the use of the starboard-inner engine, while losing all readings on the starboard-outer. The Lancaster dropped to 9,500 feet, but Sgt Parker managed to coax it back up to 11,000 feet and bring it home to a crash-landing at the emergency strip at Woodbridge, where it burst immediately into flames and was consumed. The crew emerged unscathed, but for them, it would be but a temporary reprieve. The shock and disappointment of the losses were compounded by the fact that the strong wind had driven the marking beyond the city to the east, and Nuremberg had, consequently, escaped serious damage.

During the course of the month, the squadron participated in nine operations and dispatched 123 sorties for the loss of two Lancasters and one crew.

April 1944

The winter campaign had brought the Command to its low point of the war, and it was the only time when the morale of the crews was in question. What now lay before the hard-pressed men of Bomber Command was in marked contrast to that which had been endured over the seemingly interminable winter months. In place of the long slog to Germany on dark, often dirty nights, shorter range hops to France and Belgium in improving weather conditions would become the order of the day. However, these operations would be equally demanding in their way, and would require of the crews a greater commitment to accuracy, to avoid casualties among friendly civilians. Despite this, a decree from on high insisted that such operations were worthy of counting as just one third of a sortie towards the completion of a tour, and, until this flawed policy was rescinded, the hint of a mutinous air would pervade the crew rooms. In fact, the number of sorties to complete a tour would fluctuate between this point and the end of hostilities. Despite the horrendous losses of the winter campaign, the Command was in remarkably fine fettle to face its new challenge, with 3 Group gradually changing to Lancasters, and the much-improved Hercules-powered Halifaxes equipping 4 Group and most of 6 Group. Harris was now in the enviable position of being able to achieve what had eluded his predecessor, namely, to attack multiple targets simultaneously with enough strength to be effective. Such was the hitting-power now at his disposal, that he could assign targets to individual groups, to groups in tandem, or to the Command as a whole, as dictated by operational requirements. Although invasion considerations would come first, while Harris was at the helm, his favoured policy of city busting would never be entirely shelved.

While most of the Command's heavy brigade remained on the ground for the first nine days of April, 5 Group returned to operations on the 5th, for which a force of 144 Lancasters was assembled plus a Mosquito flown by W/C Cheshire of 617 Squadron. The target was the former Dewoitine aircraft factory at Toulouse in south-western France, which, under a nationalisation plan in 1936 involving six aircraft companies, including Lioré et Olivier and Potez, was now operating under the name SNCASE, or Sud Est for short. Cheshire was to mark it with spotfires from low-level, using the system that he was instrumental in developing, and one which would become an integral part of 5 Group operations, with refinements, from this point on. This would be Cheshire's first operational flight in a Mosquito, and the first time that he marked a target for 5 Group, rather than just for 617 Squadron. Much depended upon its success if Harris were to become sold on the idea of the low-level visual marking technique and give it his backing. At Coningsby, 619 Squadron bombed up fourteen Lancasters and dispatched them between 20.17 and 20.47 with W/Cs Jeudwine and Humphreys the senior pilots on duty and an outward flight ahead of them of more than four hours. Departing from Waddington at about the same time was a 467 Squadron Lancaster captained by Wing Commander Operations, W/C James "Willie" Tait, a veteran of operations with 4 Group, former commanding officer of 51 and 10 Squadrons, future commanding officer of 617 Squadron and now a member of the 5 Group Master Bomber fraternity based at Coningsby. P/O Griffiths and crew were west of London when their radio receiver let them down, and they returned to base with their bomb load intact. The others arrived in the target area in time to watch Cheshire lob two red spotfires onto the roof of the factory at 00.17 during his third pass, and, so accurate were they, that the two 617 Squadron Lancaster backers-up were not required. The bombing took place in bright moonlight, the 619 Squadron crews delivering their loads of seven 1,000 and seven 500 pounders each from 12,250 to 15,000 feet between 00.21 and 00.31, after which they observed explosions among buildings, large fires and smoke rising through 7,000 feet. One 207 Squadron Lancaster was hit by flak over the target at 00.30 and exploded, killing all on board, and this was the only loss from an outstandingly successful operation. The 619 Squadron crews mostly landed away from Coningsby at Wellesbourne Mountford, Chipping Norton and Westcott to name but three, and they would straggle back to Lincolnshire during the course of the day. Within hours of receiving a report of the raid, Harris gave the go ahead for 5 Group to take on its own target marking force, and become, in effect, an independent entity.

It would be almost two weeks before the necessary moves took place, and, in the meantime, the pre-invasion campaign got into full swing with the posting of two operations on the 9th. Responsibility for the destruction of the Lille-Delivrance goods station in north-eastern France was handed to 239 aircraft from 3, 4, 6 and 8 Groups, while the marshalling yards at Villeneuve-St-Georges, on the southern outskirts of Paris, were to be targeted by 225 aircraft drawn from all groups. The weather conditions were excellent, and clear skies greeted the latter force as it crossed the French coast at around 14,000 feet. The target could be identified visually, but the Path Finders had placed their red and green TIs accurately onto the aiming point, and the main force crews delivered their hardware from between 13,000 and 14,500 feet in the face of little opposition. Many bomb bursts were observed along with orange explosions, and, to those high above, the raid appeared to be highly successful. In fact, many bomb loads had fallen into adjacent residential districts, where four hundred houses had been destroyed or seriously damaged, and ninety-three people killed. This was far fewer than had died in the simultaneous operation at Lille, many miles to the north-east, where over two thousand items of rolling stock had been destroyed, and buildings and installations seriously damaged, but at a collateral cost of 456 French civilian lives. Civilian casualties would prove to be an unavoidable by-product of the campaign.

619 Squadron was among a number from 5 Group not to take part in the above operation, but would be called into action on the following day, Monday the 10th, when a further five railway yards, four in France and one in Belgium, were posted as the targets for that night and assigned to individual groups. 5 Group was handed those at Tours in the Loire region of western France, for which 180 Lancasters were made ready, eighteen of them on the 619 Squadron dispersals at Coningsby. At briefing, it was revealed that W/C Jeudwine would perform the role of Master Bomber, and W/C Humphreys would operate with the squadron for the final time. S/Ls McGilvray and Whamond were also on the Order of Battle as the 619 Squadron participants departed Coningsby between 22.00 and 22.40 and W/C Tait operated again from Waddington. They set course for England's south coast and the Channel crossing, and it was when five miles short of the Normandy coast that F/L Morrison lost a starboard engine and turned back. The others arrived at the target to find bright moonlight and red spotfires marking the aiming point, and W/C Jeudwine directing the first phase of the attack against the western side of the yards, while W/C Tait oversaw the second at its eastern counterpart. The 619 Squadron crews attacked the western aiming point "A" from 5,000 to 8,000 between 01.32 and 01.55, some electing to make two passes, the first to deliver the cookie and the second the incendiaries. They described the yards as an avenue of fire, but the scene was soon confused as smoke began to spread across the site and billow into the air, rising through 8,000 feet in the later stages. The second phase crews had been instructed to approach the aiming point in a left-hand orbit from the east, during which the Master Bomber called a temporary halt as he reassessed the changing visibility, before reinstating the bombing order until the smoke forced him to end the attack at 02.48. There were mixed opinions as to the effectiveness of the operation, some gaining the impression that the eastern half of the yards had not been touched, but others claimed the attack to have been accurate and concentrated within the yards, and two large fires were observed. Post-raid reconnaissance confirmed the success of the attack, but the Germans would round up local civilians and force them into repairing the damage to get the yards working again before long.

Aachen was a major railway centre with marshalling yards at both the western and eastern ends, but the size of the force assembled for the attack planned for the night of the 11/12th was clearly designed to cause as much damage as possible within what was Germany's most westerly city. The force of 341 heavy aircraft was drawn from 1, 3, 5 and 8 Groups with sixteen of the Lancasters provided by 619 Squadron, their bomb bays mostly loaded with fourteen 1,000 pounders, the bomb of choice for marshalling yards. They departed Coningsby for what would prove to be the last time between 20.20 and 21.14 with S/L McGilvray the senior pilot on duty, and joined the bomber stream as it climbed to between 18,000 and 20,000 feet by the time it reached the Belgian coast at 3 degrees east. That altitude was maintained all the way to the target, where six to ten-tenths thin cloud was encountered at between 7,000 and 8,000 feet, through which the red and green TIs could be seen to identify the aiming point. The 619 Squadron crews attacked it from 18,000 to 20,000 feet between 22.42 and 22.55, observing many bomb bursts and fires, which suggested that the attack was accurate. The crews maintained height on the way home until fifty miles from the coast, at which position they began a gentle descent to exit enemy territory at 15,000 feet or above. Nine Lancasters failed to return, and two empty dispersals at Coningsby told a story of two highly experienced crews who would not be moving with the rest of the squadron to Dunholme Lodge. LL784 exploded over southern Holland, flinging the two survivors into space to be taken into captivity, while S/L McGilvray DFC and the rest of his crew perished. A little further to the north-west near Tilburg, F/L Moore and his wireless operator abandoned a burning EE116 to its fate, and joined their squadron colleagues in captivity as the sole survivors of their crew. Reports coming out of Aachen revealed this to be the city's worst experience of the war to date, with extensive damage in central and southern districts, disruption of its transport infrastructure and a death toll of 1,525 people. However, post-raid reconnaissance revealed that the railway yards had not been destroyed and would require further attention.

On the 14th, the squadron was told to prepare to move to Dunholme Lodge, a station situated some four miles north of Lincoln east of the A15 and opposite Scampton, which it would share with 44 (Rhodesia) Squadron. On the same day, Bomber Command became officially subject to the orders coming from the Supreme Headquarters of the Allied Expeditionary Force (SHAEF), under General Dwight D Eisenhower, and would remain thus shackled until the Allied armies were sweeping towards the German frontier at the end of the summer. The advance party of 619 Squadron moved out of Coningsby on the 16th and the main party, including the aircraft, followed on the 17th, leaving Coningsby available to receive 83 and 97 Squadrons on the 18th. They were being loaned to 5 Group from the Path Finders, on what amounted to a permanent detachment, along with the Mosquito unit, 627 Squadron, which would join 617 Squadron at Woodhall Spa. The Lancaster units were to become the 5 Group heavy markers, while the Mosquitos would eventually take over the low-level marking role currently performed by 617 Squadron. This was a major coup for AVM Cochrane and 5 Group and a bitter blow to AVM Bennett, the Path Finder chief, whose relationship had never been cordial, but this plunged it to new depths. Both were brilliant men, Bennett, an Australian, a man of the greatest intellect, who, despite his total lack of humour, commanded the deepest respect and loyalty from his men, while Cochrane enjoyed a closer relationship with Harris, having served as a flight commander under him in Mesopotamia between the wars. Each had a strong opinion on the subject of target marking, Bennett believing that a low-level method exposed the crews to unnecessary danger, while Cochrane insisted that the risks in a fast-flying Mosquito were negligible and would produce greater accuracy. Though 83 and 97 Squadrons were formerly of the elitist 5 Group, and relied on it to supply new crews, once part of 8 Group, they had come to see that as the pinnacle, and were upset at being removed from what they considered to be an elevated status. Once entitled, they were fiercely proud to wear the Path Finder badge and enjoyed the enhanced promotion opportunities, but, happily for them, as the squadrons were only officially on loan to 5 Group, these were privileges that they would retain.

Any resentment might have been smoothed over had their reception at Coningsby been handled better, but, as the newly arrived crews tumbled out of their transports, they were summoned immediately to the briefing room, to be lectured by the 54 Base commander, Air Commodore "Bobby" Sharp, a pompous and self-important link in the chain of command. Rather than welcoming them as brothers-in-arms, he harangued them over their bad 8 Group habits, and ordered them to buckle down to learning 5 Group ways. This was an insult to experienced airmen, for whom the task of illuminating targets for 5 Group would be a piece of cake in comparison with the complexities of their 8 Group duties. The fact that the insult was being delivered by a man with no relevant operational experience, made it doubly unpalatable. From this point on, 5 Group would be known in 8 Group circles somewhat disparagingly as the "Independent Air Force", or "The Lincolnshire Poachers".

The 5 Group target on the 18th was the marshalling yards at Juvisy, situated on the west bank of the Seine south of Paris, which was one of four similar targets for the night. The intention had been for the new arrivals to participate, but the disgruntled commanding officers, G/C Laurence Deane of 83 Squadron and W/C Jimmy Carter of 97 Squadron, announced that they were not yet ready, and the operation would have to go ahead without them. 202 Lancasters and four Mosquitos were made ready, the latter belonging to 617 Squadron, and 8 Group would provide three Oboe Mosquitos to deliver the initial marking. 619 Squadron made ready fourteen Lancasters, and dispatched them from Dunholme Lodge between 20.29 and 20.55 with F/L Buttar the senior pilot on duty, and all reached the target to find clear skies and ideal bombing conditions, in which they observed W/C Cheshire's red spotfires become backed up by green TIs. Despite the presence of black smoke drifting across the aiming point and upwards from the destruction of a fuel dump at 23.32, the 619 Squadron crews were able to hit the markers from 7,500 to 11,200 between 23.29 and 23.53. Returning crews were enthusiastic about the success of the operation, which was confirmed by post-raid reconnaissance, and prompted the crews to make the valid comment that, to count this operation as just one-third of a sortie was undervaluing it, and this was a sentiment shared by all whose job involved putting their lives on the line.

Briefings on 5 Group stations on the 20th informed crews of their part in the first operation to include the three newly transferred squadrons, a two-phase attack on railway yards at La Chapelle, situated in a northern suburb of Paris. Meanwhile, the night's main event was to be conducted by a force of 357 Lancasters and twenty-two Mosquitos drawn from 1, 3, 6 and 8 Groups against Cologne. A meticulous plan had been prepared for 5 Group, in which the phases were to be separated by an hour, each with its own specific aiming point, and 83 Squadron's W/C Deane was to be the Master Bomber with S/L Sparks his deputy. The plan called for 8 Group Mosquitos to drop cascading flares by Oboe to provide an initial reference, and for a Mosquito element from 627 Squadron to lay a Window screen ahead of the main force Lancasters. Once the target had been identified, the first members of the 83 Squadron flare force were to provide illumination for the low-level marker Mosquitos of 617 Squadron, which would mark the first aiming point with red spot fires for the main force element to aim at. The whole procedure would then be repeated at the second aiming point. At Coningsby, W/C Deane conducted the briefing, and, at its conclusion, wished the assembled throng good luck, before dismissing them, whereupon a voice from the back declared that the briefing wasn't over, and that the base and station commanders wanted their say. This had not been standard practice in 8 Group, and left Deane mystified and a little humiliated. The senior officers had only waffle to offer, but it made them feel important, while confirming the first impressions of A/C Sharp.

619 Squadron made ready fourteen Lancasters in an overall force of 247 Lancasters of 5 Group and twenty-two Mosquitos of 5 and 8 Groups, and they departed Dunholme Lodge between 21.45 and 22.11 as part of the first wave with S/L Whamond the senior pilot on duty. Each Lancaster was carrying fourteen 1,000 pounders, and arrived at the target to find largely clear skies, good visibility and only some ground haze to mar the view. W/C Tait was also involved in the operation, flying on this occasion in a 463 Squadron Lancaster from Waddington. Zero hour for the opening phase had been set for 00.05, but the Oboe Mosquitos were two minutes late, and some communications problems had to be ironed out before matters began to run smoothly. A large orange explosion at 00.28 sent a column of black smoke skyward, which impaired visibility to some extent, but, those attacking afterwards were able to identify a red spotfire and bomb it, observing large explosions and fires that were visible to the second phase crews as they approached. The 619 Squadron crews carried out their attacks from 7,000 to 11,000 feet between 00.24 and 00.50, but the crews of P/O Aitken and W/O Schofield were unable to pick up the aiming point through the smoke, despite making a number of passes, and returned their bombs to store. The second phase crews were drawn on by the fires, and had the glow of the burning target visible behind them for a hundred miles into the return flight. At debriefing, most expressed confidence that they had contributed to a successful operation, and post-raid reconnaissance confirmed the success of both phases of the raid, which had left the yards severely damaged for the loss of six Lancasters. Among these was 619 Squadron's veteran W4127, which crashed in the target area killing P/O French and all but the Canadian mid-upper gunner, who was spirited away by locals to retain his freedom. A congratulatory message from A-O-C Cochrane was received on all participating stations.

The real test for the 5 Group low-level marking system would come at a heavily defended German target, for which Braunschweig was selected on the 22nd, while the rest of the Command targeted the Ruhr city of Düsseldorf. 5 Group put together a force of 238 Lancasters and seventeen Mosquitos, with ten ABC Lancasters of 1 Group's 101 Squadron to provide radio countermeasures (RCM). 619 Squadron contributed sixteen Lancasters, which took off from Dunholme Lodge between 22.46 and 23.26 with S/L Whamond and the newly promoted S/L Fuller the senior pilots on duty, and they would again meet up at the target with W/C Tait in a 463 Squadron. There were no early returns among the 619 Squadron element, and all reached the target area after being guided by Path Finder route-markers. They encountered six to eight-tenths thin cloud at between 8,000 and 10,000 feet, and benefitted from accurate marking by the 617 Squadron Mosquito element. Despite this, the main force crews were unable to properly identify the aiming point, a situation again compounded by communications problems between various controllers, caused by the failure of VHF and the consequent need to pass on instructions instead by W/T. This led to confusion, and many crews were forced to orbit for up to fifteen minutes before bombing. The 619 Squadron crews carried out their attacks on green TIs and red spotfires from 19,000 to 22,000 feet between 01.57 and 02.11, before returning safely to report what appeared to be a successful operation, while also complaining about the dangers of orbiting a target with aircraft heading in a variety of directions. Although some bombs did fall in the city centre, most were directed at reserve H2S-laid TIs to the south of the city, and damage was less severe than might otherwise have been. Sgt Wadsworth and crew claimed the destruction of a Ju88, and were awaiting confirmation from other sources.

At 21.00 on the 23rd, the freshman crew of Sgt Broomfield took off from Dunholme Lodge in ME747 for a night cross-country exercise and failed to return. The thought was that they had fallen victim to an intruder, and reports came in eventually to confirm that the Lancaster had crashed into the sea two miles off Hornsea without survivors.

When Munich was posted across 5 Group as the target on the 24th for another live test of the low-level visual marking method, it might have been seen as somewhat ambitious to select such a major city, that was protected by two hundred flak guns. The main operation on this night was to be conducted by a force of 637 aircraft against Karlsruhe, 150 miles to the north-west, which, it was hoped, would help to distract the night-fighters. 234 Lancasters were made ready by 5 Group, and supplemented by ten of the ABC variety from 101 Squadron, while four Mosquitos of 617 Squadron were loaded with spotfires to carry out the marking, and twelve of 627 Squadron with Window to dispense during the final approach to the target. 619 Squadron's fifteen Lancasters took to the air between 20.34 and 21.09 with S/L Fuller the senior pilot on duty, and rendezvoused with the rest of the force as it headed for the south coast before setting course across France towards the south-east and feinting towards Italy. The 617 and 627 Squadron Mosquitos took off three hours after the heavy brigade and adopted a direct route, the latter laying a Window screen from high level six minutes from the target, masking the arrival of the flare force that was to provide seven minutes of illumination for the 617 marker Mosquitos. 619 Squadron's recent excellent record of serviceability continued, as all reached the target area to encounter clear skies and good visibility, in which W/C Cheshire dived onto the aiming point in the face of murderous light flak, before racing away across the rooftops to safety. The main force followed hard on his heels, the 619 Squadron crews bombing on the red spotfires and green TIs from 15,000 to 22,000 feet between 01.50 and 01.56 in the face of intense searchlight and flak activity. Many fires were seen to take hold, and, as the bombers pointed their snouts back towards France to eventually pass to the north of Paris, Karlsruhe could be seen burning over to starboard. Post-raid reconnaissance and local sources confirmed the success of the raid, which left 1,104 buildings in ruins and a further thirteen hundred severely damaged. It was probably this operation that sealed the award to Cheshire of the Victoria Cross at the conclusion of his operational career in July, after completing one hundred sorties. Among nine missing Lancasters was 619 Squadron's ME723, which had been brought down by flak to crash at 01.44 a mile south of the Speichersee to the north-east of Munich, killing W/O Schofield DFM and his crew.

At briefing on the 26th, thirteen 619 Squadron crews were told that Schweinfurt was to be their target that night, after the failure of the RAF to destroy it in February and the American 8th Air Force just two weeks ago. The tone was very much, "leave it to RAF Bomber Command", and, with the satisfaction of Munich still fresh in the mind, and the natural rivalry between the two forces, such attitudes were to be expected. They learned that, for this operation, 627 Squadron would act as the low-level marker force for the first time, and for a main force of 215 Lancasters, including nine from 101 Squadron to provide RCM protection. This was just one of three major operations taking place, with the main event at Essen, while the railway yards at Villeneuve-St-Georges were being attended to by a predominantly Halifax main force. The 619 Squadron element departed Dunholme Lodge between 21.03 and 21.36, with W/C Jeudwine and S/Ls Fuller and Whamond the senior pilots on duty. Stronger-than-forecast head winds delayed the arrival in the target area of the heavy brigade, which found generally clear skies and good visibility that the 627 Squadron crews failed to exploit, as their debut marking effort proved to be inaccurate. The 83 Squadron crews remarked on the lack of illumination, and those carrying hooded flares were called in a number of times to back-up. The 619 Squadron crews bombed from 14,000 to 21,000 feet between 02.25 and 02.40, aiming at red spotfires and green TIs, some following the instructions of the Master Bomber to overshoot by a thousand yards. A large white explosion was witnessed at 02.29, and many fires were reported, but, once again at this target, most of the hardware fell outside of the target area, leaving ball-bearing production more or less unaffected. Night-fighters got amongst the heavy force, and twenty-one Lancasters were shot down, a hefty 9.3%, and this time two of the victims belonged to 619 Squadron. LL905 came down somewhere in southern Germany with the eight-man crew of Sgt Whinfield on board, and the sole survivor was the Kiwi second pilot, who was taken into captivity. LL919 crashed just to the north of the Forêt du Pavillon in the Haute-Marne region of north-eastern France, killing all but the bomb-aimer in the more experienced crew of F/L Gunzi, and he joined his squadron colleague in enemy hands.

5 Group made preparations on the 28th to send a force of eighty-eight Lancasters and four Mosquitos to attack the Alfred Nobel Dynamit A.G explosives works at St-Médard-en-Jalles, situated in a wood on the north-western outskirts of Bordeaux in south-western France. A further fifty-one Lancasters and four Mosquitos would head in the opposite direction to target an aircraft maintenance facility at the Kjeller Flyfabrikk, some ten miles north-east of Oslo, which had been occupied by the Germans since April 1940 and was used by Junkers, Daimler-Benz and BMW. The latter was the destination for the 52 Base Dunholme Lodge squadrons, and ten 619 Squadron Lancasters took off between 21.06 and 21.23 with S/Ls Fuller and Whamond the senior pilots on duty. F/Sgt Paterson and crew lost their intercom and turned back, leaving the others to arrive in the target area to find clear skies and excellent visibility. They identified the target by H2S, confirmed by yellow TIs at the start of the bombing run, but the flares and red spotfires missed the aiming point, and the Master Bomber broadcast a two-thousand-yard correction to compensate for a poor marking performance. The 619 Squadron crews carried out their attacks from 5,000 to 7,500 feet between 01.29 and 01.40, observing explosions on the airfield and runway, and among barrack buildings and some of the sheds. An ammunition dump went up at 01.40, but crews were left uncertain as to the effectiveness of the attack, and 44 (Rhodesia) Squadron's commanding officer, W/C Thompson, was scathing about the quality of marking and control, and the amount of smoke given off by too many hooded flares. Meanwhile, more than eleven hundred miles to the south, the attack near Bordeaux had also been spoiled by smoke and haze from a wood burning nearby, and only twenty-six aircraft had bombed before the Master Bomber called a halt.

The operation against the dynamite works was rescheduled for the following night, when the Michelin tyre factory at Clermont-Ferrand was added to the target list, while the 52 Base squadrons remained at home. Post-raid reconnaissance confirmed that both targets had been severely damaged with a massive loss of production. During the course of the month, 619 Squadron participated in nine operations and dispatched 130 sorties for the loss of seven Lancasters and their crews.

May 1944

Twelve 619 Squadron crews joined seventeen from 44 (Rhodesia) Squadron at briefing at Dunholme Lodge on the 1st, to learn that they would be going to southern France that night to attack the Proudrerie explosives works at Toulouse. They would be part of two 5 Group forces totalling 131 Lancasters and eight Mosquitos targeting the city, the other to attack a SNCASE aircraft assembly factory at Saint-Martin-du-Touch, a western suburb. A third 5 Group force of forty-six Lancasters and four Mosquitos would be sent against an aircraft repair workshop at Tours in western France. The 619 Squadron crews took off between 21.09 and 21.38 with W/C Jeudwine and S/Ls Fuller and Whamond the senior pilots on duty, and employed Gee for the first part of the outward flight until it was jammed, relying, thereafter, on good navigation, green track markers provided by the Path Finders, and H2S. They all reached the target to find moonlight, clear skies and excellent visibility, with flares and red spotfires marking out the aiming point, backed up by green TIs, and carried out their attacks from 6,000 to 9,250 feet between 01.31 and 01.45 in accordance with the instructions of the Master Bomber. The bombing was clearly focused on the aiming point, where many detonations were observed and the glow of the burning site remained visible for a hundred miles into the return journey. All crews returned to their respective stations confident of a successful outcome, and post-raid reconnaissance revealed all three factories to have been heavily damaged.

Briefings took place on 1 and 5 Group stations on the 3rd, for what would become a highly contentious operation that night against a Panzer training camp and transport depot at Mailly-le-Camp, situated some seventy-five miles east of Paris in north-eastern France. The units based there posed a potential threat to Allied forces as the invasion unfolded and needed to be eliminated. The events of the operation proved to be so controversial, that recriminations abound to this day concerning the 5 Group leadership provided by W/Cs Cheshire and Deane. Although the grudges by 1 Group aircrew against them can be understood in the light of what happened, they are unjust, and based on emotion and incorrect information, and it is worthwhile to examine the conduct of the operation in some detail. W/C Cheshire was appointed as marker leader, and was piloting one of four 617 Squadron Mosquitos, while 83 Squadron's commanding officer, W/C Deane, was overall raid controller, with S/L Sparks as Deputy. Deane and Cheshire attended separate briefings, and neither seemed aware of the complete plan, particularly the role of the 1 Group Special Duties Flight from Binbrook, which was assigned to mark its own specific aiming point for an element of the 1 Group force.

The eleven 619 Squadron participants became airborne between 21.47 and 22.03 with S/Ls Fuller and Whamond the senior pilots on duty, and all reached the target area to find clear skies, moonlight and excellent bombing conditions, but confusion already beginning to influence events. 617 Squadron's W/C Cheshire and S/L Shannon were in position before midnight, and, as the first flares from the 83 and 97 Squadron Lancasters illuminated the target below, Cheshire released his two red spot fires onto the first aiming point at 00.00½ from 1,500 feet. Shannon backed them up from 400 feet five-and-a-half minutes later, and, as far as Cheshire was concerned, the operation was bang on schedule at this stage. A 97 Squadron Lancaster also laid markers accurately, to ensure a constant focal point, and Cheshire passed instructions to Deane to call the bombers in. It was at this stage of the operation that matters began to go awry. A communications problem arose, when a commercial radio station, believed to be an American forces network, jammed the VHF frequencies in use. Deane called in the 5 Group element, elated that everything was proceeding according to plan, but nothing happened. He checked with his wireless operator that the instructions had been transmitted, and called up S/L Sparks, who was also mystified by the lack of bombing. A few crews from 9, 207 and 467 Squadrons had heard the call to bomb, and did so, but, for most, the instructions were swamped by the interference. The 619 Squadron crews realised that R/T was jammed, and six of them, including both flight commanders, bombed between 00.01 and 00.15 from 4,900 to 6,250 feet on observing others to do so, and with smoke already beginning to drift across the target area. W/C Deane then attempted to control the operation by W/T, which also failed.

Post raid reports are contradictory, and it is impossible to establish an accurate course of events, particularly when Deane and Cheshire's understanding of the exact time of zero hour differed by five minutes. Remarkably, it also seems, that Deane was unaware that there were two marking points, or three, if one includes 1 Group's Special Duties Flight. Cheshire, initially at least, appeared happy with the early stages of the attack, and described the bombing as concentrated and accurate. It seems certain, however, that many minutes had passed between the dropping of Cheshire's markers and the first main force bombs falling, during which period, Deane was coming to terms with the fact, that his instructions were not getting through. A plausible scenario is, that in the absence of instructions, and with red spot fires clearly visible in the target, some crews opted to bomb, and others followed suit. These would have been predominantly from 5 Group, but as the 1 Group crews became increasingly agitated at having to wait in bright moonlight, with evidence of enemy night fighters all around, some of them inevitably joined in.

Now a new problem was arising. Smoke from these first salvoes was obliterating the entire camp, and Cheshire had to decide whether or not to send in Fawke and Kearns to mark the second aiming point. His feeling, and that of Deane, as it later transpired, was, that it was unnecessary. The volume of bombs still to fall into the relatively compact area of the target, would ensure destruction of the entire site. By 00.16, the first phase of bombing should have been completed, leaving a clear run for Fawke and Kearns across the target. In the event, the majority of 5 Group crews were still on their bombing run, a fact unknown to Cheshire, who asked Deane for a pause in the bombing, while the two Mosquitos went in. As far as Cheshire was concerned, there was no response from Deane, who would, anyway, have been confused by mention of a second aiming point. In the event, Deane's deputy, S/L Sparks, eventually found a channel free of interference, and did, in fact, transmit an instruction to halt the bombing, both by W/T and R/T, and some crews reported hearing something. While utter chaos reigned, Kearns and Fawke dived in among the falling cookies at 00.23 and 00.25 respectively, to mark the second aiming point on the western edge of the camp. At 2,000 feet, they were lucky to survive the turbulence created by the exploding 4,000 pounders, when 4,000 feet was considered to be a minimum safe height. They were not entirely happy with their work, but F/O Edwards of 97 Squadron dropped a stick of markers precisely on the mark, and S/L Sparks was then able to call the 1 Group main force in along with any from 5 Group with bombs still on board. Among these were the remaining 619 Squadron crews, who attacked from 5,000 to 6,000 feet between 00.27 and 00.37. Meanwhile, the night fighters continued to create havoc among the Lancasters as they milled around in the target area, and, as burning aircraft were seen to fall all around, some 1 Group crews succumbed to their anxiety and frustration. In a rare breakdown of R/T discipline, let fly with comments of an uncomplimentary nature, many of which were intended for, and, indeed, heard by Deane.

Despite the problems, the operation was a major success, which destroyed 80% of the camp's buildings, and 102 vehicles, of which thirty-seven were tanks, while over two hundred men were killed. Forty-two Lancasters failed to return, however, two thirds of them from 1 Group, while 50 Squadron was 5 Group's most afflicted unit with four Lancasters and crews unaccounted for. 619

Squadron posted missing the crew of P/O Wadsworth DFC in JB134, which crashed outbound at Courboin in the Hauts-de-France region some fifty miles north-east of Paris. There were no survivors among the eight occupants, and three were holders of the DFM. At debriefing, S/L Blome-Jones of 207 Squadron described the situation as a complete shambles and chaos, the controller as inefficient and the discipline of some crews as bad. Others voiced the opinion that this was a trip worthy of more than one-third of a sortie. On the following day, an inquest into the conduct of the raid revealed that the wireless transmitter in Deane's Lancaster had been sufficiently off frequency to allow the interference from the American network to mask the transmission of instructions and prevent the call to bomb from reaching the main force crews. The 1 Group A-O-C, AVM Rice, decided he would not participate in further operations organised by 5 Group, which was probably not a blow to Cochrane, who was confident that his group did not need back-up.

On the 6th, 1 and 5 Groups were invited to send a modest force each to attack ammunition dumps in France, 5 Group detailing sixty-four Lancasters and four Mosquitos for a site at Louailles, situated some four miles south-east of the town of Sable-sur-Sarthe, south-west of Le-Mans. Clear skies and excellent visibility provided ideal conditions, and a Master Bomber was on hand to direct the attack, which resulted in numerous bomb flashes that lit up the long storage sheds. Two enormous explosions were each followed by a large mushroom of smoke rising through 3,000 feet as the force withdrew. Dunholme Lodge sat this one out, but was alerted on the 7th to prepare for its part in five small-scale operations to be mounted against airfields, ammunition dumps and a coastal battery in support of the coming invasion. 5 Group was involved in two raids, the airfield at Tours and an ammunition dump at Salbris, some sixty miles to the east, and it was for the latter that 619 Squadron made ready thirteen Lancasters. An additional Lancaster was loaded with mines for F/O Redshaw and crew to deliver to the Nectarine I garden off the western Frisians, and all took off together between 21.47 and 22.08 with W/C Jeudwine and S/Ls Fuller and Whamond the senior pilots on duty on what turned out to be another night of perfect conditions. They headed south to pass by Reading on their way to Selsey Bill for the Channel crossing, intending to make landfall at Cabourg before setting course for the target. Gee working perfectly all the way out, and, with twenty miles horizontal visibility under bright moonlight, the red spotfires were observed well in advance of arrival at the aiming point. ND730 crashed at Champigny-en-Beauce between Tours and Orleans in north-west central France, it is believed while outbound, and S/L Fuller perished with the other seven occupants. Those from 619 Squadron reaching the target carried out their attacks from 5,300 to 8,000 feet between 00.28 and 00.36, and observed large, vivid explosions and a column of smoke rising through 11,000 feet as they withdrew. Post-raid reconnaissance confirmed that both targets had been bombed accurately and effectively to leave them severely damaged. Meanwhile, F/O Redshaw and crew had successfully delivered their mines unopposed from below the cloud base at 4,000 feet at 00.05 after establishing their position by Gee-fix. They returned safely from an uneventful sortie, but, sadly, would not survive the month.

Another small-scale operation was mounted by the group on the 8th against the airfield and seaplane base at Lanveoc-Poulmic, located on the northern side of the peninsula forming the southern boundary of the L'Elorn estuary opposite Brest. A force of fifty-eight Lancasters and six Mosquitos identified the target easily by the coastline and layout of the hangars, which they left on fire along with other buildings and the entire site enveloped in smoke. The night of the 9/10th brought attacks on seven coastal batteries in the Pas-de-Calais by four hundred aircraft. The purpose of these operations was to confirm in the mind of the enemy the belief that the Allied invasion forces would land at Calais, and right up to D-Day itself, the coastal region between Gravelines to the east of the port and Berck-sur-Mer to the south-west, would be subjected to constant bombardment. 5 Group, meanwhile, prepared fifty-six Lancasters and eight Mosquitos to attack two factories, the Gnome & Rhône aero-engine works and the Goodrich tyre factory at Gennevilliers in northern Paris, while a second force of thirty-nine Lancasters and four Mosquitos targeted a small ball-bearing factory at Annecy, situated in south-eastern France close to the frontiers with Switzerland and Italy. 52 Base was assigned to Paris for which 619 Squadron made ready a dozen Lancasters, which departed Dunholme Lodge between 22.09 and 22.31 with F/Ls Buttar and Roberts the senior pilots on duty. They rendezvoused with the other squadrons over Reading, before beginning the Channel crossing at Shoreham-on-Sea and making landfall on the French coast near Dieppe. P/O Baker and crew had dropped out by then after their starboard-inner engine and mid-upper turret failed. Moonlight and clear skies enabled the others to map read after Gee was jammed at the French coast, and H2S proved useful as they closed on Paris. Yellow TIs and red spotfires identified the aiming point, and the bombing by the 619 Squadron crews proceeded from 5,500 to 9,600 feet between 00.35 and 00.43. Local sources confirmed damage to the target, but, also, collateral damage that killed twenty-seven French civilians and injured more than a hundred. The squadron's LM446 was among five missing Lancasters, and, was established later to have crashed at Aubergenville near the south bank of the Seine some twenty miles north-west of Paris. It was another eight-man crew captained by P/O Aitken RNZAF, and only the rear gunner survived to fall into enemy hands. Post-raid reconnaissance confirmed the Annecy site also to have been severely damaged.

Five railway targets were selected for attention on the night of the 10/11th, among them the marshalling yards at Lille for 5 Group. Bomb bursts were seen across the tracks, and two large explosions were observed to confirm a successful assault on this important hub linking north-eastern France with Belgium. Night-fighters were out in force, and most of the night's casualties resulted from this operation, from which a dozen Lancasters failed to return. 5 Group put together a force of 190 Lancasters and eight Mosquitos on the 11th, to target a military camp at Bourg-Leopold in north-eastern Belgium, for which 619 Squadron made ready fifteen Lancasters. They departed Dunholme Lodge between 22.09 and 22.40 with W/C Jeudwine and S/L Whamond the senior pilots on duty, but the commanding officer was forced to turn back from what would be his final sortie with the squadron after his starboard-outer engine caught fire when approaching the Suffolk coast. The others reached the target to find hazy conditions and a little thin cloud at around 10,000 feet, despite which, they would be able to identify ground detail in the form of buildings and huts in the light of illuminating flares. Three Oboe Mosquitos were on hand to deliver the initial marking, but inaccurately forecast winds caused the 83 Squadron element to arrive late, by which time the main force crews had begun to orbit to await instructions. A communications problem prevented some crews from hearing the Master Bomber's broadcasts, but the aiming point could be seen to be marked by red spotfires and green TIs. From the Master Bomber's perspective, the initial Oboe marker had been visible only to a few crews, and quickly burned out, and so he called for another Mosquito to drop a red spot fire onto the aiming point. Before this was accomplished, however, the main force began to bomb, and seven 619 Squadron crews were among ninety-four to release their loads, doing so from 15,000 and 17,000 feet between 00.18 and 00.23. As smoke began to obscure the ground, the Master Bomber, S/L Mitchell, quickly became uncomfortable about the close proximity of civilian residential property, and called a halt to the bombing at 00.35, before sending the rest of the force home, some of them after circling for more than twenty minutes.

Minor operations occupied elements of the Command, thereafter, until the 19th, during which period W/C Jeudwine was award a DFC on the 13th, before being posted on the 15th to 54 Base at Coningsby, where he would excel as a member of the Master Bomber fraternity, rubbing shoulders with the likes of Tait, Owen, Woodroffe, Benjamin and Porter to name but a few. He had completed sixty-seven sorties, thirty-three of them by daylight in the Far East, and would carry out more as a Master Bomber, usually flying 5 Group's American P38 Lightning twin-engine fighter, which was ideal for the task. W/C Jeudwine's crew was posted to 83 Squadron, where their experience would be highly valued. 619 Squadron and W/C Jeudwine would meet up again in October at the end of his operational career, on his appointment to command Dunholme Lodge for its final two days in 5 Group, before moving with the squadron to command its new home at Strubby, some five miles from the Lincolnshire coast at Sutton-on-Sea. Until the appointment of a new commanding officer, S/L Whamond stepped into the breach.

When orders began to arrive on stations on the 19th, the teleprinters worked overtime dispensing the details of five operations that night targeting marshalling yards, two on coastal batteries and one against a radar station. 5 Group detailed 225 Lancasters, 112 to be sent to Amiens with eight Mosquitos, and 113 for Tours with four Mosquitos, and 52 Base was assigned to the former. 619 Squadron made ready sixteen Lancasters, which departed Dunholme Lodge between 22.52 and 23.19 with S/L Whamond the senior pilot on duty, and set course for north-eastern France via Hastings and Dieppe. They found the target shrouded in a layer of eight to ten-tenths cloud between 6,000 and 11,000 feet, and the aiming point apparently identified by red spotfires, but when checked on H2S, these appeared to be up to five miles away. S/L Whamond bombed from 6,000 feet at 01.21 and F/O Roberts and P/O Crawford from 6,000 and 9,200 feet at 01.22, and were among thirty-seven to carry out an attack before instructions came through by W/T at 01.25 to terminate the attack and return home. The others either jettisoned their loads on the way home across the Channel or brought them back. The Tours raid had been directed at the marshalling yards in the centre of the city, which required great precision on the part of the marker and main forces, both of which performed magnificently to leave the target severely damaged without causing collateral damage.

For the first time in a year, Duisburg was posted as the target for raid by the heavy brigade on the 21st, for which a force of 510 Lancasters was drawn from 1, 3, 5 and 8 Groups. They would be supported by twenty-two Mosquitos, and, while this operation was in progress, seventy Lancasters, including some from 5 Group, and thirty-seven Halifaxes, would undertake gardening duties in the Nectarines and Rosemary gardens around the Frisians and off Heligoland, and in the Forget-me-not, Silverthorn and Quince gardens in the Kattegat and Kiel Bay regions of the Baltic. 619 Squadron supported the main event with thirteen Lancasters, which departed Dunholme Lodge between 22.34 and 23.01 with F/L Buttar the senior pilot on duty. They had been told at briefing to adhere to the plan for the outward route, which involved a few aircraft from 3 Group gaining height as they adopted a north-westerly course as far as Sleaford, so as not to cross into enemy radar cover earlier than necessary. The groups would rendezvous at 18,000 feet over the North Sea at 3 degrees east to cross the enemy coast via the western Frisians at 20,000 feet and climb to 22,000 or 23,000 feet, before increasing speed for the run across the target. 619 Squadron lost the services of the crews of P/O Davis to an unserviceable wireless receiver and F/O Wingate to a starboard-outer engine issue, leaving the others to reach the Ruhr, which they found to be concealed beneath ten-tenths cloud with tops at between 11,000 and 20,000 feet. The Path Finder red Wanganui markers with-yellow-stars fell into the cloud tops almost before they could be seen, and this, combined with inaccurate data provided by the windfinder system, made it difficult for crews to establish their positions. The 52 Base crews used the explosion of cookies, the glow of fires and the evidence of intense flak as references and the 619 Squadron participants bombed from 18,000 to 22,500 feet between 01.15 and 01.29, before returning home with little useful information to report. NN695 was homebound over Norfolk when pounced upon by an enemy intruder, which shot it down to crash near East Wretham bomber station, and only one man survived from the crew of F/O Redshaw. The failure to return of twenty-nine Lancasters was a reminder to the Command that the Ruhr remained a dangerous destination, although most of the missing had come down onto Dutch and Belgian soil or into the sea homebound, after falling victim to night-fighters. Martin Drewes of III./NJG1 alone accounted for at least three Lancasters. Returning crews were not enthusiastic about the outcome, and post-raid reconnaissance confirmed that a modest 350 buildings had been destroyed in the southern half of Duisburg, and 665 others had been seriously damaged.

Just like Duisburg, Dortmund was posted on the 22nd to host its first large-scale visit from the Command for a year, and would face an all-Lancaster heavy force of 361 aircraft drawn from 1, 3, 6 and 8 Groups. While this operation was in progress, 220 Lancasters of 5 Group and five from 101 Squadron were to target Braunschweig, which, thus far, had evaded severe damage at the hands of the Command. 619 Squadron made ready fourteen Lancasters, which departed Dunholme Lodge between 22.24 and 22.50 with F/Ls Buttar and Roberts the senior pilots on duty. P/O Runnalls complained of dizziness, and turned back, leaving the others to press on through the clearly evident night-fighter activity from the Dutch coast all the way to the target, and negotiated the patches of ten-tenths cloud over northern Germany and intense searchlight activity as they passed between Bremen and Osnabrück. The forecast at briefings had suggested clear skies over Braunschweig, but, in fact, the marker force encountered four to seven-tenths drifting cloud with tops up to 7,000 feet. Although highly effective in the right weather conditions, the 5 Group low-level visual marking method could easily be rendered ineffective by cloud cover. The blind heavy marker crews dropped skymarkers by H2S, while the 627 Squadron Mosquito element went in at low level to release red spotfires. Some crews described "hopeless confusion" with flares and incendiaries spread over a distance, and many had to rely on their own H2S to establish their position. Some found a complete absence of marking and orbited for up to fifteen minutes until a few green TIs appeared, and bombing by the 619 Squadron element took place on these or on incendiary fires from 19,000 to 22,000 feet between 01.18 and 01.38. Considerable interference over R/T communications added to the problems, and, although the Master Bomber could be heard in discussions with his Deputies, no instructions were received from him, and the attack lacked cohesion. Post-raid reconnaissance confirmed that most of the bombing had fallen onto outlying communities, confirming in the minds of the residents that this was, indeed, an intentional ploy by the Command. It was a relatively expensive failure that cost thirteen Lancasters, although none belonging to the 52 Base squadrons.

The main operation on the 24th would involve 442 aircraft in an attack on two marshalling yards at Aachen, Aachen-West and Rothe-Erde in the east. As the most westerly city in Germany, sitting on the frontiers of both Holland and Belgium, it was a major link in the railway network that would be a route for reinforcements to the Normandy battle front. Other operations on this night would be directed at coastal batteries in the Pas-de-Calais and war-industry factories in Holland and Belgium. 5 Group detailed forty-four Lancasters to attack the Ford Motor works in Antwerp, and fifty-nine for the Philips electronics factory at Eindhoven in southern Holland, while 52 Base remained off the Order of Battle. Those bound for Eindhoven were more than an hour into the outward journey when the Master Bomber sent them home by W/T, presumably after a Met Flight Mosquito crew had found poor visibility in the target area. There were no such difficulties at Antwerp, where the target was identified by illuminating flares, a yellow TI and red spotfires, despite which, post-raid reconnaissance revealed the factory to be intact.

An immediate award of the DFC was made to S/L Whamond on the 26th, a day of preparations for minor operations, including mining in Nectarine I off the western Frisians and one of the Silverthorn gardens in the Kattegat off the eastern coast of Jutland. 44 (Rhodesia) Squadron represented 52 Base, while 619 Squadron remained at home, and its crews were fully rested when fourteen of them were called to briefing on the 27th to learn of a night of feverish activity, which would generate more than eleven hundred sorties, reflecting the close proximity of the invasion, now just ten days away. The largest operation would bring a return to the military camp at Bourg Leopold in Belgium, the previous attack on which, two weeks earlier, had been abandoned part-way through. There was also a repeat of the Aachen attack of the 24th, which had failed to destroy the Rothe-Erde marshalling yards at the eastern end of the city and needed further attention. 5 Group was not involved in either of the above, and, instead, prepared forces of one hundred Lancasters and four Mosquitos and seventy-eight Lancasters and five Mosquitos respectively to target marshalling yards and workshops at Nantes and the aerodrome at Rennes, situated some fifty miles apart in north-western France. The group would also support operations against coastal batteries, of which there were five on this night, including one at Morsalines, situated on the eastern seaboard of the Cherbourg peninsula, some ten miles north of what, during the forthcoming Operation Overlord, would be the Americans' Utah landing ground. This was the target for 52 Base, for which fourteen 619 Squadron Lancasters would join eighteen representing 44 (Rhodesia) Squadron, the former departing Dunholme Lodge between 22.28 and 22.55 with S/L Whamond and S/L Gunter the senior pilots on duty, the latter having recently arrived with his crew from 51 Base (5 Group's conversion units). All reached the target area on Gee-fix to find seven-tenths cloud at 3,000 to 4,000 feet, but fair visibility, and the aiming point was identified by flares, red spotfires and green TIs. The 619 Squadron participants carried out their attacks from 5,000 to 7,000 feet between 01.00 and 01.15 in accordance with the instructions of a Master Bomber, and observed the bombing to be concentrated around the markers. Cloud and smoke obscured much of the detail, but the consensus was, that if the markers had been accurate, the target had been hit.

On the 28th, 181 Lancasters and twenty Mosquitos continued the attacks on coastal batteries overlooking the Normandy beaches, which, a week hence, would be the scene of Operation Overlord. 52 Base was not called into action on this night, or on the following two nights, and it was on the 31st when the next operational orders were received to prepare for further operations that night against coastal batteries covering the Normandy beaches. 5 Group was to send a force of eighty-two Lancasters and four Mosquitos to attack a railway junction at Saumur in the Loire Valley, and another of sixty-eight Lancasters to a coastal battery at Maisy, overlooking what would be the Americans' Omaha Beach. It was for the latter that the Dunholme Lodge squadrons prepared a dozen Lancasters each, those from 619 Squadron taking off between 22.50 and 23.12 with W/C Maling, the new commanding officer and another to arrive from 51 Base, the senior pilot on duty.

His operational experience to date had largely been gained during a thirteen-month tour in India ending in early 1942. They had to fly through a belt of storm-bearing clouds as they flew from base to Reading, and the foul weather continued as they passed over Selsey Bill to start the Channel crossing. The leading crews were within seven miles of the French coast when they were recalled by W/T and diverted to Wing and Westcott in Buckinghamshire. During the course of the month the squadron carried out eleven operations including the recall, and dispatched 133 sorties for the loss of four Lancasters and their crews.

June 1944

June was to be a hectic month which would make great demands on the crews. The bombing of coastal batteries was to be the priority during the first few days leading up to D-Day, but 5 Group would open its account by returning to Saumur to attack a second railway junction on the 1st. The day dawned cloudy and cold, and these conditions would persist throughout the first week of the month, causing concern among the invasion planners. The 52 Base squadrons remained at home, while fifty-eight Lancasters took off in the late evening to find ten-tenths cloud covering the route out to within twenty miles of the town, where it dispersed completely to leave clear skies and good visibility under a three-quarter moon. The flare force was almost superfluous in the conditions, but the first wave was called in by the Master Bomber, W/C Jeudwine, to release from 15,000 feet at 01.08, and the first red spot fire from an Oboe Mosquito fell bang on the aiming point two minutes later. Smoke became a problem as it drifted across the area to obscure the spotfire that was still burning, and a green TI was dropped to maintain the aiming point. Apart from a few scattered sticks to the north, and on an island in the Loire to the south, the attack seemed to be accurate. Returning crews reported little opposition, fires in the yards and a large explosion at 01.35, and the success of the raid was confirmed by photographic reconnaissance, which showed severe damage to the track.

Fourteen 619 Squadron crews were among those called to briefing at Dunholme Lodge on the 2nd, when they were told that they would be joining forty-seven other Lancasters of the group to maintain the invasion deception by attacking a coastal battery at Wimereux, situated south-west of Calais. They took off between 23.36 and 00.19 with W/C Maling and S/L Gunter the senior pilots on duty, and all reached the French coast to encounter the most unfavourable weather conditions including ten-tenths cloud at 10,000 feet. The glow of red TIs greeted their arrival, but the Master Bomber was uncomfortable with the conditions and sent the force home after only a handful of crews had released their bombs, none of them from 619 Squadron. The outcome, in terms of damage, was unimportant, as long as it reinforced in the mind of the enemy, that Calais was to be the destination of the expected invasion force. The Squadron remained off the Order of Battle thereafter until D-Day Eve, while ninety-six Lancasters of the group carried out an operation on the 3rd against a listening station at Ferme-d'Urville, situated on the Cherbourg peninsula to the west of the port, which had escaped damage when attacked by Halifaxes two nights earlier. The bombing was focused within a five-hundred-yard radius of the aiming point, and was confirmed by post-raid reconnaissance to have obliterated the site.

Orders came through on the 4th to prepare for attacks that night on coastal batteries, three in the Pas-de-Calais to maintain the deception, and the one at Maisy, overlooking the Utah and Omaha beaches. 259 aircraft of 1, 4, 5, 6 and 8 Groups were made ready, the majority for the deception targets, while fifty-two of the Lancasters, all representing 5 Group, were assigned to Maisy. 52 Base was not involved in these pre-dawn attacks, which took place through ten-tenths cloud with a base at around 4,000 feet. This necessitated the use of Oboe skymarkers, and positions were confirmed by Gee-fix and a faint red glow, before the bombing was carried out from just above the cloud tops. It was impossible to assess the outcome, and similarly cloudy conditions had thwarted two of the three attempts in the Pas-de-Calais.

The night of the 5/6th was D-Day Eve, and, during the course of the night, a record number of 1,211 sorties would be flown against coastal defences and in support and diversionary operations. Sixteen crews each from 44 (Rhodesia) and 619 Squadrons attended briefing at Dunholme Lodge, where no direct reference was made to the invasion, but, unusually, they were given strict altitudes at which to fly, and were told not to jettison bombs over the sea. They learned also that they would be among more than a thousand aircraft targeting ten heavy gun batteries along the Normandy coast, and that their specific objective was at La Pernelle, some three miles north of the recently attacked Morsalines battery, which, although not disclosed to them, was close to Utah Beach. The plan called for 5 Group to provide 122 Lancasters and four Mosquitos for this site, and 115 Lancasters and four Mosquitos for a second target at Saint-Pierre-du-Mont, which was the closest to Omaha Beach. 83 Squadron would provide the illumination and the marking for the former, while 97 Squadron took care of business at the latter, led by W/C Jimmy Carter. The 52 Base squadrons loaded their Lancasters with a mixture of 1,000 and 500 pounders and the 619 Squadron element departed Dunholme Lodge between 01.19 and 01.54 with W/C Maling and S/L Gunter the senior pilots on duty. They all arrived in the target area to find a layer of ten-tenths cloud with a base at around 7,000 feet and tops at 12,000 feet, with broken cloud below, through which the glow of the red and green TIs and red spotfires could be seen. The bombing was carried out by twelve of the 619 Squadron crews from 8,000 to 11,500 feet between 03.40 and 04.01, while four others still had their bombs on board when the Master Bomber called a halt to proceedings and sent them home. Any homeward-bound crews looking down through the occasional gaps in the clouds were rewarded by the incredible sight of the greatest armada in history, ploughing its way sedately southwards towards the French coast. A total of five thousand tons of bombs was dropped during the night, and this was a new record. Only seven aircraft failed to return from these operations, three of them from Sainte-Pierre, including the one containing 97 Squadron's W/C Carter and seven highly experienced crewmen, all but one of whom held either a DFC or DFM.

As the beachheads were being established during the course of the 6th, preparations were put in hand to support the ground forces by attacking nine road and railway communications centres through which the enemy could bring reinforcements. 5 Group was assigned to two targets, Argentan supply depot and railway centre located some thirty miles south-east of Caen, and a road bridge in Caen itself, for which forces of 112 Lancasters and six Mosquitos and 120 Lancasters and four Mosquitos respectively were assembled. 619 Squadron made ready seventeen Lancasters for the latter, and they departed Dunholme Lodge between 00.24 and 00.55 with S/L Gunter the senior pilot on duty. They began the Channel crossing at Bridport on the Dorset coast, and headed for the Channel Islands before turning sharply to the east to cross the Cherbourg peninsula. All reached the target area to find ten-tenths cloud with a base at 5,000 to 6,000 feet, below which, 627

Squadron Mosquitos ran in at low-level to drop red spotfires. These were then supplemented by red TIs from the heavy marker element, after which, the 619 Squadron crews attacked the aiming point from below the cloud base from 2,500 to 5,000 feet between 02.39 and 02.51, in accordance with the Master Bomber's instructions, and were able to clearly pick out the river, marshalling yards and town detail. Six Lancasters failed to return from the Caen raid, largely as the result of the need for the force to orbit while the markers were assessed. 619 Squadron's LL783 came down between Baupt to the west and Carentan to the east, taking with it the experienced F/L Roberts DFC RAAF and four of his crew, and delivering the flight engineer and bomb-aimer into enemy hands.

Four railway targets were earmarked for attention by a force of 337 aircraft on the 7th, while elements of 5 Group were being prepared to join forces with 1 and 8 Groups to attack a six-way road junction at Balleroy, situated fifteen miles west of Caen on the approach to the Foret-de-Cerisy, where it was believed the enemy was concealing a fuel dump and tank units. The 52 Base squadrons were not involved in the operation, which took place in conditions of ten-tenths cloud with a base at 8,000 to 10,000 feet and haze below. The initial Oboe markers appeared to be accurate and on time, but another marker fell simultaneously some five miles to the south-west and attracted some bomb loads. The Master Bomber quickly gained control of the situation and directed the bombing to the correct marker, which was pounded by concentrated bombing. Dense clouds of black smoke and one particularly large explosion were evidence of a successful outcome, during which the gunners in the crew of the 207 Squadron commanding officer shot down three enemy fighters in a twenty-minute period.

The night of the 8/9th was devoted to the disruption of railway communications, for which 483 aircraft were detailed and assigned to five centres. Orders were received at Dunholme Lodge for 44 (Rhodesia) and 619 Squadrons to prepare a dozen and fourteen Lancasters respectively as part of a 5 Group force of fifty-four Lancasters and four Mosquitos assigned to railway installations at Pontabault, while a second force of ninety-seven Lancasters and four Mosquitos attended to a similar objective at Rennes in Brittany, thirty miles to the south-west. 617 Squadron would also operate on this night to deliver the very first Barnes Wallis-designed 12,000lb Tallboy earthquake bombs against the railway tunnel at Saumur. The 619 Squadron element took off between 22.12 and 22.43 with W/C Maling and S/L Whamond the senior pilots on duty, but lost the services of P/O Molinas and crew to the failure of their hydraulics system. The others reached the target area to encounter up to six-tenths stratocumulus cloud at 6,000 feet and a layer at 2,000 feet, and the first attempt to mark was cancelled with yellow TIs. The second attempt with red spotfires and TIs was successful, and the bombing took place in accordance with the instructions of the Master Bomber from 4,000 to 8,000 feet between 00.45 and 01.08. Returning crews reported concentrated bombing on or near the markers, and the operation was deemed to have been successful.

401 aircraft from 1, 4, 6 and 8 Groups were detailed on the 9th to target airfields in the battle area, while 5 Group concentrated on a railway junction at Etampes, south of Paris. 108 Lancasters and four Mosquitos were to take part, fourteen of them representing 619 Squadron, which departed Dunholme Lodge between 21.35 and 22.01 with S/L Gunter the senior pilot on duty. Those reaching the target found eight to ten-tenths cloud with a base at 8,000 feet, and patches of two to three-tenths lower down at 4,000 feet, but this had no effect on the marking with red spotfires, backed up with green and yellow TIs and illumination flares. Some crews thought that they had

picked up a recall signal, and others a message at around midnight to orbit, until being called in to bomb. The 619 Squadron participants carried out their attacks from 5,000 to 7,200 feet between midnight and 00.21, three crews after the Master Bomber had called an end to bombing at 00.17, while F/Sgt Buckley and crew heard the order and withheld their bombs. It appeared to be a successful operation, at a cost of six Lancasters, and photo-reconnaissance confirmed that all tracks had been cut for a distance of four hundred yards to the north-east of the junction. It also revealed that the town had sustained collateral damage, which had caused many civilian casualties.

5 Group detailed 108 Lancasters and four Mosquitos on the 10th, and briefed the crews for an attack on a railway junction at Orleans, situated some thirty miles south-west of Paris. 52 Base was not involved in this operation, which took place under clear skies and in good visibility, and appeared to be successful. The campaign against communications targets continued on the 12th at six locations, including Caen and Poitiers, for which 5 Group detailed forces of 109 Lancasters and four Mosquitos and 112 Lancasters and four Mosquitos respectively. 52 Base was assigned to the former, where road bridges were the specific targets, and the 619 Squadron element of sixteen Lancasters departed Dunholme Lodge between 23.45 and 00.19 with W/C Maling the senior pilot on duty. All reached the Caen area, where they encountered six to ten-tenths cloud with tops at between 4,000 and 6,000 feet, which provided difficult conditions in which to spot the TIs on the ground. A strict timing was imposed for the duration of the attack, and eleven 619 Squadron crews delivered their loads from 4,500 to 10,000 feet between 02.21 and 02.29, before the Master Bomber called a halt and sent more than thirty Lancasters home without bombing. In contrast, clear conditions attended the raid on Poitiers, and photo-reconnaissance revealed the Paris to Bordeaux line to have been cut in seven places. A new oil campaign began on this night, prosecuted by 286 Lancasters and seventeen Mosquitos of 1, 3 and 8 Groups, whose target was the Nordstern (Gelsenberg A.G.) plant at Gelsenkirchen. Such was the accuracy of the attack, that all production of vital aviation fuel was halted for a number of weeks at a cost to the Germans of a thousand tons per day.

The 14th brought Bomber Command's first daylight operation since the departure of 2 Group twelve months earlier. The target was Le Havre, from where the enemy's E-Boats and other fast, light marine craft were posing a threat to Allied shipping supplying the Normandy beachheads. The two-phase operation was conducted by predominantly 1 and 3 Groups with 617 Squadron representing 5 Group, and took place in the evening under the umbrella of a fighter escort. The attack was highly successful, and few craft survived the onslaught. Other operations on this night were directed against railway installations at three locations in France, while elements of 4, 5 and 8 Groups attended to enemy troop and vehicle concentrations at Aunay-sur-Odon and Évrecy near Caen. 5 Group assembled a force of 214 Lancasters and five Mosquitos for the former, of which sixteen of 619 Squadron departed Dunholme Lodge between 22.15 and 22.53 with S/L Whamond the senior pilot on duty and undertaking the final sortie of his second tour. The weather was generally clear with some low cloud, but this did not hamper the marking process, which proceeded punctually and accurately. W/C Jeudwine was the Master Bomber, with 83 Squadron's W/C Northrop as Deputy, and the latter made four passes over the target, at 00.30 at 8,000 feet, 00.41 at 10,000 feet, and at 00.54 and 01.00 at 11,000 feet, dropping clusters of flares on the first two, green TIs on the third and red TIs on the fourth. The 619 Squadron crews bombed the above-mentioned TIs from 5,800 to 10,000 feet between 00.37 and 01.04, observing what appeared to be a concentrated attack that produced numerous fires and much black smoke.

Although S/L Whamond would not leave Dunholme Lodge immediately, his successor as a flight commander, S/L Smith, had already arrived from 51 Base and carried out his first familiarisation flight on the 15th. A force of 297 aircraft from 1, 4, 5, 6 and 8 Groups was assembled on this day to try to do to Boulogne what had been done to Le Havre twenty-four hours earlier. It was again left to 617 Squadron to represent 5 Group, and the operation was concluded with equal success. While this was in progress, 5 Group dispatched 110 Lancasters and four Mosquitos to deal with a fuel dump at Châtellerault, situated between Tours and Poitiers in western France. 52 Base was not involved in the operation, which took place under clear skies and in good visibility, after which, post-raid reconnaissance confirmed that eight out of thirty-five individual fuel storage sites within the target had been destroyed.

Plans were put in hand on the 16th, to launch 829 sorties that night against a number of targets. Just three days earlier, the first V-1 flying bombs had landed on London, and this prompted a response in the form of a second new campaign to open during the month, this one against the revolutionary weapon's launching and storage sites in the Pas-de-Calais. Four targets were earmarked for attention, 5 Group assigned to a storage site at Beauvoir, located some twenty miles inland from Berck-sur-Mer. The large storage sites, many in various stages of construction, were referred to in Bomber Command parlance as "constructional works", while others, called "ski sites", were small buildings in the shape of a hockey stick and were attached to launching ramps. 112 Lancasters were detailed, seventeen each provided by the Dunholme Lodge squadrons, and the 619 Squadron element took off between 22.50 and 23.21 with W/C Maling the senior pilot on duty. They all reached the target area to find nine to ten-tenths cloud with tops at 6,000 to 8,000 feet, and bombed on the faint glow of red Oboe markers from 10,000 to 13,000 feet between 00.40 and 00.49. It was impossible to assess the outcome, which left crews with little to pass on to the Intelligence Section at debriefing.

The oil campaign continued on this night, when elements of 1, 4, 6 and 8 Groups carried out an attack on the Ruhr-Chemie synthetic oil plant at Sterkrade-Holten, a district of Oberhausen in the Ruhr, but cloudy conditions caused the bombing to be scattered, and there was little impact on production. With the exception of 617 Squadron, 5 Group remained inactive over the ensuing days, leaving the "specialists" to attack constructional works at Watten and Wizernes with Tallboys in daylight on the 19th and 20th. Cloudy conditions affected accuracy at the former and caused the latter to be aborted, so as not to waste the precious, highly engineered and inordinately expensive Tallboys.

5 Group had to wait until Mid-Summer's Night, the 21st, before becoming involved in the oil offensive, and was handed two targets to attack simultaneously. A force of 120 Lancasters from 52 and 55 Bases and six Mosquitos from 54 Base was assembled for the refinery at Wesseling, or to give it its full name, the Union Rheinische Braunkohlen-Kraftstoff Aktien Gesellschaft, situated on the east bank of the Rhine south of Cologne. On the 53 and 54 Base stations, meanwhile, 120 Lancasters and four Mosquitos were made ready for the Hydrierwerke-Scholven plant in the Buer district of Gelsenkirchen, and both operations would benefit from a sprinkling of ABC Lancasters of 101 Squadron for RCM duties, while a number of Path Finder Oboe Mosquitos would provide the initial marking at the Ruhr target. 619 Squadron made ready sixteen Lancasters for Wesseling, and they departed Dunholme Lodge between 22.59 and 23.31 with F/L Saunders the senior pilot

on duty, before heading into the greatest disaster to befall 5 Group in the war. F/O Morcom and crew abandoned their sortie because of DR compass failure, leaving the others to make landfall on the enemy coast over the Western Schelde, before crossing Belgium to enter Germany south of Aachen. They arrived in the target area having observed many combats as they made their way inland and expected to find clear skies, instead of which, they encountered up to ten-tenths low cloud at 2,500 to 4,000 feet, which was the Achilles heel in the otherwise highly effective 5 Group low-level marking method. It created impossible conditions for the Mosquito crews, who were unable to do their job, and faced with this situation, the Master Bomber, W/C Tait, ordered a blind attack, which required the Lancaster crews to bomb on their own H2S or on the red and green TIs dropped by 83 Squadron also on H2S. The 619 Squadron crews bombed from 17,000 to 20,000 feet between 01.39 and 01.46 in the face of heavy predicted flak, and a large explosion at 01.46 caused an extensive red glow in the cloud, before another one was witnessed at 01.51. There was shock at Dunholme Lodge when twelve of the Lancasters that had taken off from there just a few hours earlier failed to return, and each squadron had six empty dispersals to contemplate in dawn's early light. After the war, a secret German report would suggest a 40% loss of production at the site, but this was probably of very short duration as the limited number of casualties on the ground pointed to a scattered and largely ineffective raid. Whatever the degree of success, it was gained at the high cost of thirty-seven Lancasters, a massive 28%, and all but two of them belonged to 5 Group Squadrons. 44, 49, 57 and 619 Squadrons each lost six Lancasters, although one from 57 Squadron ditched off the English coast and the crew was rescued, while 207 and 630 Squadrons each posted missing five Lancasters and crews.

An analysis concluded that the Wesseling force had been hacked to pieces by night-fighters benefitting from the excellent visibility above the cloud, and it was the worst night of the war for both 44 (Rhodesia) and 619 Squadrons. It is not possible to determine the sequence of 619 Squadron's losses, as the outward and inbound routes each crossed Belgium and Holland, but, the likelihood is, that most were on their way to the target when their end came. LL808 was carrying the eight-man crew of P/O Johnson, who died with two others when it came down in the general target area and delivered the five survivors into enemy hands. LL977 was hit by flak near Aachen and exploded, flinging clear the pilot, F/L Saunders, who was the sole survivor among the eight occupants. ME846 crashed near Antwerp killing P/O Davis and both gunners, while ED859, the squadron's oldest Lancaster with seventy-one sorties behind it, was a night-fighter victim and crashed at Hetzerath, twenty-five miles east of Luxembourg with no survivors from the crew of F/Sgt Buckley. ND986 was almost certainly homebound when it was brought down by flak to crash into the Rhine at Duisburg, and took with it to their deaths the crew of P/O Crawford RAAF, which contained members of the RCAF, RNZAF and RAF. Finally, P/O Baker and four of his crew lost their lives when NE151 came down in the target area and the survivors fell into enemy hands. The sad fact was that thirty-two 619 Squadron airmen had been killed and twelve taken prisoner, and, when added to the forty-three absentees from the 44 (Rhodesia) Squadron ranks, this meant that eighty-seven members of the Dunholme Lodge community had gone in a single night.

Similar conditions had thwarted any chance of low-level marking at Scholven-Buer, but the preliminary Mosquito-borne Oboe markers had been backed up by red and green TIs from 97 Squadron Lancasters, and the glow from these was observed dimly through the cloud. The crews aimed for these, but it was impossible to assess the outcome, and the operation cost eight 5 Group aircraft, most falling to the night-fighters waiting to greet them as they crossed Holland outbound. A secret German report would suggest a 20% loss of production for a limited period.

While more than four hundred aircraft of 3, 4, 6 and 8 Groups targeted four flying-bomb sites on the 23rd, 1 and 5 Groups were sent respectively against railway yards at Saintes and Limoges in western France. Ninety-seven Lancasters and four Mosquitos were detailed for the latter, and they found clear skies and good visibility in the target area, in which ground features like the River Vienne and the railway sidings stood out prominently. Red spotfires and green TIs marked out the aiming point, and a number of large explosions were observed with much smoke. Another very large explosion was witnessed by some crew when one hundred miles into the return flight at 02.46, and post-raid reconnaissance would confirm a highly accurate and concentrated attack.

617 Squadron had attempted to continue the Tallboy assault on the constructional works at Wizernes in daylight on the 22nd, but the attack had been abandoned in the face of ten-tenths low cloud. The squadron returned the bombs to store, and brought them back to France on the 24th to score a number of direct hits. Eleven 619 Squadron crews were also called to briefing on the 24th to learn of their part in a busy night of operations involving more than seven hundred aircraft targeting seven flying-bomb sites. 5 Group was assigned to Pommeréval and Prouville, situated respectively some fifteen miles south-east of Dieppe, and east of Abbeville, and detailed 103 Lancasters and four Mosquitos for each. The 52 Base squadrons from Dunholme Lodge and Fiskerton were among those assigned to the former, and the 619 Squadron participants took off between 22.12 and 22.32 with S/L Smith the senior pilot on duty for the first time. All reached the target area to be greeted by the favourable conditions of clear skies and twenty-mile visibility, and W/C Tait was again on hand in the role of Master Bomber to watch the Oboe marker go down on time at 23.50. He assessed that it was five hundred yards south of the aiming point, and directed the flare force to illuminate another one that was much closer, before sending in the low-level Mosquitos. The main force Lancasters followed close on their heels and delivered concentrated bombing around the aiming point, which the 619 Squadron crews identified by green TIs. They delivered their bombs from 6,000 to 9,000 feet between 00.06 and 00.13, observing the bursts to be concentrated within a few hundred yards of them. There was little defence from the ground, but night-fighters were evident, and four Lancasters failed to return, two of them belonging to 44 (Rhodesia) Squadron.

At Prouville, the preliminary Oboe Mosquito was punctual, but the subsequent marking was hampered by intense searchlight activity working in co-operation with flak and night-fighters, and bombing was delayed while the aiming point was positively identified and marked. It took until all of the illuminator flares had been expended before the low-level Mosquitos dropped red spotfires and the heavy brigade from 97 Squadron backed up with red and green TIs. The bombing was controlled by the Master Bomber, but the impression was of a somewhat haphazard attack that lacked concentration, and cost thirteen Lancasters, possibly as a result of the delay in opening the attack.

More than seven hundred aircraft were detailed for operations against six flying-bomb sites on the 27th, while two railway yards would occupy the attention of other elements. There were two targets for 5 Group, a flying-bomb site at Marquise, situated some five miles inland from Cap Gris-Nez, and railway yards at Vitry-le-Francois south-east of Reims. The Dunholme Lodge squadrons of 52

Base contributed twenty-nine Lancasters between them to the force of eighty-six assigned to the former, and the fourteen belonging to 619 Squadron took off between 22.53 and 23.17 with W/C Maling the senior pilot on duty. There were no early returns, and the outward flight was completed within seventy-five minutes under clear skies and in good visibility. The marking was punctual and accurate, and the 619 Squadron crews delivered their eleven 1,000 and four 500 pounders each onto red TIs from 15,500 to 19,000 feet between 00.50 and 00.55, before returning to report a successful operation. On their return, P/O Warner and crew were declared tour-expired after completing thirty-six sorties.

The 103 Lancasters and four Mosquitos assigned to the Vitry marshalling yards were greeted at the target by varying amounts of cloud, reported as between zero and seven-tenths at around 7,000 feet, but the visibility was good, and the aiming point was clearly marked by red spot fires and green TIs. Not all had bombed when the Master Bomber called a halt and ordered crews with bombs still aboard to take them home, after smoke obscured the aiming point. There were no further operations for 52 Base in a month that had involved 619 Squadron in eleven operations, which generated 175 sorties for the loss of seven Lancasters and their crews.

July 1944

The new month began as June had ended, with flying-bomb sites providing employment for over three hundred aircraft on both the 1st and 2nd. It was the 4th before the Independent Air Force was invited to re-enter the fray, when it was called upon to attack a V-Weapon storage site in caves at St-Leu-d'Esserent, some thirty miles north of Paris. The caves had originally been used for growing mushrooms, and they were protected by some twenty-five feet of clay and soft limestone, to say nothing of the anti-aircraft defences brought in by the Germans. The operation involved not only seventeen Lancasters, a Mustang and a Mosquito from 617 Squadron, but also 211 other Lancasters and eleven Mosquitos from 5 Group, with three ABC Lancasters to provide RCM cover and three Path Finder Oboe Mosquitos to carry out the marking of an initial reference-point. Some accounts suggest that 617 Squadron attacked early in the evening, and was followed by the group later on, when, in fact, both elements took off at the same time. There were actually two aiming points, the road and railway communications to the area dump for the main force, and the tunnel complex at Creil, a settlement located three miles north-east of St Leu, for 617 Squadron and thirty-two Lancasters from Dunholme Lodge. The eighteen-strong 619 Squadron took off between 23.06 and 23.37 with F/Ls Johnston and Squibbs the senior pilots on duty, and only F/O Brown and crew returned early with an engine issue. The others pressed on to reach the target area under clear skies and in good visibility, which was of equal assistance to the night-fighters. There were no searchlights, but the expected volume of flak was thrown up as the two elements ran across their respective aiming points, the 619 Squadron crews carrying out their attacks with 1,000 and 500 pounders from 15,000 to 18,000 feet between 01.33 and 01.45. Night-fighters pounced on the bombers over the target and on the route home, and thirteen Lancasters failed to return, 619 Squadron's ND932 almost becoming a fourteenth after sustaining damage during a night-fighter attack before bombing. P/O Donnelley landed at Ford on the south coast with a wounded mid-upper gunner, who was detained in hospital. Post-raid reconnaissance revealed that a large area of subsidence had blocked the side entrance to the caves at St-Leu and that the road and railway links had been cut over a distance of four hundred yards.

On the 6th, more than five hundred aircraft were engaged on operations against V-Weapons targets, and 617 Squadron was assigned to a V-3 super-gun site at Mimoyecques. Originally planned as one of two sites near Cap Gris Nez containing twenty-five barrels each, angled at 50 degrees and aimed at London, test failures and delays meant that a single three-barrel shaft stretching a hundred metres into the limestone hill, five miles from the coast and 103 miles from its target, was all that existed at the time. Each fifteen-metre-long smooth-bore barrel, which was designed on the multiple-charge principle to progressively boost the acceleration of the one-ton projectile as it travelled towards the muzzle, was to be capable of pounding London at the rate of hundreds per day without let-up. It was protected by a concrete slab thirty metres wide and five-and-a-half metres thick, which was correctly believed by the designers to be impervious to conventional bombs. It had been attacked on a number of occasions without success, but 617 Squadron scored direct hits with Tallboys, and provisional reconnaissance revealed four deep craters in the immediate target area, one causing a large corner of the concrete slab to collapse. The extent of the damage underground would not be apparent to the planners at Bomber Command, but the shafts and tunnels had been rendered unusable and would remain so. Although Cheshire did not know it, this was to be his final operation, not only with 617 Squadron, but also of the war in Europe. His successor needed to be someone of stature, and the job was handed to W/C James "Willie" Tait, who would continue Cheshire's outstanding work.

The authorities were not convinced that the site at St-Leu-d'Esserent had received terminal damage, and scheduled another attack on it for the late evening of the 7th. Before the operation got under way, more than 450 aircraft from 1, 4, 6 and 8 Groups had carried out the first major operation in support of the Canadian 1st and British 2nd Armies, which were trying to break out of Caen. The target had been changed from German-fortified villages to an area of open ground north of Caen, where almost 2,300 tons of bombs was dropped somewhat ineffectively, and, ultimately, that decision proved to be counter-productive by causing damage to the northern suburbs of the city rather than to German forces. 5 Group detailed 208 Lancasters and fifteen Mosquitos for St-Leu, the 619 Squadron element of sixteen departing Dunholme Lodge between 22.09 and 22.40 with S/L Smith the senior pilot on duty. They arrived in the target area to find medium-level cloud, which prevented the moonlight from providing illumination, although below the cloud level, the visibility was good. The Master Bomber was W/C Ed Porter, formerly of 207 Squadron, and he oversaw the delivery of the Oboe yellow TI at 01.06, which was followed by the first stick of flares four minutes later. The first red spot fire went down at 01.08, a hundred yards south of the aiming point, but in line with the direction of the bombing run, and backing-up by red and green TIs continued until 01.13. The marking was assessed as sufficiently accurate to call in the main force at 01.15, and the 619 Squadron crews dropped their loads of eleven 1,000 and four 500 pounders from 11,000 to 15,000 feet between 01.17 and 01.21. The Master Bomber's VHF was indistinct, so 83 Squadron's S/L Eggins assumed control, and sent the force home at 01.25. Twenty-nine Lancasters and two Mosquitos failed to return after night-fighters got amongst them, and this represented 14% of the force. It was another sobering night for Dunholme Lodge, after three 44 (Rhodesia) Squadron Lancasters and one from 619 Squadron were found to be absent from their dispersals. ME745 crashed at 01.45 in the target area with both gunners on board, while F/L Johnston and the others at the front of the Lancaster escaped by parachute and, thanks to local people, retained their freedom. Photo-reconnaissance revealed that both ends of the tunnel complex had collapsed, as had a section in the middle, and the approach road and rail links had been heavily cratered and blocked.

There was no immediate opportunity for the afflicted squadrons, particularly 106 and 207, which had lost five crews each, to "get back on the horse", and there must have been a sombre air, while the populations of RAF Metheringham and Spilsby each came to terms with the loss of thirty-five familiar faces in one night. A special congratulatory message arrived on the participating stations from A-O-C, AVM Sir Ralph Cochrane, who considered it the finest effort by the group to successfully press home the attack in the face of the fiercest opposition. Operations were posted on 5 Group stations on the 10th and 11th, and then cancelled, before the 12th, when fifteen crews each from 619 and 44 (Rhodesia) Squadrons were called to briefing to be given the details about that night's operation against railway installations at Culmont-Chalindrey in eastern France. Two aiming points were planned, at the western and eastern ends, for which a force of 157 Lancasters and four Mosquitos was made ready. While this operation was in progress, another by elements of 1 Group further south at a railway junction at Revigny would, hopefully, help to dilute the night-fighter response. The 619 Squadron element departed Dunholme Lodge between 21.36 and 22.05 with S/L Gunter the senior pilot on duty, and headed for Bridport to begin the Channel crossing as far as the Channel Islands, before turning east-south-east to pass south of Paris to reach the target. Eight-tenths low cloud attended the outward flight until shortly before reaching the target area, where the conditions improved to provide clear skies, and, promisingly, no sign of defensive activity from the ground. The controller at the eastern aiming point experienced VHF communications problems, which delayed that part of the attack, and eventually, the entire force was directed to the western aiming point. The 619 Squadron crews delivered their mixed loads of 1,000 and 500 pounders onto two red spotfires from 5,500 to 8,000 feet between 01.51 and 01.57, and explosions were observed, followed by fires that remained visible for fifty miles into the return flight. The high proportion of delayed action fuses in use prevented an immediate assessment of results, but post-raid reconnaissance would confirm an effective operation.

A new policy was introduced on the 14th that raised every pilot officer to flying officer rank, which meant that a flight sergeant, on commission, would progress directly to flying officer. Despite this, there appeared to be no consistency and squadron ORBs still listed some as pilot officers, but, with the exception of a handful of warrant officers, all aircraft would be captained by a commissioned pilot. Whether this was a uniform and permanent arrangement is difficult to establish. Thirteen 619 Squadron crews were detailed to operate on the 14th, and were informed at briefing that their target was to be the huge marshalling yards at Villeneuve-St-Georges, situated on the southern rim of Paris. They would be part of a force of 111 Lancasters, six Mosquitos and an American twin-engine P38 Lightning containing the Master Bomber, W/C Jeudwine. They departed Dunholme Lodge between 21.56 and 22.14 led by W/C Maling, and followed a similar route to that of forty-eight hours earlier. W/C Jeudwine was having compass trouble, and would arrive on target twelve minutes late, so contacted his Deputy, 83 Squadron's W/C Joe Northrop, to take matters in hand. A large amount of cloud lay over the target area with a base at 5,000 feet, but clear conditions below enabled Joe to identify the aiming point, and he judged the Oboe marker to be within fifty yards of it. He called in the 5 Group marker force, which lobbed the TIs within the confines of the yards, and the operation appeared to be proceeding smoothly and precisely according to plan. The 619 Squadron crews bombed on red and green TIs from 6,000 to 9,000 feet between 01.36 and 01.54, and most of it hit the yards, while a proportion also fell outside to the east. Meanwhile, 1 Group had returned to Revigny, but had been thwarted by ground haze, which forced the Master Bomber to abandon the attack before any bombing could take place. Seven Lancasters were lost for no gain, and it would fall to 5 Group to finish the job a few nights hence at great expense.

Flying-bomb sites and railways dominated the target list on the 15th, and 5 Group was handed a railway junction at Nevers, a city on the north bank of the Loire in central France. 44 (Rhodesia) Squadron alone represented Dunholme Lodge and contributed eight Lancasters to the force of 104 with four Mosquitos to carry out the low-level marking. They reached the target after an outward flight of more than three-and-a-half hours to find clear skies and a little haze, and the marker force exploited the favourable conditions to mark promptly and accurately with a red spotfire and green TIs. The entire force was carrying delayed-action ordnance, and no immediate assessment could be made, but a large explosion suggested, perhaps, that an ammunition train or dump had been hit. Photographic reconnaissance later in the day revealed that the Nevers site had been all but obliterated, and there was much damage to rolling stock.

Thirty-two crews were called to briefing at Dunholme Lodge at midnight on the 17/18th to learn of their part in a tactical support operation to be carried out at dawn by a force of 942 aircraft, of which 201 of the Lancasters were to be provided by 5 Group. It was the start of the ground forces' Operation Goodwood, which was General Montgomery's plan for a decisive breakout into wider France as a prelude to the march towards the German frontier. The aiming points were five enemy-held villages to the east of Caen, Colombelles, Mondeville, Sannerville, Cagny and Manneville, all of which stood in the path of the advancing British 2nd Army. The 619 Squadron element of eighteen departed Dunholme Lodge between 04.01 and 04.25 with W/C Maling and S/L Gunter the senior pilots on duty, and all reached the target area to find their aiming point, the Mondeville steel works, which the Germans had converted into a strongly defended fortress, already marked by red and yellow TIs, but about to be swallowed up and obscured by drifting smoke. Bombing took place from 6,000 to 10,000 feet between 06.05 and 06.17 in accordance with instructions from the Master Bomber, and, as far as could be determined, fell accurately onto the markers. The RAF dropped five thousand tons of bombs to good effect onto the two German divisions in just half an hour, and the Americans followed up with a further two thousand tons.

Operations were not done for the day, and, that night, following two failed attempts by 1 Group to cut a railway junction at Revigny at a combined cost of seventeen Lancasters, the job was handed to a 5 Group element of 109 Lancasters, four Mosquitos and a P38 Lightning containing the Master Bomber, W/C Jeudwine. It was to be a busy night of operations, which included another railway and two oil targets, along with support and diversionary activities involving a total of 972 sorties. 44 (Rhodesia) Squadron remained at home while 619 Squadron represented Dunholme Lodge, taking off between 22.50 and 23.04 with no senior pilots on duty, and crossing the French coast near Dieppe, before passing through an intense searchlight belt some twenty miles inland. They were harried all the way into eastern France by night-fighters, which had been fed into the stream shortly after it entered enemy airspace, and, in just forty-five minutes, sixteen Lancasters fell victim to night-fighters and one to flak. The carnage began for 619 Squadron with the shooting down of JB186 at 01.01 near Auger-St-Vincent, killing F/O Begernie and all but his bomb-aimer, who was rescued by locals. Within minutes, LM378 and LM640 were blazing wrecks on the ground, victims of the "Schräge Musik" upward firing cannons, and only the flight engineer survived from the crew of F/O Molinas DFC RAAF in the former, while none survived from the predominantly Canadian crew of F/O Wilson RCAF in the latter. PB245 became another night-fighter victim at about the same time, and F/O Donnelley RNZAF perished with his entire crew, although not before his gunners had dispatched the fighter. The survivors pressed on, and shortly after reaching the final turning point, LL969 succumbed to a night-fighter attack, from which only the rear gunner in F/O

Morcom's crew emerged alive to find sanctuary among the local populace. The remnants of the bomber stream reached the target to find clear skies, but haze obscuring ground detail, and this target continued to present problems, beginning with the first wave of flares, delivered at about 01.30, which were too far to the east. More flares were ordered, and the bombing was put back by five minutes, while Wanganui markers were dropped by Mosquito, and the situation was assessed. The 619 Squadron crews carried out their bombing runs from 8,000 to 10,000 feet between 01.47 and 01.52, but F/O Neilson and crew arrived just after W/C Jeudwine had called a halt, and they jettisoned their load. The whole attack seemed chaotic, and the use of many delayed-action bombs meant that it was difficult to see what was happening on the ground. Photo-reconnaissance revealed, that the operation had been successful in cutting the railway link to the battle front, but had cost twenty-four Lancasters, almost 22% of those dispatched. 619 Squadron had been the most severely afflicted, while 49 and 630 Squadrons had lost four each, 207 Squadron three, and three other squadrons two. *(For a full and highly detailed account of the three Revigny raids read the amazing book, Massacre over the Marne, by Oliver Clutton-Brock.)*

5 Group crews stood-by on the 19th for a possible daylight operation, and it was evening before orders came through to prepare for an attack on a flying-bomb storage site at Thiverny, situated just to the north of St-Leu-d'Esserent. A force of 103 Lancasters and two Mosquitos was detailed, fifteen of the former provided by 44 (Rhodesia) Squadron, which represented Dunholme Lodge, while 619 Squadron licked its wounds. The attack was to take place in daylight under the protection of a Spitfire escort, with which the bombers rendezvoused at the south coast, before making their way to the target. They arrived to find fine weather conditions, but the presence of ground haze to create challenging conditions in which to identify the aiming point. Late preliminary marking by the Path Finder element and communications problems between the Master Bomber and his Deputy added to the frustrations and led to most crews having to orbit for five minutes before bombing visually in the face of moderate to intense heavy flak bursting as high as 18,000 feet. Post-raid reconnaissance revealed some loose bombing, but sufficient aiming point photographs were brought back to suggest a successful outcome, and there had been no losses.

Railway yards and a triangle junction at Courtrai (Kortrijk) in Belgium provided the targets for a joint effort by 1, 5 and 8 Groups on the 20th, for which 619 Squadron contributed fifteen Lancasters to the 5 Group force of 190 Lancasters and five Mosquitos. They departed Dunholme Lodge between 22.54 and 23.17 with S/L Gunter the senior pilot on duty, but lost the services of F/O Parker and crew to intercom failure. The others reached the target area to find it free of cloud and slightly obscured by ground haze, but the Oboe marking was well-placed in the marshalling yards, and backed up by green TIs, onto which the squadron participants delivered their eleven 1,000 and four 500 pounders each from 10,000 to 14,000 feet between 00.58 and 01.01. They returned home safely to report a large orange explosion at 00.57 and a successful outcome, which was confirmed by post-raid reconnaissance that revealed both aiming points to have been obliterated in return for the loss of nine Lancasters.

Following two nights at home for 5 Group and a two-month break from city busting, Harris sanctioned a major raid on the naval port of Kiel on the 23rd, for which a force of 629 aircraft was made ready. 619 Squadron carried the Dunholme Lodge flag, dispatching a dozen Lancasters between 22.50 and 23.05 as part of a 5 Group force of ninety-nine Lancasters. W/C Maling and S/L Gunter were the senior pilots on duty as they headed for the rendezvous point to form up behind an elaborate "Mandrel" jamming screen laid on by 100 Group, before setting course for Denmark's western coast. *(In November 1943, 100 Group had been formed to take over the Radio Countermeasures (RCM) role, which had been the preserve of 101 Squadron since its introduction a number of months earlier. 101 Squadron, however, would remain in 1 Group and continue to provide RCM for the remainder of the war.)* When they arrived unexpectedly and with complete surprise in Kiel airspace, they rendered the enemy night-fighter controller confused and unable to bring his night-fighter resources to bear. Kiel was covered by a nine to ten-tenths veil of thin cloud with tops at 4,000 feet, and a skymarking plan was put into action, which enabled the main force crews to bomb on the glow, first of the flares, and then of fires. The 619 Squadron contingent carried out their attacks from 16,000 to 20,000 feet between 01.27 and 01.36, but it was not possible to determine the outcome, although the glow of fires visible for a hundred miles into the return journey suggested an effective raid. This was confirmed by local reports, which conceded that this had been the town's most destructive raid of the war, and had inflicted heavy damage on the port and shipyards, and cut off water supplies for three days and gas for three weeks. Many delayed-action bombs had been dropped, and these continued to cause problems for some time. Among four missing Lancasters was 619 Squadron's PB208, which crashed into the Baltic, and there were no survivors from the crew of F/O Parker.

5 Group divided its forces on the 24th to enable it to support the first of a three-raid series in five nights on the city of Stuttgart, and an oil refinery and fuel dump at Donges. Situated on the north bank of the Loire to the east of St Nazaire, the latter target had been attacked successfully by elements of 6 and 8 Groups on the previous night, but clearly required further attention. 5 Group detailed ninety-nine Lancasters for southern Germany in an overall force of 614, while 104 Lancasters and four Mosquitos were made ready for western France, with five 8 Group Mosquitos in attendance. 619 Squadron supported the Donges operation with nine Lancasters and Stuttgart with six, and, with a greater distance to travel, dispatched the latter from Dunholme Lodge first between 21.27 and 21.46 with S/L Gunter the senior pilot on duty. The Donges-bound element took off between 22.24 to 22.36 led by S/L Smith, and, soon afterwards, the Stuttgart element had become depleted by the early return of F/O Fleck and crew because of the failure of their W/T and H2S equipment. The others reached the target area to find nine to ten-tenths cloud cover with tops at 4,000 to 7,000 feet, which required the employment of Wanganui flares (skymarking) to mark the aiming point. The 619 Squadron crews bombed on the red glow on the cloud base from 17,000 to 19,000 feet between 01.51 and 01.57 in accordance with the instructions of the Master Bomber, and set course for home fairly satisfied with the outcome, although it was impossible to make an accurate assessment. Meanwhile, some five hundred miles to the west, the modest force had left the oil refinery in a state of devastation for the loss of three Lancasters, one of which was 619 Squadron's LM643, in which F/O Orbell and crew lost their lives after it crashed four miles north-east of St-Nazaire. At debriefings across the Command, the Stuttgart crews reported a glow of fires covering an area of perhaps five square miles, which remained visible for eighty miles into the return journey. No local report came out of Stuttgart for this night, but it had been a successful and destructive raid, although gained at a cost of seventeen Lancasters and four Halifaxes.

5 Group split its forces again on the 25th to support the second of the raids on Stuttgart with eighty-three Lancasters, and a daylight attack on an aerodrome and signals depot at Saint-Cyr involving ninety-four Lancasters and six Mosquitos. *(There are at least four locations called Saint-Cyr, and it is believed that the one targeted on this night was in the Ile-de-France to the west of Paris.)* 619

Squadron briefed fourteen crews for Stuttgart, which departed Dunholme Lodge between 21.06 and 21.38 with W/C Maling and S/L Smith the senior pilots on duty, and headed for landfall on the French coast between Fecamp and Dieppe. They entered Germany north of Strasbourg accompanied by layers of cloud, which, over the target, was at five to ten-tenths with tops in places as high as 20,000 feet. There was haze below the cloud level to create further challenges for the marker force, and the red and green TIs appeared to the main force crews to be somewhat scattered. Bombing by the 619 Squadron crews took place from 15,500 to 21,000 feet between 01.56 and 02.17, but it was impossible to assess the outcome, and there was little optimism at debriefings that a successful operation had taken place. In fact, this was probably the most destructive of the three raids in this current series, but it would be only after the third one that cumulative reports came out of the city to confirm much destruction and heavy casualties. It had cost eight Lancasters and four Halifaxes, and among the former was 619 Squadron's ND935, which crashed at around 02.30 while homebound, delivering W/C Maling and three of his crew into enemy hands, while the wireless operator and both gunners failed to survive. Post-raid reconnaissance confirmed a successful attack at the Saint-Cyr site, which had left all of the buildings severely damaged.

The hectic round of operations continued for 5 Group on the 26th with preparations for an attack on two aiming points in the marshalling yards at Givors, situated on the west bank of the River Rhône in south-east-central France. 178 Lancasters and nine Mosquitos were made ready, eleven of the former by 619 Squadron, and they departed Dunholme Lodge between 21.57 and 21.26 with S/Ls Gunter and Smith the senior pilots on duty, and a round trip of eleven hundred miles ahead of them. Bad weather had been anticipated, but the conditions during the outward leg over France were even worse than forecast, with icing and electrical storms, and fourteen aircraft turned back. There were no "boomerangs" from the Dunholme Lodge squadrons as they covered the almost five-hour outward flight to reach the target to be greeted by severe weather conditions in the form of rain, thunderstorms and lightning. The cloud was down to around 7,000 feet with poor visibility below, and the flare force made a number of runs across the target between 01.42 and 02.07, and orbited in between, awaiting instructions. There were occasional glimpses of the ground, but the Master Bomber was experiencing great difficulty in getting Mosquito TIs onto the two aiming points. Eventually, one of the Deputies managed to put a green TI onto the southern aiming point, and the main force began to bomb at around 02.00. The 619 Squadron crews carried out their attacks from 4,000 to 8,000 feet between 02.13 and 02.26, using the light from flares and aiming at green TIs, all in accordance with instructions. They could offer little to the Intelligence Section at debriefing, where the crew of F/O Turvey RAAF was conspicuous by its absence. LM484 crashed at Saint-Loup, some fifteen miles north-west of the city of Lyon, and there were no survivors from the mixed RAAF, RCAF and RAF crew. 44 (Rhodesia) Squadron had borrowed PB346 from 619 Squadron, and it was now a burned-out wreck three miles north-north-west of the small town of Montrevault in north-western France. Post-raid reconnaissance revealed that the attack at Givors had fulfilled its aims in closing the tracks to the north of the junction and damaging the locomotive depot in the yards.

The night of the 28/29th would prove to be busy, eventful and expensive, as the Command prepared for major operations against Stuttgart and Hamburg and a number of smaller undertakings involving a total of 1,126 aircraft. The final raid of the series on Stuttgart was to be an all-Lancaster affair of 494 aircraft drawn from 1, 3, 5 and 8 Groups, while 307 Lancasters and Halifaxes of 1, 6 and 8 Groups carried out the annual last-week-of-July attack on Hamburg, a year and a day after the devastating firestorm of Operation Gomorrah. 5 Group put up 176 Lancasters, thirteen of them made ready by 619 Squadron, and they were each loaded with a 2,000 pounder and thirteen or fourteen 500lb J-Cluster bombs. They departed Dunholme Lodge between 21.47 and 22.15 with F/Ls Jordan and Squibbs the senior pilots on duty, and joined other elements of the force over Reading. They lost the services of P/O Scripps and crew to a defective aileron, but the remainder made landfall on the French coast south of Fécamp and flew on across France in bright moonlight above the cloud layer. However, the forecast medium cloud at 18,000 feet was absent, which left them exposed to the night-fighter hordes that had infiltrated the bomber stream as it closed on the target. It was the Luftwaffe's Nachtjagd that would gain the upper hand on this night, but the Dunholme Lodge participants must have been in a section of the bomber stream that remained unmolested, as none reported contact with a night-fighter. There was a layer of up to ten-tenths thin cloud over the city, with tops in places at around 10,000 feet, and the Path Finders initially employed skymarker flares (Wanganui), and then green TIs, at which the 619 Squadron crews aimed their bombs from 14,000 to 18,000 feet between 01.50 and 02.15. LM536 was homebound when it came down at 02.30 some five miles west-south-west of Pforzheim, ending the lives of W/O Paterson and his crew. Thirty-nine Lancasters failed to return, fourteen of them from 5 Group, and night-fighters also caught the Hamburg force on its way home, bringing down a further twenty-two aircraft to raise the night's casualty figure to sixty-one aircraft. Although it was difficult to make an accurate assessment of this final Stuttgart raid, the series had severely damaged the city, leaving its central districts devastated, with most of its public and cultural buildings in ruins, and 1,171 of its inhabitants dead.

W/C Milward had been posted in from 51 Base to fill the void left by the failure to return of W/C Maling, and he was among fourteen 619 Squadron crews and a dozen from 44 (Rhodesia) Squadron who were briefed and put on stand-by at Dunholme Lodge late on the 29th. This was in anticipation of an early-morning tactical support operation in the Villers Bocage-Caumont region of the Normandy battle area south-west of Caen, in which they were to be part of an overall force of 692 aircraft to attack six enemy positions facing predominantly American forces. The 619 Squadron element took off for their aiming point at Cahagnes between 05.59 and 06.25 with the new commanding officer, W/C Milward, leading from the front and supported by S/Ls Smith and Gunter. They approached the target over ten-tenths cloud with tops at 5,000 feet and a base at 3,500 feet, and were five minutes from the bombing run at 07.59, when the Master Bomber sent them home with their bombs.

5 Group prepared for two daylight operations on the 31st, one of them an evening attack on a flying bomb storage tunnel at Rilly-la-Montagne, some five miles south of Reims, for which a force of ninety-seven Lancasters and three Mosquitos was assembled, that included sixteen Lancasters of 617 Squadron, led by its recently appointed successor to Cheshire, W/C Tait. A second operation was to be directed at locomotive facilities and marshalling yards at Joigny-la-Roche, situated north of Auxerre and some ninety miles south-east of Paris, for which a force of 127 Lancasters and four Mosquitos was drawn from 1 and 5 Groups. 619 Squadron briefed seven crews for each operation, and sent them on their way together between 17.19 and 17.57 with W/C Milward and S/L Smith the senior pilots on duty in the Rilly element and F/Ls Jordan, Squibbs and Wingate in that assigned to Joigny. They made their way south to rendezvous with the rest of the two forces, 83 Squadron forming into two vics, one at 15,000 and the other at 18,000 feet, to lead the Rilly force to the target under a fighter escort. They arrived to find clear skies over the target, and the 619 Squadron crews

bombed the northern tunnel entrance from 15,100 to 18,000 feet between 20.18 and 20.20. Meanwhile, the Joigny-la-Roche force had arrived in the target area, also with a fighter escort, to find no more than three-tenths cloud with tops at 7,000 feet, and good enough visibility to enable a visual identification of the aiming point. The marking was concentrated, and the 619 Squadron crews delivered their bomb loads onto the red TIs from 12,000 to 14,500 feet between 20.26 and 20.28. Post-raid reconnaissance confirmed both operations to have been successful for the loss of a single Lancaster from Joigny and two from Rilly, one of the latter containing the 617 Squadron crew of F/L Bill Reid VC, who survived with one of his crew after their Lancaster was hit by bombs from above.

During the course of the month, the squadron took part in sixteen operations and dispatched 201 sorties for the loss of eleven Lancasters and their crews.

August 1944

August would bring an end to the flying bomb offensive, and also see a return to major night operations against industrial Germany. Flying bomb sites were to dominate the first half of the month, however, and would be targeted in daylight on each of the first six days. It began with the commitment of 777 aircraft to operations against numerous flying bomb-related sites on the afternoon of the 1st, although there were serious doubts about the weather conditions, which were poor over England. 5 Group's targets were at La Breteque, situated in Normandy, some ten miles east-south-east of Rouen, Mont Candon, a mile or two south-west of Dieppe, and Siracourt, located some thirty miles east of the coastal town of Berck-sur-Mer. Forces of fifty-three Lancasters, fifty-nine Lancasters and a Lightning and Mosquito and sixty-seven Lancasters and four Mosquitos respectively were made ready, the first and last-mentioned supported by 619 Squadron with seven and five Lancasters. The five Siracourt-bound crews departed Dunholme Lodge between 15.01 and 15.16 with S/L Smith the senior pilot on duty, and they were followed into the air between 16.26 and 16.59 by the La Breteque element of seven led by F/L Squibbs. They joined forces with the others of their respective formations as they made their way towards the south, and lost the cloud as they began the Channel crossing, only for it to build again to nine to ten-tenths stratocumulus with tops at between 2,000 and 5,000 feet over the Pas-de-Calais region. One Lancaster bombed at La Breteque, before the Master Bomber called a halt to proceedings, and the other two attacks were abandoned before any bombing took place. It was a similar story for the other groups, and, in total, only seventy-nine aircraft bombed.

On the following afternoon, 5 Group contributed 194 Lancasters, two Mosquitos and a P38 Lightning to operations by 394 aircraft against one flying bomb launching and three supply sites. Ninety-four Lancasters and two Mosquitos were assigned to a storage site at Trossy-St-Maximin, situated north of Paris and close to St-Leu d'Esserent, and a hundred Lancasters and the P38 to the Bois-de-Cassan facility. 619 Squadron loaded thirteen Lancasters with a mix of 1,000 and 500 pounders destined for the latter, some with a delay fuse of up to thirty-six hours, and dispatched them from Dunholme Lodge between 14.42 and 14.55 with W/C Milward the senior pilot on duty. Some crews from other squadrons complained that the leaders flew too fast, and there were comments about excessive weaving, but all reached the target area to find three to five-tenths patchy cloud. Few saw the Oboe proximity markers go down over the target, and most crews bombed on visual reference, nine of the 619 Squadron crews aiming for the centre of the smoke from 15,000 to 18,000 feet between 17.18 and 17.20. The lead aircraft turned suddenly at the last moment and caused a number of crews from another squadron to overshoot the aiming point, and they withheld their bombs, while some other bomb loads were seen to fall wide of the mark. At Trossy-St-Maximin, the Oboe proximity markers went down on time, and were backed up with TIs, and, once the bombing started, the defences opened up with accurate flak that caused damage to twenty-seven aircraft. Despite that, most of the formation passed over the aiming point and plastered it from 15,000 to 18,000 feet. Post-raid reconnaissance at Trossy revealed many new craters, a large rectangular building stripped of its roof and sides, and the southern end of two road-over-rail bridges demolished and, at Bois-de-Cassan many new craters were evident.

Despite the effectiveness of the operation, the Trossy-St-Maximin site was included among targets for more than eleven hundred aircraft on the following day. The 1 and 5 Group crews were told at briefing, that the importance of the site to the Third Reich demanded that no building be left intact, and one or two may have escaped damage during the previous day's attack. 187 Lancasters, one Mosquito and the P38 Lightning were made ready as 5 Group's contribution to the operation, the thirteen 619 Squadron participants departing Dunholme Lodge between 11.43 and 12.07 with S/L Smith the senior pilot on duty. Each Lancaster was loaded with a dozen 1,000 pounders and four of 500 pounds, all of which reached the target area intact. The 5 Group element was to attack about fifteen minutes after 1 Group, and, as they reached the target, smoke could be seen rising to 8,000 feet, and this, combined with a fierce flak defence, presented the crews with challenging conditions. The 619 Squadron element bombed on a visual reference from 15,000 to 16,000 feet between 14.31 and 14.33, under instruction from the Master Bomber, having been prevented by the smoke from seeing the markers. Many aircraft returned to their respective stations bearing flak damage, although the 52 Base crews were more concerned about the dense concentration of aircraft over the aiming point, which put them in danger of being hit from above and led to a scattering of bombs. 619 Squadron's ME568 failed to return, and there were no survivors from the crew of W/O Bennett. Photo-reconnaissance was unable to confirm that the site had been obliterated, and it would need to be attacked again on the following day, a job that would be handed to 6 Group, while most of 5 Group stayed at home.

The 5th dawned bright and clear, and brilliant sunshine glinted off the Perspex of fourteen 619 Squadron Lancasters as they took off from Dunholme Lodge between 10.46 and 11.13 bound for familiar airspace over St-Leu-d'Esserent with F/Ls Jordan, Squibbs and Wingate the senior pilots on duty. They were part of a 5 Group force of 189 Lancasters and one Mosquito, which, in turn, represented about 25% of the effort by 4, 5, 6 and 8 Groups against two flying-bomb sites, the other in the Forét-de-Nieppe, close to the Belgian frontier. It was an almost intact force that homed in on the target to find it partly protected by up to six-tenths patchy cloud with tops at about 12,000 feet. This prevented the Master Bomber from picking up the aiming point until thirty seconds from it, which meant a very late course change to bring the bombers into position. This was achieved, however, although smoke and cloud hid the markers from view, and most crews picked up the aiming point by means of ground features. They ran through a spirited flak defence to the point of bomb release, and a shell burst just under the nose of F/L Jordan's LM420, mortally wounding the bomb-aimer, Sgt Speckman. The flight engineer released the bombs with the rest of the 619 Squadron element from a uniform 15,000 to 15,500 feet between 13.32 and 13.35. Returning crews reported a fairly concentrated attack, which PRU photos seemed to confirm with views of fresh damage, and heavily cratered approaches.

The squadron detailed thirteen crews for operations on the morning of the 6th, and they were in their Lancasters before 09.00 to carry out the checks before departing for another swipe at the flying-bomb launching site at Bois-de-Cassan in the L'Isle-Adam, a few miles to the south-west of St-Leu. F/O Dickenson and crew were in PB222, a Lancaster borrowed from 44 (Rhodesia) Squadron. The 52 Base element was part of a 5 Group force of ninety-nine Lancasters and the P38 Lightning, and those from 619 Squadron took off between 09.36 and 10.16 with W/C Milward and S/L Smith the senior pilots on duty. They made their way south to join up with the rest of the formation, with 83 Squadron's G/C Deane performing the role of Master Bomber and F/L Drinkall acting as his deputy. Deane began to experience problems with his navigation homing equipment as he crossed the English coast outbound, and decided to hand over to F/L Drinkall while remaining with the formation. When about forty miles inland of the French coast, a large cumulus cloud barred the way up to 20,000 feet, and F/L Drinkall communicated his intention to take the force below it, descending to 16,000 feet. G/C Deane warned him not to go below 15,000, and advised him not to enter the cloud, but to turn to starboard. However, they were immediately enveloped in cloud, and G/C Deane did his best to hang on to F/L Drinkall's tail, as he continued to descend, and the two eventually became separated. Emerging on the other side of the cloud, Deane saw a large formation in the distance, and followed it. Passing through the cloud had caused the formation to become widely scattered, and it could not be reformed. Only thirty-eight aircraft bombed after picking up the aiming point visually, while fifty-eight others, including the entire 619 Squadron element, withheld their loads, but still had to contend with a fierce flak and fighter defence. Three Lancasters failed to return, and among them was that of F/L Drinkall and crew, who all lost their lives. Photo-reconnaissance revealed some fresh damage to the eastern side of the target, but two large buildings on the main roadway immediately south of the aiming point remained intact, and further operations would be required.

Other than night flying tests (NFTs), there was little activity during the day on the 7th, the first time during the month that no daylight operations had been mounted. At Woodhall Spa, former 619 Squadron navigator, F/O Phill Ingleby, joined 617 Squadron's F/O Warren Duffy DFC, RCAF for a jaunt in Mosquito NT202, which had been used by W/C Tate two days earlier during a daylight raid on U-Boot pens at Brest. Duffy had just completed his tour, and was awaiting his posting, while Ingleby, it is believed, was on the station staff at either Woodhall Spa or Coningsby. They took off shortly before 11.00 to drop a few practice bombs on the Wainfleet bombing range on The Wash, just south of Skegness, and as they carried out a climbing turn to port at the end of their third run at 11.12, the starboard engine failed, and the starboard wing broke away, causing the Mosquito to crash into shallow water on the foreshore, killing both occupants. It was from teatime onwards that the feverish activity began, to prepare 1,019 aircraft for attacks on five enemy positions facing Allied ground forces in the Normandy battle area. The aiming point for 179 Lancasters and one Mosquito from 5 Group was the fortified village of Secqueville, situated some fifteen miles east of Le Havre. Thirteen 619 Squadron Lancasters departed Dunholme Lodge between 21.15 and 21.52 with S/L Smith the senior pilot on duty, and joined up with the others as they travelled south. The target could be seen by the approaching bombers to be under clear skies, although haze shrouded ground detail to an extent, and star shells were fired from the ground to illuminate the aiming point. This enabled the Path Finder aircraft to drop red TIs onto it for the main force crews to aim at, and the first phase of bombing proceeded according to plan in concentrated fashion, lasting fifteen minutes. Nine of the 619 Squadron crews carried out their attacks from 6,500 to 9,000 feet between 23.23 and 23.34, and, it was then that smoke began to obscure the markers, and the Master Bomber called a halt to proceedings before the remaining four had bombed.

The 8th provided the 619 squadron crews with a day off, while just four 44 (Rhodesia) Squadron crews were sent mining in the Gironde estuary that night. The 9th was also operation-free until late afternoon, and it was on this day that F/O Duffy was laid to rest in the Canadian Stonefall Cemetery at Harrogate, while Ingleby was interred in Coningsby churchyard. Later, briefings took place for that night's operation against an oil storage dump in the Forét-de-Châtellerault, situated south of Tours in western France. It was to be predominantly a 5 Group show involving 171 Lancasters and fourteen Mosquitos, but with five 101 Squadron Lancasters to provide RCM cover. 619 Squadron dispatched thirteen Lancasters between 20.30 and 20.57 with F/L Wingate the senior pilot on duty, but lost the services of F/O Bateman and crew at the south coast with a defective rear turret. The remainder arrived in the target area under clear skies, but the presence of considerable ground haze created poor visibility for the marker crews attempting to identify the two aiming points, and the flares dropped by the first two waves of the marker force were scattered, prompting the Mosquito marker leader to drop a Wanganui flare as a guide to the third flare-force crews. This meant that some main force crews had to orbit for up to twenty minutes before the Master Bomber was satisfied that the green TIs were in the right spot and called them in to bomb. They produced an accurate attack, that resulted in three large explosions and volumes of black smoke, which, within five minutes, completely obscured the aiming point. A pause in the bombing was called, before it recommenced, until the lack of a verifiable marker compelled the Master Bomber to call a halt. All of the 619 Squadron crews carried out an attack from 5,500 to 8,000 feet between 23.53 and 00.18, and all but one returned home safely to make their reports. ME866 had crashed within yards of a 50 Squadron Lancaster in the village of Thure, some four miles north-west of Châtellerault, killing F/O Hall and all but his navigator, who evaded capture.

The mighty Gironde estuary, situated on France's Biscay coast, narrows as it leads inland towards the south-east, before dividing to become the Garonne River to the west and the Dordogne to the east. Its banks and islands were home to a number of important oil production and storage sites at Pauillac, Blaye, Bec-d'Ambe and Bordeaux, and the region was a frequent destination for gardening activities. Bordeaux itself was a vitally important port to the enemy, containing U-Boot pens, and was, therefore, heavily defended along the entire length of the waterway. Orders were received on 52, 54 and 55 Base stations at teatime on the 10th to prepare sixty-two Lancasters and five Mosquitos to bomb oil storage facilities at Bordeaux, and 619 Squadron responded with six of its own, which departed Dunholme Lodge between 18.41 and 18.58 with S/L Smith the senior pilot on duty. They headed towards the south, joining up with the other elements, which included nine Lancasters from 83 Squadron to act as the flare and marker force. The flight out was in daylight, which enabled the Deputy Master Bomber to recognise that the formation had become somewhat disorganised. There were about twenty main force aircraft ahead of the flare force, and the remainder behind it to starboard, but they were catching up, and veering further and further to starboard, until they were some ten to twenty miles off track. Fortunately, the situation rectified itself, and the force arrived in the target area to find clear skies with a little ground haze. As they ran in on the aiming point, a limited amount of heavy flak began to burst at 16,000 to 18,000 feet, while the considerable light flak fell short, and neither proved to be troublesome. Within thirty seconds of the flares illuminating the ground, the TIs were burning close to the aiming point, and the 619 Squadron crews bombed from 16,000 to 19,000 feet between 22.34 and 22.39. Returning crews were confident of a successful attack, but, as few explosions were observed, it was difficult to accurately assess the outcome.

On the 11th, while 617 Squadron took care of the U-Boot pens at La Pallice, thirty-nine other Lancasters and two Mosquitos from 5 Group attacked a similar target at Bordeaux under the protection of six "Serrate" Mosquitos of 100 Group. *(Serrate was a highly effective and successful radar device that enabled 100 Group Mosquito night-fighters to home in on enemy night-fighters, and turn the hunters into prey).* For the evening operation, 5 Group was switched to communications targets at Givors, located about twenty miles to the south of Lyon in south-east-central France. There were to be two aiming points, the town's marshalling yards to the north, and a railway junction to the south, and 619 Squadron's thirteen-strong element was assigned to the former in an overall force of 175 Lancasters and ten Mosquitos. They departed Dunholme Lodge between 20.11 and 20.59 with S/L Gunter the senior pilot on duty, but soon lost the services of F/O Brown and crew to an engine issue. The others arrived in the target area to find favourable conditions in the form of clear skies and a little haze, which the seemingly usual organised chaos of contradictory or confusing instruction via VHF and W/T threatened to waste. Unaccountably, and contrary to the opinions of the crews, the 5 Group ORB described the W/T control as excellent and the VHF R/T as good. Permission to bomb was not received until 01.12, by which time some crews had been forced to spend fifteen minutes orbiting three times, while the Master Bomber and his Deputy discussed the accuracy of the markers. Despite the wrinkles, both aiming points were well-illuminated and marked, and the bombing was concentrated in the correct place. The 619 Squadron crews confirmed their positions by Gee and H2S-fix before carrying out their attacks on red TIs in accordance with the Master Bomber's instructions from 6,500 to 8,500 feet between 01.15 and 01.23. They all returned to home airspace critical of some aspects of the raid, but confident that it had been concluded successfully. Photo-reconnaissance revealed heavy damage to both aiming points, with the ground badly-cratered and many tracks severed, and the middle span of the railway bridge over the River Rhône was revealed to have received a direct hit.

The main operation on the 12th was an experiment to gauge the ability of main force crews to locate and attack an urban target on the strength of their own H2S equipment in the absence of a Path Finder element. This resulted from the huge volume of operations generated by the four concurrent campaigns, each of which called upon the finite resources of 8 Group, compelling it, in the short term at least, to spread itself more and more thinly. The conclusion of the flying-bomb campaign at the end of the month, together with the end of tactical support for the ground forces, would remove the pressure, and the planned independence of 3 Group through the G-H bombing system from the autumn would solve the problem altogether. In the meantime, however, no one knew what demands might be made of the Command, and it would be useful to see what main force crews could do when left to their own devices. The target was to be Braunschweig, for which a force of 379 aircraft was assembled, seventy-two of the Lancasters provided by 5 Group. 619 Squadron's contribution amounted to just three Lancasters, captained by S/Ls Gunter and Smith and F/O Neilson, which departed Dunholme Lodge between 21.01 and 21.05. It was a night of heavy Bomber Command activity at numerous locations involving more than eleven hundred sorties. A second large operation over Germany was directed at the Opel tank works at Rüsselsheim two hundred miles to the south, and involved 297 aircraft, but, as events were to prove, this would not weaken the enemy night-fighter defences, and powerful elements of the Nachtjagd were waiting for the Braunschweig force as it crossed the German coast at around 18,000 feet. Night-fighter flares were in evidence from then until the coast was crossed again on the way home, and it would prove to be an expensive night for the Command as a whole. As the Braunschweig force made its way eastwards under clear skies, 619 Squadron's ME855 was engaged by a night-fighter, the cannon fire from which smashed the rear turret and killed the occupant. The crew of S/L Gunter was left with no choice but to abandon the Lancaster to the inevitable, and all six survivors floated down into the arms of their captors. The others pressed on to encounter nine to ten-tenths thin cloud in the target area with tops at 7,000 feet, which was not a problem, as the whole purpose of the operation was to locate and bomb the target blind by H2S. 619 Squadron's F/O Neilson and S/L Smith delivered their attacks from 19,500 and 21,000 feet at 00.03 and 00.10 respectively, and observed the glow of fires beneath the cloud. Some of the bombing did, indeed, hit Braunschweig, but there was no concentration, and many outlying towns also reported bombs falling. Twenty-seven aircraft failed to return from this operation and a further twenty from a disappointing tilt at the Opel factory, demonstrating that the Nachtjagd still had sufficient resources to effectively divide its strength.

While the above was in progress, a "rush job" called upon the services of 144 crews to attack German troop concentrations and a road junction north of Falaise. 5 Group supported the attack with twenty-five Lancasters, the crews of which found a blanket of ten-tenths stratus cloud with tops at 2,000 feet, through which the green TIs were clearly visible and bombed. Post-raid reconnaissance confirmed that the area around the junction was heavily cratered and the roads leading from it were mostly blocked.

5 Group began the 13th with an attack by elements of 617 and 9 Squadrons on the derelict French cruiser *Gueydon* at berth at Brest, which, it was believed, the enemy might sink strategically along with other ships in the harbour, to render it unusable if liberated. In the early evening, fifteen Lancasters from 53 Base took off to target an oil storage depot at Bordeaux, and, later on, 619 Squadron dispatched five Lancasters from Dunholme Lodge between 21.10 and 21.18 for mining duties in the Deodars garden in the Gironde estuary. F/O Leonard and crew turned back when west of Guernsey after their H2s failed, leaving the others to press on to the target area, where they delivered their vegetables into the briefed locations from 10,000 feet between 00.26 and 00.45.

The main activity during the afternoon of the 14th was an operation in support of Canadian divisions in the Falaise area, which involved 805 aircraft targeting seven enemy troop positions. 5 Group took part, by sending sixty-one Lancasters to the village of Quesnay, where accurate bombing left the village in ruins. Master Bombers were on hand to control the bombing at each aiming point because of the close proximity of the opposing armies, but, despite the most stringent efforts to avoid friendly fire incidents, some bombs did fall into a quarry occupied by Canadian troops, killing thirteen men, injuring fifty-three others and destroying a large number of vehicles. In the evening, 128 Lancasters and two Mosquitos were made ready to send back to Brest for another go at the *Gueydon*, a tanker and a hulk, and among those taking part were fifteen crews representing 619 Squadron, who departed Dunholme Lodge between 17.46 and 18.08 with W/C Milward and S/L Smith the senior pilots on duty. F/O Neilson and crew were thwarted by an engine issue, which forced them to abort their sortie, while the others arrived over the port to find clear skies and excellent visibility, but also a fierce flak defence, which would inflict scars of battle on a number of aircraft. The 619 Squadron crews bombed from 14,500 to 17,500 feet between 20.21 and 20.32, and a number of direct hits were observed on both vessels, with smoke issuing out of the tanker. Photo-reconnaissance revealed that the tanker had settled on the bottom, and the cruiser had suffered a similar fate with its decks now awash.

In preparation for his new night offensive against Germany, Harris called for operations against enemy night-fighter airfields in Holland and Belgium. In response, a list of nine such targets was prepared for attention by daylight on the 15th, and they would involve a thousand aircraft. 5 Group was handed Deelen in central Holland and Gilze-Rijen in the south, and prepared forces of ninety-four Lancasters and five Mosquitos for the former and 103 Lancasters, four Mosquitos and the P38 Lightning for the latter. The P38 contained S/L "Count" Ciano and W/C Guy Gibson, who was desperate to get back onto operations. 52 Base was assigned to Deelen, and 619 Squadron dispatched fourteen Lancasters between 09.27 and 09.53 with S/L Smith the senior pilot on duty. They found the target under clear skies in excellent visibility, and were able to identify the aiming point visually. The Lancasters were each loaded with eleven 1,000 and four 500 pounders, which the 619 Squadron crews dropped onto yellow TIs almost as one from 14,800 to 17,000 feet between 12.10 and 12.13, in accordance with instructions from the Master Bomber. Many bomb bursts were observed on the aerodrome, and post-raid reconnaissance confirmed 230 craters on the runways and damage to hangars and other buildings.

The new offensive began with simultaneous attacks on Stettin and Kiel on the night of the 16/17th, 5 Group contributing 145 aircraft to the overall all-Lancaster force of 461 assigned to the former. 619 Squadron made ready sixteen Lancasters, which departed Dunholme Lodge between 21.00 and 21.27, with S/L Smith the senior pilot on duty. F/O Pettigrew and crew turned back with a dead starboard-outer engine, leaving the others to complete the three-and-a-half hour outward flight, where they were greeted by up to nine-tenths high cloud with a base at 18,000 to 20,000 feet and sufficient breaks to register clear visibility below. Concentrated red and green TIs could be seen marking out the aiming point, and the 619 Squadron crews bombed these from 17,000 to 20,000 feet between 01.05 and 01.22 and reported fires taking hold. Not all returning crews were confident about the outcome, some suggesting the raid had been scattered, when, in fact, it had been highly successful, destroying fifteen hundred houses, numerous industrial premises, and sinking five ships in the harbour, while seriously damaging eight more. The attack on Kiel had been less successful, but had caused extensive damage in the docks area and among the shipbuilding yards, while wasting much of the effort outside of the town to the north-west.

Seventeen 619 Squadron crews were called to briefing early on the 18th to be told of that morning's operation against two flying-bomb dumps in the Forét-de-L'Isle Adam, north of Paris. 158 Lancasters, six Mosquitos and the P38 Lightning were to be involved, with 83 Squadron leading, and providing the back-up marking on the heels of the low-level Mosquitos at the two aiming points in the east and west. The 619 Squadron element departed Dunholme Lodge between 11.27 and 11.57 with W/C Milward and S/L Smith the senior pilots on duty, and each Lancaster carrying ten 1,000 and four 500 pounders. They headed south in squadron formation to rendezvous with the rest of the force and pick up the fighter escort, and, when over the mid-point of the Channel at 13.15, sixty or seventy American Liberators passed across the bows of the gaggle, heading east a thousand feet higher, prompting the lead Lancaster to change course. This may have been the cause of comments by some crews on return, that not all had observed station keeping as set out at briefing, a situation that would result in aircraft bombing out of the planned sequence and on incorrect headings. On arrival in the target area, they encountered five to seven-tenths cloud with tops at around 8,000 feet, which hampered identification of both aiming points, and instructions were issued to not bomb unless a clear view of the target had been established. Some were able to pick out the aiming points assisted by smoke markers, and the 619 Squadron crews bombed almost as one from 10,750 to 11,500 feet between 14.09 and 14.10, observing a number of bursts. Bombing photos suggested that the attack had overshot to the north, and this was confirmed later by PRU photos.

53 Base was called into action on the 19th to provide fifty-two Lancasters for an attack on La Pallice, and reached the target area to find six to nine-tenths cloud hanging over the western aiming point, and seven to eight-tenths over the eastern one, with tops at 15,000 feet. This created challenging conditions in which to identify the targets, made more so by intense light flak, but crews claimed to have done so visually before carrying out their attacks. This was the first day of a spell of wet, cloudy and, sometimes, windy weather, which would last for the next week, and, apart from a number of small-scale operations, 5 Group remained largely on the ground. The 619 Squadron crews of F/Os Leonard, Neilson and O'Neill were called to briefing on the 20th while their Lancasters were being loaded with vegetable to take to the Cinnamon II garden off La Pallice. They departed Dunholme Lodge between 20.07 and 21.09 and delivered their stores into the allotted locations from 9,000 to 11,500 feet between 23.16 and 00.27, before returning safely from uneventful sorties.

Major operations resumed on the 25th, when preparations were put in hand to make ready more than nine hundred aircraft to launch against three main targets, the Opel tank works at Rüsselsheim and the nearby city of Darmstadt in southern Germany, and the port of Brest, while a further four hundred would be engaged in a variety of smaller endeavours. The largest operation was to be the all-Lancaster affair involving 461 aircraft from 1, 3, 6 and 8 Groups in a return to the Opel works, while 334 others attended to eight coastal batteries around Brest. 5 Group was assigned to Darmstadt, a university city and centre of scientific research and development, and one of a few almost virgin targets considered to be worthy of attention. 5 Group assembled a force of 191 Lancasters and six Mosquitos, nineteen of the former made ready by 619 Squadron, which departed Dunholme Lodge between 20.24 and 20.58 with W/C Milward the senior pilot on duty. The Master Bomber was one of five crews to return early, leaving his two Deputies from 83 Squadron, F/L Meggeson DFC and S/L Williams DFC to step into the breach. The target area was found to be free of cloud, and some ground haze was present, but this was not responsible for matters going awry early on. VHF communication proved to be weak, which made it difficult for the Deputy Master Bombers to pass on instructions, and five aircraft dropped flares at 01.05, which turned out to be too far to the west, and the low-level Mosquitos reported at 01.07, that they were unable to find the aiming point. H-hour was pushed back to 01.22, although bombing actually began at 01.19, and, soon after, someone left their VHF on transmit, creating a noise that drowned out all voice communications at the same time that W/T became jammed. One of the Deputies was heard indistinctly instructing the crews to "bomb on the box" (H2S), and then he and the other Deputy were shot down. The main force crews did their best to comply, among them the 619 Squadron element, who were over the target at 8,000 to 10,000 feet between 01.21 and 01.39 and described a widely scattered attack. The lack of marking persuaded some of the force to seek alternative targets, and some joined in at Rüsselsheim, while other chose targets of opportunity.

The German port of Königsberg, now Kaliningrad in Lithuania, is located on the eastern side of the Bay of Danzig, and was being used by the enemy to supply its eastern front. It lay some 860 miles in a straight line from the bomber stations surrounding Lincoln, which increased to a round trip of 1,900 miles when the routing across Denmark was taken into account. This made it the most distant location ever targeted by the Command, and was exceeded only by SOE flights to Poland. Such a distance required sacrificing bombs for fuel, and it was a reduced load of a single 2,000 pounder and twelve 500lb J cluster bombs that was loaded into each of 619 Squadron's fifteen Lancasters, which were part of an overall heavy force of 174. Having been briefed for this target twice before without going, there was some doubt as to whether or not this one would take place, but it did, and the first 619 Squadron Lancaster began to roll at Dunholme Lodge at 19.48 to be followed by the others over the ensuing forty-five minutes with no senior pilots on duty. Ahead of them lay a ten-hour marathon, and all from 619 Squadron would complete the outward flight to arrive at the target after flying through electrical storms and icing conditions over Denmark. In contrast, the skies in the target area were clear and the visibility good, and the force was greeted by around a hundred searchlights and an intense flak defence. The flare force went in at 14,000 to 15,000 feet between 01.05 and 01.12, to be followed minutes later by the heavy markers at a lower level. The 619 Squadron crews identified the aiming point by red TIs, and bombed them from 6,000 and 9,500 feet between 01.16 and 01.27, the latter time three minutes after the Master Bomber had issued the order to cease bombing. Returning crews were fairly enthusiastic about the outcome, reporting punctual marking, concentrated bombing and fires that could be seen, according to some, from 250 miles into the return journey. Photo-reconnaissance revealed that the main weight of the attack had fallen into the town's north-eastern districts, where fire had ripped through many building blocks at a cost of just four Lancasters. However, the job was not yet done, and a second operation would have to be mounted. Three of the gardeners returned to report delivering their mines successfully from 10,000 to 12,000 feet between 01.13 and 01.24, but the crew of S/L White was absent from debriefing. News eventually arrived via the Red Cross that NE138 had disappeared into the sea in the target area, and that only S/L White had survived to be taken into captivity.

The final operations in the long-running flying-bomb campaign were conducted by small Oboe-led forces against twelve sites on the 28th, and Allied ground forces took control of the Pas-de-Calais a few days later. It was clear, that a decisive blow had not been delivered on Königsberg, and, at 17.30 on the 29th, briefings took place on the participating 5 Group stations for the return. Eighteen 619 Squadron crews learned that they were to be part of a 5 Group force of 189 Lancasters, and departed Dunholme Lodge between 20.06 and 20.36 with F/L Squibbs the senior pilot on duty, and, because of the extreme range, they again carried between them only 480 tons of bombs to deliver onto four aiming points. The bomber stream made its way across the North Sea and Denmark and reached the target to encounter eight to ten-tenths cloud with a base at around 10,000 feet. The Master Bomber, W/C Woodroffe, one of 5 Group's most experienced raid controllers, having decided on a visual attack, instructed the first flare force wave to drop below the cloud, and kept the spearhead of the main force circling for twenty minutes before the marking began. The later arrivals could see the markers going down as they approached for what was a complex plan of attack that proceeded with the first flares going down at around 01.05 and continuing at regular intervals thereafter. At 01.24, the third flare force wave was instructed to illuminate the red spot fire, and a minute later an instruction was given to overshoot by 400 yards to the east of the aiming point. At 01.26, a marker aircraft was told to run over the red marker and overshoot by 300 yards, while, at 01.27, another was ordered to overshoot by 600 yards east of the aiming point, before the visual backers-up were sent to track over the reds and greens and overshoot by 300 yards. The flare force was invited to go home at 01.30, and, at 01.34, the visual marker crews were instructed first to back up the greens by 600 yards on a westerly heading, and, two minutes later, the concentrations of reds and greens. The 619 Squadron crews identified the target by the red and green TIs and searchlight concentrations, and confirmed their positions by H2S before bombing from 6,000 to 10,500 feet between 01.34 and 01.49. The Master Bomber called a halt to bombing at 01.52 and sent the crews home, where the absence of four 50 Squadron Lancasters at Skellingthorpe prompted a scathing review of W/C Woodroffe's performance, blaming his stubbornness for the high casualty rate of fifteen Lancasters, 7.9% of those dispatched. They maintained that the backers-up had confirmed the marking to be on the mark, despite which, he kept some crews orbiting for up to forty minutes. 619 Squadron's LM696 disappeared without trace, probably in the Baltic, and took with it the crew of F/O Eley. Post-raid reconnaissance confirmed that the operation had been an outstanding success, which destroyed over 40% of the town's residential and 20% of its industrial buildings.

The flying-bomb campaign may now have ended, but a new one against V-2 rocket storage and launching sites began on the 31st with raids on nine suspected locations in northern France. 5 Group sent three forces, of forty-nine, forty-six and fifty-two Lancasters with two Mosquitos each to respectively target sites at Auchy-les-Hesdin, Rollancourt and Bergueneuse, all situated some twenty miles inland from the coast at Berck-sur-Mer. 52 Base was assigned to the first-mentioned, for which 619 Squadron made ready sixteen Lancasters, and dispatched them from Dunholme Lodge between 15.36 and 16.11 with every pilot of flying officer rank. All reached the target area to find five to eight-tenths cloud with a base at 6,000 feet and tops as high as 18,000 feet, out of which issued occasional heavy rain showers. The force was told to orbit until the cloud bank moved away to allow the Mosquitos to drop smoke markers, which failed to ignite. The Master Bomber directed the bombing to be carried out visually, and the 619 Squadron crews complied from 9,000 to 12,500 feet between 18.01 and 18.20, and a large explosion was witnessed at 18.10. The operation appeared to be a little scattered, but largely successful, as were those at the other sites.

This concluded a month of feverish and record activity for most heavy squadrons, during which, 619 Squadron took part in twenty-one operations, and dispatched 251 sorties for the loss of three Lancasters and their crews.

September 1944

The destructive power of the Command was now almost beyond belief. Each of its heavy bomber groups was capable of laying waste to a German town and city at one go, and, from now until the end of the war, this would be demonstrated in awesome and horrific fashion. Much of the Command's effort during the new month would be directed towards the liberation of the three French ports remaining in enemy hands, but operations began for 5 Group with an attack on shipping at Brest on the 2nd, for which sixty-seven Lancasters were detailed from 52 and 55 Bases.

619 Squadron made ready sixteen Lancasters and sent them on their way from Dunholme Lodge between 11.03 and 11.37 with F/L Squibbs the senior pilot on duty. They had to negotiate thunderstorms on the way out, and, on arrival in the target area, initially found a layer of five to seven-tenths cumulus cloud between 2,000 and 9,000 feet affording a range of visibilities between good and poor. However, as the cloud appeared to be drifting away, they were ordered to orbit until the aiming point could be identified visually. The bombing was carried out unopposed by the 619 Squadron element from 10,000 to 12,000 feet between 14.36 and 15.05, and was observed to straddle the quays, in which vessels were berthed. Post-raid reconnaissance revealed damage to a number of the vessels, and additional destruction within the town.

Preparations were put in hand on the following morning to launch attacks on six Luftwaffe-occupied aerodromes in southern Holland. A total of 675 aircraft were to be involved, 5 Group detailing 103 Lancasters and two Mosquitos for its target at Deelen, 619 Squadron dispatching seventeen Lancasters between 14.58 and 15.23 with F/L Jordan the senior pilot on duty. F/O Lean and crew turned back from fifty miles out from the Lincolnshire coast after their starboard-outer engine let them down, but the others reached the target area without incident, although cloud on the way out had created challenging conditions for formation-keeping. Over enemy territory they encountered varying amounts of cloud up to nine-tenths with tops at 7,000 feet, and orbited while they awaited gaps through which to identify the aiming point visually. The marking was assessed to be accurate, and a dozen of the 619 Squadron crews bombed from 10,500 to 16,000 feet between 17.28 and 17.40 in the face of a spirited flak defence from the airfield. When the Master Bomber called a halt to bombing, four of the 619 Squadron crews were still waiting to carry out an attack, and they jettisoned part of their loads. There were no losses, but almost every Lancaster from Dunholme Lodge returned with flak damage to some degree. At debriefing, crews expressed themselves to be relatively confident that they had fulfilled their brief, although some described the smoke-puff markers as inadequate. It would be the 6th before photo-reconnaissance provided a partial cover of the target area and revealed at least sixty craters around runway intersections and taxiways.

Most of 5 Group remained at home over the ensuing five days, while enemy strong-points in and around Le Havre received daylight visitations from other elements of the Command on the 5th, 6th, 8th and 9th. These operations took place during a spell of unhelpful weather conditions, and the attacks of the 8th and 9th were not fully pressed home. Mönchengladbach was posted as the target for 113 Lancasters and fourteen Mosquitos on the 9th, for which, briefings took place at 13.30. The sixteen 619 Squadron crews learned, that they were to attack the centre of this town, which, with Operation Market Garden looming, was expected soon to be within striking distance of the advancing Allied forces. They would have to wait until the early hours of the 10th before departing Dunholme Lodge between 02.37 and 03.16 with S/L Smith the senior pilot on duty. There would be no early returns as they made their way via Ostend to the target on the heels of the flare forces, which had started dispensing illumination a little early at 05.05 and had continued until 05.14, at which point they were sent home. The main force crews were called in to attack under clear skies and in good visibility, those from 619 Squadron identifying the aiming point by means of red TIs, which they bombed from 15,000 to 16,000 feet between 05.20 and 05.27. A number of large explosions occurred at 05.21 and 05.23, and a heavy pall of smoke was rising to meet the crews as they turned away to find the glow of fires still visible from the Dutch coast up to eighty miles away.

There were no losses, and photo-reconnaissance confirmed the claims of the crews, revealing a highly successful raid, which had left the town centre in ruins.

A further attack on German positions around Le Havre was carried out on the 10th and involved almost a thousand aircraft, 5 Group supporting the effort with 108 Lancasters and two Mosquitos. Ten of the former were provided by 619 Squadron, and departed Dunholme Lodge between 15.24 and 15.50 with S/L Smith and the newly promoted S/L Squibbs the senior pilots on duty. There were no early returns, and the crews were greeted at the French coast by clear skies and just a little ground haze, which enabled them to identify the target visually. They released their bombs almost as one and entirely unopposed onto red TIs from 10,000 to 11,000 feet between 17.26 and 17.27, and, by the time that they turned back, the area had become enveloped in smoke. The 11th would bring the final attacks on the environs of the port, and would involve 218 aircraft drawn from 4, 5, 6 and 8 Groups. 5 Group contributed ninety-three Lancasters from 53, 54 and 55 Bases, which arrived in the target area under clear skies with slight haze, and, just after dawn, located their respective aiming points to the north and south of the outer defences, each named after a car manufacturer, like Cadillac. Initially, there were no markers on the northern aiming point, and nothing was heard from the Master Bomber, which left the crews to their own devices. Photo-reconnaissance confirmed accurate and concentrated bombing, and, within hours of this operation, the German garrison surrendered to British forces.

Many of the crews involved in the morning activity, found themselves on the Order of Battle and back in the briefing room later in the day to learn of their part in 5 Group's return to Darmstadt, which had escaped serious damage at its hands during the last week of August. A force of 221 Lancasters and fourteen Mosquitos was made ready, and the 619 Squadron element of eighteen departed Dunholme Lodge between 20.41 and 21.09 with S/L Squibbs the senior pilot on duty. They began the Channel crossing at Beachy Head, aiming for the French coast near Berck-sur-Mer, before traversing France to enter Germany in the Strasbourg area and turning north to the target. They arrived to find the skies over southern Germany clear of cloud, and, despite some ground haze, good visibility prevailing as the flare force went in at 17,000 feet at 23.52, homing in on a green TI delivered by a Mosquito. The Master Bomber seemed satisfied with the illumination, and required no further flares, leaving the backers-up to drop their TIs over the ensuing four minutes, before being sent home at 23.59. The main force crews followed up with extreme accuracy and concentration, those from 619 Squadron bombing on red and green TIs from 14,500 to 15,500 feet between 23.58 and 00.06. The city centre became engulfed in flames, which spread outwards to consume large parts of the built-up area, and the glow, according to some, could be seen from the French coast, 250 miles away. The operation cost the group twelve Lancasters, among which were 619 Squadron's LM191 and LM209, both of which were on their way home when the end came. The former crashed at 00.15 some four miles south-south-west of Bad Schwalbach, and the latter fifteen minutes later between the target and the town of Griesheim, and there were no survivors from the crews of F/O Dockrey RCAF and S/L Squibbs respectively. The conditions had been ideal for the 5 Group marking method, and photo-reconnaissance confirmed the main weight of the attack to have fallen in the central and surrounding districts to the south and east. It was learned after the war, that the attack had resulted in a genuine firestorm, only the third to be recorded after Hamburg and Kassel in 1943, although a number of local ones may have occurred in other cities like Berlin and Stuttgart. More than twelve thousand people died in the inferno, and a further seventy thousand, 60% of a total population of 120,000, were made homeless.

Orders were received on 5 Group stations on the 12th to prepare for a return to southern Germany that night, this time to target Stuttgart. Fourteen 619 Squadron crews attended the briefing at Dunholme Lodge, and learned that they were to be part of a force of 195 Lancasters and fourteen Mosquitos, which would be accompanied by nine ABC Lancasters from 1 Group's 101 Squadron. A simultaneous operation by 378 Lancasters and nine Mosquitos of 1, 3 and 8 Groups would take place at Frankfurt, a hundred miles to the north. The 619 Squadron element took off between 18.36 and 19.07 with no senior pilots on duty, and joined the bomber stream as they headed south to adopt a course similar to that of twenty-four hours earlier. They mostly enjoyed an uneventful flight across France to Stuttgart, which was found to be under clear skies with moderate visibility and ground haze, and, therefore, ideal conditions for the low-level markers. The marking and backing up was very accurate, and the main force bombing concentrated upon the city centre, with a slight tendency to creep back towards the north-eastern district of Bad Canstatt and beyond into Feuerbach. The 619 Squadron crews bombed on red TIs from 15,800 to 16,750 feet between 23.11 and 23.20, and all returned safely to report a successful operation. A huge explosion was reported at 23.25, which lasted for about five seconds, and, when a PRU aircraft photographed the city on the following morning, the entire centre was obscured by the smoke from numerous and widespread fires. Local reports from Stuttgart described the central districts as "erased", and it seems that a firestorm erupted in northern and west-central districts, wiping them from the map. Almost twelve hundred people lost their lives, the highest death toll ever in this much-bombed city, in exchange for which only four Lancasters were missing.

Other than the first of 617 Squadron's three attacks on *Tirpitz* on the 15th, launched from Yagodnik in Russia, 5 Group undertook no further operations until the morning of the 17th, when contributing to a total of 762 aircraft assembled to attack troop positions at seven locations around the port of Boulogne. The raids would be staggered over a four-hour period and benefit from a 5 Group effort of 195 Lancasters and four Mosquitos, sixteen of the former representing 619 Squadron and departing Dunholme Lodge between 06.56 and 07.21 with F/L Jordan the senior pilot on duty. The 52 Base squadrons were part of the first wave of aircraft to attack one of two aiming points assigned to 5 Group, and were an hour ahead of the second wave. They found clear skies with good visibility and no opposition, and saw red TIs marking out the aiming point. The Master Bomber's instructions were a little indistinct, but sufficient to direct the bombing, and six of the 619 Squadron crews delivered their eleven 1,000 and four 500 pounders each from 8,000 to 8,750 feet between 08.37 and 08.46. The remaining ten were either orbiting or on their bombing run when the Master Bomber halted the attack at 08.45, and most of them jettisoned part of their load. The following waves completed the job, although some crews were hampered by drifting smoke, and a total of three thousand tons of bombs was sufficient to pave the way for Allied ground forces to move in shortly afterwards to accept the surrender of the German garrison. This left only Calais of the major French ports still under enemy occupation.

5 Group stations received orders on the 18th to prepared for an operation that night against the port of Bremerhaven, located on the east bank at the mouth of the River Weser, some thirty miles north of Bremen. It was to be a classic 5 Group-style attack, employing the low-level visual marking method and involved 206 Lancasters and seven Mosquitos. At Dunholme Lodge, 619 Squadron loaded sixteen Lancasters with a mix of 2,000 pounders and 500lb J-Cluster bombs plus incendiaries, and sent them on their way between 17.55 and 18.25 with W/C Milward the senior

pilot on duty. There were no early returns, and both Dunholme Lodge squadrons arrived intact in the target area to find favourable weather conditions and good visibility. They ran in on the aiming point at medium level to release their loads onto red TIs from 13,800 to 16,500 feet between 20.59 and 21.07, mostly in accordance with the Master Bomber's instructions. A number of huge explosions were witnessed at 21.02 and 21.07, and, as they headed out of the target area, they could see many large fires spreading throughout the built-up area, the glow from which remained visible for at least 150 miles. Post-raid reconnaissance revealed that this first major attack on the port, carried out by what, at the time, could be considered to be a modest force, had devasted the built-up areas north and south of the harbour entrance, wiping out installations and warehousing, and only the most northerly and southerly suburbs had escaped complete destruction. Local reports produced a figure of 2,670 buildings reduced to rubble and thirty-thousand people bombed out of their homes, all at the modest cost to 5 Group of a single Lancaster and a Mosquito.

Sixteen 619 Squadron crews assembled for briefing at Dunholme Lodge on the 19th, and learned that they were to be part of a predominantly 5 Group attack on the twin towns of Mönchengladbach and Rheydt. This represented a shallow penetration into Germany, just ten minutes from the Dutch border, and, therefore, a short round trip of four-and-a-half to five hours, followed by a night in bed. 217 Lancasters and ten Mosquitos were made ready, along with ten ABC Lancasters from 101 Squadron, and the 619 Squadron participants took off between 18.43 and 19.09 with F/L Jordan the senior pilot on duty, each Lancaster carrying a 2,000 pounder and eleven 500lb J-Cluster bombs. The Master Bomber for the operation was W/C Guy Gibson VC, DSO, DFC, who had been agitating to get back into the war before it was over, and didn't want his service to end in a backwater, while others gained the glory by being in at the death. Gibson was a warrior, and the war had brought out of him qualities, which, in peacetime, may have lain dormant. War had also given him a direction, and he revelled in the company of fellow operational types, particularly those of the officer class. Having been torn away from the operational scene following the success of the Dams operation, his purpose had gone, and he had become listless, frustrated and discontented. His time in the operational wilderness had not, however, deprived him of his arrogance and self-belief, and, when the opportunity to fly as Master Bomber on the coming raid presented itself, he grabbed it. He was driven the three miles from Coningsby to Woodhall Spa to collect his 627 Squadron Mosquito, which, for whatever reason, he rejected, and swapped with F/L Mallender, causing a degree of resentment. Gibson had already set the tone for the evening by rejecting the advice of W/C Charles Owen, who had been Master Bomber at this target ten nights earlier. Owen had advised him to leave the target by a south-westerly route, and cross north-eastern France to the coast, and also to observe orders to remain above 10,000 feet. Gibson insisted that he would fly home via a direct route across Holland at low level and would not be dissuaded. He took off ahead of the 627 Squadron element at 19.51, to meet up with the main force over the target, where two aiming points were to be marked.

Some crews reported icing clouds at around 9,000 feet as they made their way to the target over Belgium at around 9,000 feet, and chose to keep below, before climbing fast to 15,000 feet as the cloud dispersed. The marking was complex, with a green marker to be dropped on a factory in a western district of Mönchengladbach, and a yellow marker on railway yards in the north, while a red marker was to be placed on railway yards in Rheydt, two miles to the south. It would have been a demanding plan even for an experienced Master Bomber, which Gibson was not, but, even so, his instructions were heard clearly. All seemed to be going to plan, with accurate and punctual marking for the green and yellow forces, but late, though accurate marking for the red force, and some of the red force crews were diverted to the green aiming point. The 619 Squadron crews were assigned to the green force, and identified it by flares and TIs, before bombing from 13,000 to 13,500 feet between 21.45 and 21.51, and observing the target to be well ablaze with the glow visible for at least a hundred miles into the return flight. Five Lancasters failed to return, three of them from 106 Squadron, one from 467 Squadron RAAF and 619 Squadron's PB405, which crashed in Holland with no survivors from the eight-man crew of F/O Leonard. Post-raid reconnaissance confirmed a highly destructive attack on both towns for the loss of four Lancasters and a Mosquito. Gibson had returned low over Holland, just as he said he would, and crashed on the outskirts of Steenbergen in south-western Holland, with fatal consequences for him, and Coningsby's recently appointed station navigation officer, S/L James Warwick. The cause of the crash is unresolved, but the general belief is that Gibson's lack of familiarity with the Mosquito led to his failure to locate fuel transfer taps and the engines became starved of petrol.

It was now time to turn attention upon Calais as the final port still under enemy occupation. Only one 5 Group Lancaster was involved in the first round of attacks on enemy positions on the 20th, after which, the group remained inactive until the 23rd. Orders came through on that morning to prepare 136 Lancasters and five Mosquitos for an attack that night on the aqueduct section of the Dortmund-Ems Canal south of Ladbergen. It was the scene of a disaster for 617 Squadron in September 1943, when five of eight crews had failed to return. An element from 617 Squadron would be on scene also on this night to open the attack with Tallboys, to which the raised banks containing the waterway were particularly vulnerable. Germany's canal system was a vital component in the transport network, and facilitated the import of raw materials and the export of finished goods to support the war effort. Its wide thoroughfares allowed the passage of large barges, and, as the slack in Germany's war production was taken up during 1944, traffic was being pushed through at increasing levels. While this operation was in progress, a second 5 Group force of 108 Lancasters, four Mosquitos and the P38 Lightning would hit the Handorf night-fighter airfield some ten miles to the south to prevent it from interfering. The main operation on this night, however, would be conducted by 549 aircraft from 1, 3, 4 and 8 Groups seventy miles to the south-west at Neuss, situated across the Rhine opposite Düsseldorf, and this, hopefully, might help to split the enemy defences.

619 Squadron prepared sixteen Lancasters to attack Handorf aerodrome, and they departed Dunholme Lodge between 18.24 and 18.57 with F/Ls Jordan and Wingate the senior pilots on duty. All reached the target area to encounter a layer of ten-tenths cloud between 8,000 and 9,500 feet, but with good visibility beneath. The Master Bomber found himself unable to direct the attack, and experienced great difficulty in communicating the fact to his Deputy because of intense interference on VHF. Identification and marking of the aiming points proved to be difficult, and only two green TIs could be seen by a few crews. There would be complaints later that there was no control, and some crews orbited and remained in the target area for up to thirty-five minutes before bombing either on green TIs at Handorf or on yellows at Münster, which was selected as the last-resort target. Seven 619 Squadron crews carried out their attacks on Handorf from 18,000 to 18,500 feet between 21.55 and 22.03, while nine were unable to establish a pinpoint and had not carried out an attack before the Master Bomber called a halt. Fourteen Lancasters failed to return after the Canal-Busters were badly mauled by night-fighters on the way home, but post-raid reconnaissance revealed that breaches in both branches of the canal, probably caused by Tallboys,

had left a six-mile stretch drained and unnavigable. It also revealed no new damage at Handorf, where only twenty-two aircraft had bombed.

The second of the series of raids on enemy positions around Calais was mounted by 188 aircraft on the 24th, for which 5 Group detailed thirty Lancasters from the 53 Base stations of Skellingthorpe and Waddington. In the event, only 126 aircraft bombed, eight of them from 5 Group, and they attacked either on a reference provided by Oboe skymarkers or came below the cloud base to bomb visually. At such a height, they were sitting ducks for the heavy and light flak batteries, which accounted for seven Lancasters and a Halifax. It was a similar story on the following day, when only a third of more than eight hundred aircraft were able to deliver their bombs, before the Master Bomber called a halt to proceedings in the face of low cloud. The campaign continued on the 26th, with two separate raids against seven enemy positions around Cap Gris Nez and nearer Calais involving more than seven hundred aircraft. This time the conditions were favourable, and bombing was observed to be concentrated around the aiming points.

On the afternoon of the 26th, eighteen 619 Squadron crews attended briefing, and learned that the night's operation was to be against the city of Karlsruhe in southern Germany, for which 216 Lancasters of 5 Group were made ready, along with ten of the ABC variety from 101 Squadron and eleven Mosquitos. It was to be a two-phase attack with a two-hour gap between, and the 52, 53 and 55 Base elements assigned to the second phase. This meant a late take-off, and it was between 00.10 and 00.56 when the 619 Squadron crews departed Dunholme Lodge with S/L Smith the senior pilot on duty. They flew out over France with ten-tenths cloud beneath them, which persisted all the way to the target, but thinned to a narrow band with the base estimated to be at between 6,000 and 7,000 feet. The plan was to bomb through the cloud on H2S, guided by Wanganui flares, and some approaching crews observed a red TI cascade above the cloud at 03.54. The 619 Squadron crews focused on the glow of red and green TIs, and bombed them from 11,500 and 14,000 feet between 04.00 and 04.10 in accordance with the instructions of the Master Bomber. All returned safely to report what appeared to be a city in flames and the glow of fires visible for up to 150 miles into the return journey. There were no plottable bombing photos, but reconnaissance confirmed that the attack had been spread throughout the city and had left a large part of it devastated. Only two Lancasters failed to return, and one of them was 619 Squadron's ED602, which was lost without trace with the eight-man crew of F/O Pettigrew RCAF.

As the crews returned to their stations after 07.00, elements of 1, 3, 4 and 8 Groups were preparing to leave theirs for a further attack on the Calais area. On arrival, the Master Bomber ordered the 340-strong force to come below the cloud base to bomb visually, and another successful operation ensued. Later that day, an advance party headed east by road to establish a squadron presence at Strubby, a station located three miles north of Alford, west of Sutton-on-Sea, which had opened in April as a sub-station of 55 Base at East Kirkby. It had been occupied first by Coastal Command as a base for its Warwick air-sea rescue operations, and then elements of the 2nd Tactical Air Force, but was now to be home for the remainder of the war to 619 Squadron. Meanwhile, at Dunholme Lodge, sixteen 619 Squadron crews attended briefing for an operation that night against Kaiserslautern, an historic city on the edge of the Palatinate Forest, some thirty miles west of Mannheim. It would be the first major attack of the war on this location, for which a force of 217 Lancasters, including ten from 101 Squadron, and ten Mosquitos, was made ready. The 619 Squadron Lancasters were loaded with 2,000 pounders, 500lb J-Cluster bombs and 4lb incendiaries, which they lifted into the air between 21.36 and 22.14 with F/Ls Jordan and O'Neill the senior pilots on duty. Clear skies over England gave way to a build-up of cloud over the Channel, and, from the French coast to near the target, they encountered ten-tenths cumulus with a base at 2,800 feet. The target was partially covered by a thin layer of five to eight-tenths cloud with tops at 3,000 feet, with a further layer at 6,000 to 7,000 feet. The marking with red and green TIs was punctual and accurate, and a green TI visible in the centre of the town became the objective for the main force crews in accordance with the Master Bomber's instructions at 00.58. The 619 Squadron crews attacked from 4,000 to 5,500 feet between 01.02 and 01.10 and observed the bombing to be concentrated. Two yellow explosions were seen at 01.02, and fires were beginning to take hold as the force retreated towards the west. Reconnaissance revealed massive damage within the city, caused by more than nine hundred tons of bombs, and an estimated 36% of the built-up area was reduced to ruins.

The final raids on German positions around Calais were carried out by 490 aircraft of 1, 3, 6 and 8 Groups on the 28th, and the garrison surrendered to Canadian forces shortly thereafter. 619 Squadron completed its move to Strubby on this day, while 44 (Rhodesia) Squadron joined 207 Squadron at Spilsby, and, together with East Kirkby, this constituted the new 55 Base, while 52 Base was disbanded. W/C Black was posted in from 51 Base on the 29th for a temporary attachment to gain operational experience before being appointed to command 207 Squadron at Spilsby in mid-October. Dunholme Lodge, like nearby Scampton, was transferred to 1 Group, and welcomed the recently reformed 170 Squadron with its Lancasters. However, because of its close proximity to Scampton, Faldingworth, Wickenby and Fiskerton with overlapping circuits, it was decided to take Dunholme Lodge out of the front line, and 170 Squadron would move out at the end of November. The crews of siblings F/O G McMorran RCAF and F/O A McMorran RCAF were posted in from 51 Base on the 30th. During the course of the month the squadron participated in twelve operations and dispatched 189 sorties for the loss of four Lancasters and their crews.

October 1944

A theme running throughout October was a campaign against the island of Walcheren in the Scheldt estuary, where heavy gun emplacements were barring the approaches to the much-needed port of Antwerp some forty miles upstream. Attempts to bomb these positions in September had proved unsuccessful, and it was decided to flood the land, both to inundate the batteries, and to render the terrain difficult to defend when the ground forces moved in. 252 Lancasters were drawn from 1, 5 and 8 Groups and made ready on the 3rd to attack the seawalls at Westkapelle, the most westerly point of the island. 5 Group contributed 128 Lancasters, allotted to four of eight waves of thirty aircraft each, with the Tallboy-carrying 617 Squadron Lancasters standing off to be called in only if required. A breach was opened by the fifth wave, which was extended by those following behind, and the flood waters had reached the town by the time the last Lancasters turned for home. 619 Squadron had not been invited to take part, and it was the 4th before orders were received to prepare five Lancasters for mining duties in the Silverthorn III garden in the Kattegat as part of a seventeen-strong 5 Group force. They departed Strubby between 17.20 and 17.25 with S/L Smith the senior pilot on duty and bound for Sejerø Bay off the north-western coast of Denmark's Sjælland island. They reached the target area to find good visibility and varying amounts of cloud between zero and eight-tenths, and P/O Peck and F/Os Coop and Scripps each delivered their six vegetables into the briefed locations from 12,000 to 13,000 feet between 20.51 and 20.57. S/L Smith and crew returned their mines to store after failing to locate the drop zone in the absence of a functioning H2S set. F/O Strachan's LM681 was hit either by a cannon shell or a rocket, which burned a three-foot hole just forward of the mid-upper turret, peppering the bomb doors and causing the ammunition to explode, while knocking out the hydraulics, intercom and emergency oxygen. The gunners fought the fire, the mid-upper sustaining serious burns, and a crash-landing was carried out at Carnaby without wheels and flaps and without further damage to the crew.

5 Group's first major outing of the month was posted on the 5th, and was a daylight attempt to bomb the port of Wilhelmshaven through ten-tenths cloud on H2S. A force of 227 Lancasters, one Mosquito and the P38 Lightning was assembled with 619 Squadron providing twenty aircraft, which set out from Strubby between 07.54 and 08.19 with W/C Milward the senior squadron pilot on duty and W/C Black undertaking his first sortie. Whether or not it was part of the plan, the controller led the force around the northern side of Heligoland, before heading for Jade Bay, where they found the forecast layer of ten-tenths cloud between 3,000 and 5,000 feet with good visibility above. The 619 Squadron crews established their positions by H2S-fix or by observing others, and delivered their ten 1,000 pounders and four 500lb J-Cluster bombs each from 15,000 to 18,000 feet between 11.03 and 11.12. No results were observed, and there was no possibility of making an assessment, but the impression of a scattered attack was confirmed later when photo-reconnaissance became possible.

From this point until the end of the war, German towns and cities were to be subjected to a new and terrible bomber offensive, beginning with a second Ruhr campaign, which was to open at Dortmund, and for which a 3, 6 and 8 Group force of 523 aircraft was made ready on the 6th. 5 Group, meanwhile, had its own target, and prepared 237 Lancasters and seven Mosquitos for what would prove to be the thirty-second and final raid of the war on the city of Bremen. 619 Squadron loaded twenty Lancasters with a mixture of high explosives and incendiaries and dispatched them from Strubby between 17.31 and 17.56 with W/C Milward and S/L Smith the senior pilots on duty and W/C Black also on the Order of Battle. Having climbed out and set course, they left the cloud behind and headed into crystal clear skies over the North Sea with a three-quarter moon. The others found the target area to be free of cloud, which was ideal for the 5 Group low-level marking method, and the conditions handed the hapless city on a plate to the bombers. The 619 Squadron crews carried out their attacks in the face of many searchlights and the usual flak response, and aimed for the red and green TIs from 18,000 to 19,500 feet between 20.26 and 20.36, before turning away from a city in flames, the glow from which remained visible for a hundred miles and more. The success of the operation was confirmed by post-raid reconnaissance and local reports, which described a huge area of fire, and catalogued the destruction of more than 4,800 houses and apartment blocks, and severe damage to war industry factories, all achieved at the modest cost of five aircraft. Now that the focus of operations had moved from France to Germany, the number of sorties to complete a tour had been reduced from thirty-five to thirty-three, and this meant an unexpected bonus to some.

Following the failure of Operation Market Garden, the German frontier towns of Cleves (Kleve) and Emmerich were earmarked for attention by daylight on the 7th. Five miles apart and separated by the Rhine, both would suffer massive damage at the hands of large forces from 1, 3, 4 and 8

Groups. 5 Group, meanwhile, was to return to Walcheren, to target the seawalls near Flushing, and made ready 121 Lancasters and three Mosquitos. Many of the bombs contained a thirty-minute delay fuse, while others detonated on impact, and the dyke was already beginning to crumble as the bombers headed home, where confirmation of a successful outcome would catch up with them. Focus remained on the Scheldt defences, and the gun battery at Fort Frederik Hendrik near Breskens on the East Scheldt was targeted by elements of 1 and 8 Groups on the 11th, while 115 Lancasters from 5 Group were assigned to others near Flushing on the north bank of the West Scheldt. At the same time, sixty-one Lancasters from 55 Base and two Mosquitos were to attempt to breach the seawalls at Veere, situated on the eastern side of Walcheren opposite Westkapelle. 619 Squadron contributed fourteen Lancasters, and they departed Strubby between 13.11 and 13.28 with F/L Brown the senior pilot on duty. On arrival at their respective targets, crews encountered varying amounts of cloud between two and seven-tenths with tops at 4,000 to 5,000 feet, through which the 619 Squadron crews carried out their attacks from 6,000 to 7,500 feet between 14.46 and 14.55. Post-raid reconnaissance revealed an area of flooding of 800 x 250 yards at Veere, but no new damage to the gun positions.

The 14th was the day on which were fired the opening salvoes of Operation Hurricane, a terrifying demonstration to the enemy of the overwhelming superiority of the Allied air forces ranged against it. Bomber Command ordered a maximum effort from all but 5 Group to attack Duisburg, for which 1,013 Lancasters, Halifaxes and Mosquitos answered the call. The American 8th Air Force would also be in business on this day, targeting the Cologne area further south with 1,250 bombers escorted by 749 fighters. The RAF force took off at first light, picked up its own fighter escort, and delivered 4,500 tons of high-explosives and incendiaries into Duisburg shortly after breakfast time, causing unimaginable destruction. That night, similar numbers returned to press home the point about superiority, bringing the total weight of bombs over the two raids to 9,000 tons from 2,018 sorties in fewer than twenty-four hours. The only involvement by 5 Group were single sorties by a Lancaster and a Mosquito to conduct a photo-reconnaissance of the operation.

However, 5 Group took advantage of the evening activity over the Ruhr to return to Braunschweig, the scene of quite a number of unsatisfactory previous attempts to land a really telling blow. A force of 232 Lancasters and eight Mosquitos was made ready, of which twenty of the former were provided by 619 Squadron. They departed Strubby between 22.21 and 23.05 with W/C Milward and the newly promoted S/L Jordan the senior pilots on duty, but lost F/O Martin and crew early on to port-outer engine failure. The others reached the target area to find conditions ideal for low-level marking, but had to approach the aiming point at 18,000 feet from the south-west, passing over Hallendorf and Salzgitter, the latter the home to the Reichswerke Hermann Göring steelworks. This forced them to run the gauntlet of searchlight cones and heavy flak for the three minutes it took to pass through, but, on the other side, they were greeted by clear skies and good visibility, which facilitated accurate marking with red and green TIs. Although the early stages of bombing tended to undershoot, the Master Bomber quickly brought the attack back on track, calling for crews to overshoot by up to nineteen seconds. The 619 Squadron contingent passed over the aiming point at 18,250 to 19,000 feet between 02.30 and 02.36, and delivered their loads accurately to contribute to a highly effective raid. 83 Squadron's F/O Price complained that main force crews were jettisoning incendiaries all the way back as far as the Rhine, and thereby illuminating the track for any stalking night fighters. In the event, only a single Lancaster failed to return from what was, indeed, confirmed to be an outstanding result, which had wiped out the entire centre of this historic city, and visited damage on almost every district.

On the following night, 5 Group sent five Lancasters to mine the waters of the Silverthorn garden in the Kattegat region of the western Baltic. F/O Coop and crew alone represented 619 Squadron, departing Strubby at 18.35 and returning at 00.25 to report planting their vegetables into the briefed location from 15,000 feet at 21.32. Stubborn resistance by the occupiers on Walcheren demanded further operations against the seawalls at Westkapelle, for which 5 Group detailed forty-seven Lancasters and three Mosquitos on the 17th. 619 Squadron briefed the crews of S/L Jordan and F/Os Clapham and Smith, while the armourers loaded each of their Lancasters with fourteen 1,000 pounders fitted with delay fuses of varying lengths. They departed Strubby between 12.53 and 13.01, and arrived at the target to find favourable conditions, before bombing within seconds of each other at 14.01 from 5,000 feet. They returned safely home with an aiming point photo each, leaving a reconnaissance aircraft over the target from 14.55 to 15.10 to record the delayed-action bomb blasts. Once developed, the photos would reveal no extension to the breach in the dyke.

Following a night off, twenty 619 Squadron crews assembled in the Strubby briefing room on the 19th, to receive details of the 5 Group operation that night against Nuremberg, while 560 aircraft from the other groups plied their trade at Stuttgart, some ninety miles to the south-west. A new record 5 Group force of 263 Lancasters and seven Mosquitos stood ready in the early evening, and the 619 Squadron element began taking off at 17.10, each bearing aloft a 2,000 pounder and twelve 500lb J-Cluster bombs. They were all safely airborne within twenty-four minutes, with F/L O'Neill the senior pilot on duty, but lost the services of F/O Chambers and crew to W/T failure shortly after they crossed the French coast near Abbeville. For the others, the outward flight across France was uneventful, and they found the target to be covered by a wedge of eight to ten-tenths cloud between 3,000 and 10,000 feet, with poor visibility below. The marker force laid down flares and backed them up with others along with red and green TIs, which were observed to be somewhat scattered, and bombing had to take place on their glow seen through the cloud. The 619 Squadron crews carried out their attacks from 15,500 to 19,200 feet between 20.56 and 21.04 in accordance with the Master Bomber's instructions, before returning home uncertain as to the outcome. The impression given by the glow of fires was of an effective attack, but post-raid reconnaissance revealed the bombing to have fallen not on the intended city centre aiming point, but predominantly into the more industrial southern districts, where almost four hundred houses were destroyed, along with forty-one industrial buildings.

W/C Black and his crew were posted to Spilsby on the 23rd, where he would take command of 207 Squadron. It was back to Walcheren on this day for 112 Lancasters of 5 Group, this time to target the coastal battery at Flushing. The 619 Squadron crews of S/L Purnell and F/Os Martin, Proctor and Runnalls attended briefing, while their Lancasters were being loaded with fourteen 1,000 pounders each. S/L Purnell had arrived around a week earlier from 51 Base to fill the vacancy for a flight commander left by the loss of S/L Squibbs. They departed Strubby between 15.09 and 15.14, and were greeted at the target by eight to ten-tenths cloud with a base at between 3,000 and 5,000 feet, and poor visibility below caused by haze and rain. The force was led in on what appeared to be a decent approach, but was ordered to "orbit port" as the lead crews experienced great difficulty in identifying their respective aiming points. A second run was no more revealing, even for those crews who ventured down as low as 2,000 feet, and twenty would still have their bombs on board when ordered to go home. The crews of F/Os Martin and Proctor carried out their attacks from 4,000 feet at 16.29, and were among eighty-eight crews to do so, while F/O Runnalls and crew were ordered home. S/L Purnell's introduction to 619 Squadron operations was somewhat challenging, as a flak hit during the bombing run set off a fire in the bomb bay. The load was jettisoned, but a second flak hit caused another fire, and the order was issued to abandon the aircraft. Four crew members took to their parachutes over the target, before S/L Purnell regained control and completed the sea crossing to allow his two remaining crewmen to jump out over Suffolk. They were taken to hospital suffering from burns, while their captain crash-landing ME787 at Woodbridge. Post-raid reconnaissance revealed evidence of seventy bomb bursts, including four near-misses, and the destruction of a number of buildings on the site.

That evening, a new record force of 1,055 aircraft was sent against Essen as part of the Hurricane "message", and dropped 4,538 tons of bombs, more than 90% of which was high explosive. This number was achieved without 5 Group, which took the night off, and committed only twenty-five Lancasters to gardening duties in northern waters on the following night. Essen was pounded again by more than seven hundred aircraft in daylight on the 25th, by which time it had ceased to be an important source of war production. Operation Hurricane moved on to Cologne on the 28th, when two districts east of the centre were totally devastated by more than seven hundred aircraft.

5 Group occupied the day with the preparation of a force of 237 Lancasters and seven Mosquitos for an operation that night against the U-Boot pens at Bergen in Norway. 619 Squadron made ready a dozen Lancasters for the main event and a further six for mining duties in the Onions/Tomato gardens in Oslo Fjord. The gardeners took off first between 20.34 and 20.39 with F/L O'Neill the senior pilot on duty, leaving the bombing brigade on the ground until their departure from Strubby between 22.46 and 23.00, each captained by a junior officer. The gardeners were an hour away from their drop zone by this time, and all reached it, five to deliver their stores as briefed from 3,600 to 10,000 feet between 00.02 and 00.13. F/O Coop and crew experienced the frustration of reaching the target area, only for their H2S to fail and prevent them from identifying the precise release point. Meanwhile, the bombing force had battled its way through electrical storms, having lost only two of its number to early returns during the three-and-a-half-hour outward flight. They had been told to expect clear conditions, although some doubts had been expressed about the forecast, and these were confirmed when the force was met by eight-to ten-tenths cloud between 4,000 and 14,000 feet, which obscured the aiming point. This would not have been a problem over Germany, but the risk to Norwegian civilians was uppermost in the mind of the Master Bomber as he pondered his options before calling for the main force to descend. Even then, most were unable to pick out any markers, and the situation was exacerbated by intermittent VHF reception, which persuaded 83 Squadron's F/L Cornish to fly up and down the coast acting as a communications link between the Master Bomber and the main force. The flare force contingent did what they could from between 12,500 and 15,000 feet, and some main force crews flew as low as 4,500 feet, without being able to identify the target. The operation was abandoned after only forty-seven aircraft had bombed, and F/O Proctor and crew were the only ones from 619 Squadron to do so, from 6,750 at 02.18.

The final operations against Walcheren were undertaken by 5 Group on the 30th, when two forces of fifty-one Lancasters and four Mosquitos each were sent against coastal batteries at Westkapelle and Flushing. 619 Squadron contributed nine Lancasters to the Westkapelle attack, and they departed Strubby between 10.37 and 11.00 with F/Ls Osborne and Tanner the senior pilots on duty. They ran into four to seven-tenths cloud at 6,000 feet over the target, despite which, visibility was good, and the aiming point was identified visually and marked by red TIs. Some of these became buried in the dunes and were partially concealed, leading to a little overshooting, but the 619 Squadron crews were able to deliver their loads accurately from 3,100 to 5,100 feet between 12.00 and 12.06. Ground forces went in on the following day, and a week of heavy fighting preceded the island's capture. Even then, the clearing of mines from the approaches to Antwerp kept the port out of commission for a further three weeks. On the evening of the 30th, nine hundred aircraft returned to Cologne, and almost five hundred went back again twenty-four hours later to complete the destruction of the Rhineland capital. During the course of the month the squadron carried out twelve operations and dispatched 134 sorties without losing a Lancaster, and it was assumed that four crew members were in enemy hands.

November 1944

The new month began with a daylight operation on the afternoon of the 1st, against the Meerbeck synthetic oil refinery at Moers/Homberg, or, to give it its full title, the Gewerkschaft Rheinpreussen A.G. plant, located on the west bank of the Rhine opposite Duisburg on the western edge of the Ruhr. The name of this target would strike fear into the hearts of 3 Group crews, who had suffered heavy casualties while attacking the plant during the summer, but it meant nothing to 5 Group crews, who were less familiar with it, and would have found the name Wesseling more unsettling. 619 Squadron briefed eighteen crews as part of an overall 5 Group force of 226 Lancasters and two Mosquitos, which were to be joined by fourteen 8 Group Mosquitos to provide the Oboe marking. They took off from Strubby between 13.55 and 14.12 with S/L Jordan the senior pilot on duty, and reached the target to find it completely obscured by cloud with tops at between 6,000 and 9,000 feet. Wanganui flares from earlier arrivals were well scattered over a circle with a ten-mile radius, prompting a backer-up from 83 Squadron to drop a yellow TI over the built-up area in the hope of attracting some bombing. The problem seemed to be, that crews at the head of the stream had seen no markers or were past them by the time that they became evident, and had taken their bombs home. Some 619 Squadron crews caught a glimpse of the target area through a chink in the cloud, while others carried out a time-and-distance run from the last visual pinpoint, before aiming at red skymarkers to deliver their fourteen 1,000 pounders each from 17,000 to 18,000 feet between 16.05 and 16.12. The attackers had faced an intense flak response, and 619 Squadron's PB540 was hit, but made it back to England where it crashed and burst into flames on landing at Woodbridge at 18.00. F/L Tanner and three others at the front of the Lancaster lost their lives, while the wireless operator and both gunners sustained injuries, the rear gunner serious burns. At debriefing, many crews reported difficulty in hearing the Master Bomber, after his VHF transmissions became jammed by someone in another aircraft leaving the transmit button on. Ultimately, the conditions rendered the whole attack ineffective, and, although 159 crews released their bombs, it is unlikely that any hit the intended target.

Düsseldorf's turn to face a massive force came on the 2nd, when 992 aircraft were made ready for what would prove to be the final major raid of the war on this much-bombed city. The "Lincolnshire Poachers" put up 187 Lancasters for this rare experience to operate with the rest of the Command. The 619 Squadron element of eleven departed Strubby between 16.12 and 16.29 with no senior pilots on duty, and arrived at the target to find clear skies, moonlight and only ground haze to slightly mar the vertical visibility. The moonlight nullified the searchlights ringing the city, but, of greater concern was the heavy flak bursting at 17,000 to 20,000 feet. The main force crews found the aiming point to be well illuminated and marked with red and green TIs, onto which each of the 619 Squadron participants dropped a cookie, six 1,000 pounders and six 500 pounders from 14,000 to 21,000 feet between 19.13 and 19.20. It was the crew of F/Sgt Webster who had ventured so low after diving to escape the clutches of a searchlight cone. Returning crews reported fires beginning to take hold and smoke rising to 2,000 feet as they turned away, and were confident of a successful raid. This was confirmed by post-raid reconnaissance, which revealed that the northern half of the city had received the main weight of bombs, and that five thousand houses had been destroyed or seriously damaged.

The continuing campaign against Ruhr cities would be prosecuted by 749 aircraft at Bochum on the 4th, while 5 Group renewed its acquaintance with the Dortmund-Ems Canal, which had been repaired following the successful breaching of its banks near Ladbergen in September. Now that Germany's railways were being pounded, the Dortmund-Ems and the nearby Mittelland Canal, took on a greater significance as vital components in the transportation system, particularly with regard to the movement of raw materials to and from the Ruhr region. A force of 168 Lancasters and two Mosquitos contained thirteen 619 Squadron aircraft, which took off between 17.39 and 17.58 with F/L Osborne the senior pilot on duty. They were headed for the familiar aqueduct section of the canal south of Ladbergen, and hoped to sneak in under cover of the main operation sixty miles to the south, hopefully, thereby, to avoid the attentions of night-fighters. The first marker aircraft of 83 Squadron arrived at the target at 19.19, after making a GPI run (ground position indicated) by means of H2S from Münster, and encountered clear skies with ground haze. A blind-dropped green TI burst on the canal bank four hundred yards short of the aiming point, and the flare force went in between 19.20 and 19.28. Red TIs were observed to fall between the two aqueducts, after which, the Master Bomber cancelled the third wave of flares and sent them all home to leave the way clear for the main force crews. The first bombs tended to overshoot, but, thereafter, the crews produced an accurate and concentrated attack, those from 619 Squadron bombing from 10,000 to 13,000 feet between 19.32 and 19.36. Photo-reconnaissance confirmed that both branches of the canal had been breached and drained, leaving barges stranded and the waterway unnavigable, and the success had been achieved for the loss of just three Lancasters.

To capitalise on the success, an attack was planned for the 6th against the Mittelland Canal at Gravenhorst, a point about a mile north of Das Nasse Dreieck, the "Wet Triangle" at Bergeshövede. This is a triangular basin, where the two waterways converge about ten miles north of Ladbergen, before the Dortmund-Ems continues on to the west, and the Mittelland north and then to the east. It was a 5 Group show involving 239 Lancasters and seven Mosquitos, sixteen of the former representing 619 Squadron. They departed Strubby between 16.19 and 16.37 with F/L Osborne the senior pilot on duty, and all reached the target area to find clear skies but haze up to around 4,000 feet affecting the visibility. The Master Bomber called in the flare force, despite which, the low-level Mosquito markers experienced great difficulty in identifying the aiming point. A single Mosquito eventually did deliver its target indicator accurately onto the aiming point, where it fell into the water and was extinguished. The Master Bomber called a halt to proceedings after thirty-one aircraft had bombed, and the 619 Squadron participants jettisoned the delayed-action 1,000 pounders, before setting course for home and encountering not only night-fighter activity, but also very challenging weather conditions of electrical storms and low cloud. PB205 crash-landed at Bethel on return, but F/O Lavigne and crew emerged unscathed, and the Lancaster would be returned to active service. Ten Lancasters and their crews were less fortunate, four of them from 467 Squadron RAAF alone. 619 Squadron's LM742 crashed somewhere in the target area, killing the wireless operator and both gunners, while F/O Hookings and the others fell into enemy hands. NN723 came down in the North Sea with no survivors from the crew of F/Sgt Webster.

Earlier on the 6th, a series of raids on Ruhr oil refineries had begun with a heavy area attack at Gelsenkirchen, and this was followed by smaller-scale operations at Homberg on the 8th, the Krupp Treibstoffwerke at Wanne-Eickel on the 9th and the Klöckner Werke A.G. refinery at Castrop-Rauxel on the morning of the 11th. Sixteen 619 Squadron crews attended briefing at Strubby later in the day to learn that they would shortly be attacking the Rhenania-Ossag synthetic oil refinery at Harburg, situated on the south bank of the Elbe opposite Hamburg. 237 Lancasters and eight Mosquitos were to take part in another all-5 Group show, while elements of 1 and 8 Groups targeted the Hoesch-Benzin plant a dozen miles further east in the Wambel district of Dortmund. Most of the Lancasters were loaded with a cookie, six 1,000 and five 500 pounders, while a few would carry fourteen N°14 cluster bombs with their cookie. Another early evening take-off had the 619 Squadron element airborne between 16.27 and 16.41 with S/L Purnell leading the way. F/O McMorran and crew lost their port-outer engine and turned back, leaving the others to press on and reach the target area to find largely clear conditions, with only a thin layer of stratus at 8,000 feet and another at 17,000 to 18,000 feet between them and the aiming point. This they identified either by H2S or red and green TIs, before delivering their loads from 14,000 to 19,000 feet between 19.16 and 19.30. The low height belonged to F/L Osborne and crew, whose starboard-outer engine caught fire and had to be feathered. The defenders threw up a heavy flak barrage, which reached as high as 23,000 feet, and this is almost certainly what accounted for 619 Squadron's PB356, which crashed in the target area with no survivors from the eight-man crew of F/O Clapham. At debriefing, crews reported a large explosion at 19.28, followed by an oil fire, and local reports would confirm that heavy damage had been inflicted upon the town's residential and industrial districts.

The 16th was devoted to the destruction of the three small towns of Heinsberg, Jülich and Düren, located respectively in an arc from north to east of Aachen, and close to the German lines being advanced upon by American ground forces. A total of 1,188 aircraft was involved, and 1, 5 and 8 Groups provided the heavy bombing and marking force of 485 Lancasters for the last-mentioned. 619 Squadron contributed sixteen aircraft to the 5 Group effort of 214, and they took off from Strubby between 12.38 and 13.00 with W/C Milward the senior pilot on duty, and each carrying eleven 1,000 and four 500 pounders. F/O McMorran and crew had the town of Boston on the horizon when the oil pressure in the port-inner engine plummeted, and they abandoned their second sortie in a row. The others flew to the target over ten-tenths cloud, which cleared to three-tenths stratus above 6,000 feet as they approached the aiming point in the final wave of the attack. They bombed in accordance with the instructions of the Master Bomber from 10,000 to 13,000 feet between 15.34 and 15.42, and observed smoke rising through 9,000 feet as they turned for home, confident in the success of the attack. All of the Strubby crews believed that they had hit the target, but most of the photos were unplottable because of the smoke covering the area. The operation was a complete success at a cost of just three aircraft, and post-raid reconnaissance confirmed that the town had been all but erased from the map, local sources claiming a death toll in excess of three thousand inhabitants. In the event, unfavourable ground conditions prevented the American advance from succeeding.

Twenty 619 Squadron crews attended briefing at Strubby on the 21st, to be told that they were going back to the Mittelland Canal on a night of multiple operations involving 1,345 sorties. Three operations, each by 270 aircraft, were to be directed at railway yards at Aschaffenburg, situated about twenty miles south-east of Frankfurt, and oil plants at Castrop-Rauxel and Sterkrade in the Ruhr. 5 Group prepared two forces of 137 and 123 Lancasters respectively, with Mosquito support, for the Mittelland and Dortmund-Ems Canals, while a whole host of minor operations would complete the Order of Battle. 55 Base was assigned to the former at Gravenhorst, for which the 619 Squadron element took off between 17.23 and 17.41 led by S/L Jordan. The crew captained by South African, Lt Meter, turned back after losing their Gee signal, while the rest pressed on to encounter a layer of six to ten-tenths cloud in the target area between 4,000 and 8,000 feet. This did not inhibit the accuracy of the marking, but the instructions of the Master Bomber caused some confusion, a situation exacerbated by a weak VHF signal. At first, he ordered the crews to come below the cloud base, to which some responded, before he changed his mind and told them to return to the briefed bombing height. This led to bombing heights among the 619 Squadron participants ranging from 2,000 to 9,000 feet. He issued instructions to aim for the more southerly of two red TIs, and they complied as best they could between 21.01 to 21.11, observing what appeared to be a good concentration of bomb bursts. Post-raid reconnaissance revealed that the Mittelland Canal had been breached over a distance of fifty feet on the western bank, south of the road bridge, and this had left a thirty-mile stretch of the waterway drained with fifty-nine barges stranded in one small section.

Reconnaissance at Ladbergen revealed success also, showing the left-hand channel, which was the only one repaired since the last attack, to have been breached again where it crossed the River Glane, which had been unable to cope with the volume of water released and extensive flooding occurred on both sides of the canal. The two operations were concluded for the loss of just two 49 Squadron Lancasters. The Germans recognised that repairing the canals was an open invitation to Bomber Command to return, but, so vital were they to the transportation system, that they could not be abandoned. The answer was to complete repairs, but to leave the sections drained and apparently still under repair, until sufficient traffic had built up to push through in one night. They would then be flooded and re-emptied to dupe RAF reconnaissance flights and maintain the deception. W/C Tomes arrived from 5LFS during the last week of the month, having undergone a heavy conversion course to prepare him for operational duties and the command of 57 Squadron early in the New Year. One wonders what operational crews thought of being commanded by an officer who had faced the enemy less than they, when there were so many among their ranks who had earned the right to command but were not rewarded with the opportunity.

On the following night, 5 Group dispatched 171 Lancasters and seven Mosquitos to attack the U-Boot pens at Trondheim in Norway, a distance of more than eight hundred miles. 619 Squadron launched a dozen Lancasters into the air between 15.50 and 16.24 with W/C Milward the senior pilot on duty, and all arrived in the target area to find clear skies and excellent visibility. Unfortunately, they were thwarted by an effective smoke screen that prevented the marker force from finding the aiming point, and the Master Bomber had no option but to send the force home.

The Strubby crews were probably about to fall into their beds when the crews of F/Os May, McMorran, Runnells and Strachan took off between 0.4.42 and 04.50 bound for the Young Eglantine garden in the Elbe Estuary in company with thirteen others. They flew out over ten-tenths cloud with tops up to 12,500 feet, and planted their vegetables as briefed from 12,000 to 14,000 feet between 06.43 and 06.51.

The weather was mainly responsible for curtailing operations over the next few days until the 26th, when briefings took place on 5 Group stations at 20.00. The eighteen attending 619 Squadron crews learned that Munich was to be their target for an all-5 Group affair involving 270 Lancasters and eight Mosquitos, which represented a maximum effort. After the take-off time was pushed back, they departed Strubby between 23.33 and 00.05 with S/L Purnell the senior pilot on duty, and each carrying a 1,000 pounder and thirteen Nº4 J-Cluster bombs. Forming up and climbing to operational altitude was a time-consuming business, and it would be five hours before the target was reached. Lt Meter and crew were some fifty miles out from the Lincolnshire coast when a fire in the starboard-inner engine ended their interest in proceedings, leaving the rest to find the target area under clear skies with good visibility. They confirmed their positions by means of H2S, while the low-level marking was being carried out, and, aside from one errant red TI, it was accurate, and the Master Bomber ensured that the crews focused upon the reds and greens on and close to the planned aiming point. The 619 Squadron crews bombed from 16,000 to 17,300 feet between 05.00 and 05.15, and returned safely to praise the quality of the route and target marking and the concentration of the attack. The last-mentioned was confirmed by post-raid reconnaissance and a local report that singled out railway installations as being particularly hard-hit.

This was the final operation of the month for 5 Group, but among others taking place before the end was an attack by 1 and 8 Groups on Freiburg in southern Germany. It was a minor railway centre within thirty-five miles of advancing American and French ground forces, and was thought to be harbouring large numbers of enemy soldiers. The force of over 330 Lancasters delivered 1,900 tons of bombs, missing the railway yards, but destroying two thousand houses and killing over two thousand inhabitants. During the course of the month, the squadron took part in ten operations and dispatched 144 sorties for the loss of four Lancasters, three complete crews and most of a fourth.

December 1944

There were no operations for 5 Group for the first three nights of the new month, largely because of the weather, and, in the meantime, 1, 4, 6 and 8 Groups pounded the Ruhr town of Hagen on the night of the 2/3rd. Worthwhile targets were becoming more and more scarce at a time when the Command was at its most powerful, and this final period of the war would bring the most devastating attacks to date on the German homeland. When the 55 Base squadrons returned to action in the early evening of the 4th, it was to contribute towards a 5 Group force of 282 Lancasters and ten Mosquitos. Their target was the city of Heilbronn, situated thirty miles due north of Stuttgart, which had the River Neckar and a north-south rail link running through it, but, otherwise, had no genuine strategic importance, and would not have been expecting to be attacked. The main operation on this night was actually by 535 aircraft of 1, 6 and 8 Groups at Karlsruhe, some fifty-six miles west-south-west of Heilbronn, and the concentration of aircraft in this area would be certain to bring out the night-fighters. The 619 Squadron element of eighteen Lancasters departed Strubby between 16.28 and 16.46 with W/C Milward and S/L Purnell the senior pilots on duty, and each carrying a cookie and either five 1,000 pounders or twelve SBCs of 4lb incendiaries. F/O Flockhart and crew were well on their way when the rear turret became unserviceable and forced them to abandon their sortie, leaving the others to continue their flight across France in good conditions to find three to five-tenths thin stratus over the target at around 12,000 feet. Some crews were able to pick out the Neckar through the cloud, and the aiming points, the marshalling yards and the built-up area, were illuminated by the flare force ahead of the low-level Mosquitos' run to drop red TIs for the visual markers to back up. The marshalling yards were marked with yellows, which the main force element was unable to distinguish in the burgeoning fires, and this persuaded them to focus on the red and green TIs in the city itself instead. The 619 Squadron crews attacked mostly from 11,000 to 11,500 feet between 19.30 and 19.43, adding to the general destruction, and, as the force retreated westwards into electrical storms, 82% of the city's built-up area was in the process of being destroyed by what probably amounted to a firestorm. The post-war British Bombing Survey estimated 351 acres of destruction, and a death toll of at least seven thousand people. It cost 5 Group twelve aircraft, two of which, LM791 and ND932, had departed Strubby in the late afternoon captained by F/O Schaefer RCAF and F/O Chambers RCAF respectively. Each was a predominantly Canadian crew from which both gunners in the former and the rear gunner in the latter survived to be taken into captivity after coming down in the general target area.

On a night of heavy Bomber Command activity on the 6/7th, 475 Lancasters of 1, 3 and 8 Groups were to target the oil refinery at Leuna (Merseburg) in the east, while 450 aircraft from predominantly 4 and 6 Groups attacked railway installations at Osnabrück in the north. 5 Group's target was the town of Giessen, situated some eighty-five miles south-east of Cologne in west-central Germany, and thirty-five miles north of Frankfurt. A force of 255 Lancasters was assembled, eighteen of them at Strubby, where the armourers loaded each of them with a cookie and thirteen SBCs of 4lb incendiaries. They took off between 16.55 and 17.25 with F/L Willitts the senior 619 Squadron pilot on duty and W/C Tomes undertaking his first sortie. The main force crews had been assigned to two aiming points, two-thirds of them to the town, and the remainder to the marshalling yards, and those arriving in the target area found up to eight-tenths thin cloud and good visibility. F/O Flockhart and crew were not among them, having been led astray by a faulty compass, and then almost lost due to severe icing conditions as they turned back. The flare force began illuminating three minutes early and to the west of the target, but the Mosquito-laid red TIs fell close to the aiming point and the Master Bomber ensured that they were backed up by greens. The 619 Squadron crews bombed from 10,000 to 11,600 feet between 20.14 and 20.26, and all returned safely to report another successful raid, which would be confirmed by reconnaissance photographs.

The Urft Dam was one of a number of similar structures in the beautiful Eifel region of western Germany, close to the Belgian frontier. There was a fear that the enemy might strategically release flood water to hamper the American advance into Germany, and it was decided to attempt to breach the dam, to allow any excess water to drain away. The first of a number of attacks on the region took place on the 3rd at Heimbach, the small town nestling against the northern reaches of the reservoir, but the 1 and 8 Group force failed to identify it, and no bombs fell. On the following day, a small 8 Group effort against the dam was unsuccessful, as was a 3 Group attack on the nearby Schwammenauel Dam on the 5th. The job was handed to 5 Group on the 8th, for which a force of 205 Lancasters was made ready, fourteen of them by 619 Squadron, while nineteen from 617 Squadron would be carrying Tallboys. The Strubby element took off between 09.01 and 09.33 with S/L Purnell the senior pilot on duty and W/C Tomes undertaking his second sortie. They were greeted at the target by six to nine-tenths cloud at between 6,000 and 8,000 feet and moderate visibility, and most crews made multiple runs across the target area seeking out the dam. Four from Strubby, including W/C Tomes, failed to identify the aiming point through the cloud and withheld their bombs. The remaining ten carried out their attacks from 8,500 to 10,200 feet between 11.02 and 11.11, and, after 129 aircraft had bombed, the Master Bomber called a halt and sent the force home. Poor weather conditions over Lincolnshire demanded a diversion, and all but four of the Strubby crews, who failed to pick up the signal, landed at Boscombe Down, from where they straggled back up to the north on the following day.

The conditions had prevented any assessment of results, which meant that another attempt on the dam would be necessary, and preparations were put in hand on the 10th to return with a force of 217 Lancasters. 619 Squadron detailed fifteen Lancasters, but F/Os McMorran and Curran conspired to collide while taxiing, and their participation had to be scrubbed. The remaining thirteen took to the air at around 04.30 on a cold and frosty morning, but the entire force was recalled before it reached the English coast. The operation was rescheduled for early on the following morning, when 233 Lancasters and a Mosquito were to join five 8 Group Mosquitos at the target, but take-off was postponed until midday. The fifteen 619 Squadron participants departed Strubby between 12.36 and 12.48 with W/C Milward and S/L Jordan the senior pilots on duty. F/L Brown and crew turned back early on after their starboard-outer engine caught fire and ended their interest in proceedings, leaving the others to encounter icing conditions at the French coast, and find that the weather in the target area was hardly an improvement on the previous day. Up to nine-tenths cloud with tops at 8,000 feet made life difficult for the Master Bomber, who tried to bring the crews down below the cloud base, some complying, while others were able to identify the aiming point through a four-mile-long gap. Eleven of the 619 Squadron crews attacked from 3,700 to 9,500 feet between 15.00 and 15.14, while three others responded to the Master Bomber's "Dewdrop" instruction to cease bombing and go home. Post-raid reconnaissance revealed a number of hits on the stepped apron of the dam, and cratering all around, but no actual breach had occurred.

W/C Tomes was posted to East Kirkby on the 13th, ultimately to assume command of 57 Squadron. 619 Squadron was put on standby to operate twice on the 14th, but only the crews of F/Os Franks and Strachan were called upon, taking off shortly after 15.30 for mining duties in the Silverthorn III garden of the Kattegat. The drop zone lay between the east coast of North Jutland and the north-western tip of Sjaelland Island, an area covered by ten-tenths cloud between 2,000 and 8,000 feet. Positions were established by H2S and the vegetables delivered into the briefed locations from 15,000 feet at 18.46 and 18.49.

The main operation on the night of the 15/16th was directed at Ludwigshafen in southern Germany, home to a number of I. G. Farben factories, which were among the most blatant exploiters of slave workers in the production of synthetic oil. The attack by 327 Lancasters and fourteen Mosquitos of 1, 6 and 8 Groups landed 450 high explosive bombs and incendiaries in the Ludwigshafen plant, causing massive damage and fires, and was the greatest setback to production during the war. Further north, the Oppau factory ceased production completely for an extended period, and five other industrial concerns also sustained severe damage, as did some residential areas. It was on the 16th that German ground forces began a new offensive in the Ardennes, in an attempt to break through the American lines and reach the port of Antwerp in what would become known as the Battle of the Bulge.

Munich had become something of a 5 Group preserve during the year, and a further operation against it was planned for the night of the 17/18th, which would turn out to be another night of heavy Bomber Command activity. The main raid was to be by more than five hundred aircraft, predominantly of 4 and 6 Groups, on Duisburg, while 1 Group targeted Ulm with over three hundred Lancasters, leaving 5 Group to send 280 Lancasters some seventy miles beyond to the Bavarian capital City. 619 Squadron briefed seventeen crews, while their Lancasters were being prepared for the 1,300-mile round trip, and they departed Strubby between 16.07 and 16.40 with S/L Purnell the senior pilot on duty. It turned out to be a night of poor serviceability for 55 Base, with six Spilsby crews and three from 619 Squadron returning early with a variety of technical issues. F/L Osborne and F/Os Hatten and Curran all suffered engine-related issues, leaving the others to cross the French coast near Berck-sur-Mer, and reach the target to find generally clear skies and good visibility. They bombed on red and green TIs from 12,000 to 14,750 feet between 20.02 and 20.09 in accordance with the instructions of the Master Bomber, who declared himself satisfied with the results. F/O Hickmott and crew endured the frustration of reaching the target only for their bomb doors to remain resolutely shut, and they had to bring their load home. They confirmed that the attack appeared to be effective and that the resultant fires were visible from a hundred miles into the return journey, but, as usual, at this target, no local report emerged. Bomber Command claimed severe and widespread damage to the city.

On the following night, it was the turn of the distant Baltic port of Gdynia to play host to 5 Group, for which 619 Squadron put up eleven Lancasters in an overall force of 236 of the type. The intention was to catch elements of the German fleet at anchor, in particular, the *Lützow*, and also to destroy harbour installations, as well as cause damage within the town. *(The original* Lützow *was actually never completed, and had been sold to the Russian navy in 1940 as a hull minus superstructure. The pocket battleship,* Deutschland, *was renamed* Lützow, *to avoid humiliation for the nation should she be lost in battle.)* While this operation was in progress, fourteen other Lancasters of the group were to sneak in under cover of the main activity to deliver mines to the Privet and Spinach gardens in Danzig (Gdansk) Bay. 619 Squadron supported this undertaking with the crews of F/Os Franks, Proctor and Runnalls, who were assigned to Privet, and the two elements departed Strubby together between 17.06 and 17.24 with F/Ls Osborne and Smith the senior pilots on duty. F/O Cowling and crew were an hour out when the first of a number of technical issues persuaded them to turn back, while the others pressed on to reach the target area after an outward flight of almost five hours. They found clear skies and good visibility in which the harbour and town could be picked out visually until a smoke screen was activated, but, in keeping with standard practice, the initial identification was by H2S. The illumination and marking proceeded according to plan, and the 619 Squadron crews delivered their eight 1,000 pounders on red and green TIs from 11,750 to 14,000 feet between 21.56 and 22.16 in accordance with the Master Bomber's instructions, and, in the face of intense light flak. The smoke screen eventually obscured the *Lützow*, and crews with bombs still to deliver turned their attention to the port area and town. It was not possible to make an accurate assessment of results, but bomb bursts were seen across the docks and quaysides. Reconnaissance photos confirmed that damage had been inflicted upon shipping, port installations and residential property in the waterfront districts, at a cost of four Lancasters. Meanwhile, the gardeners were experiencing some difficulties in identifying the drop zone by H2S, but all three from Strubby planted their vegetables into the briefed locations from 15,000 feet between 21.58 and 22.05, probably after pinpointing on Point Hel.

Thick fog kept the crews on the ground on the 20th, and threatened to do so also on the 21st, but an operation was called on the basis that the weather over Scotland after midnight would be clear for returning aircraft, even if Lincolnshire remained fogbound. Seventeen 619 Squadron Lancasters were detailed for the 5 Group operation that night, and briefings took place while the ground crews did their best to get the aircraft ready in time. In briefing rooms across southern and south-eastern Lincolnshire, crews learned that their target would require them to retrace their recent steps to Germany's eastern Baltic region, although the I. G. Farben-owned Wintershall oil refinery at Politz, situated less than ten miles north of the port of Stettin, was some two hundred miles short of their trip to Gdynia. *(This location is often wrongly spelled Pölitz, which is a town in Germany's Schleswig-Holstein region at the western end of the Baltic. Politz is now Police in Poland.)* A force of 207 Lancasters and a single Mosquito was assembled, and, unusually, it included an element from 617 Squadron carrying Tallboys. The 619 Squadron element departed Strubby between 16.35 and 17.07 with F/Ls May and Smith the senior pilots on duty, each crew sitting on a cookie and twelve 500 pounders. F/O Bateman and crew were about an hour out when he became indisposed and had to turn back, but the others reached the target, many after cutting corners to keep up with the stream, and found clear skies with ground haze, which may have been a smoke screen. This important war-industry asset was protected by around fifty searchlights, and heavy flak accompanied the Lancasters as they ran in on the aiming point. The markers fell some two thousand yards north-north-west of the plant, a situation recognised by the Master Bomber, but he was unable to persuade the backers-up to shift the point of aim accordingly, and most of the bombing would miss the mark. The 619 Squadron element bombed on red and green TIs from 15,500 to 19,700 feet between 22.02 and 22.12, and observed most of the bomb bursts to be around the markers. Fires remained visible for almost a hundred miles into the return journey, but the plant had not been destroyed, and it would be necessary to mount further raids.

The final wartime Christmas period was celebrated on 5 Group stations in traditional style and undisturbed by operational activity between the 22nd and Boxing Day, which was not the case for some other groups. The peace came to an end on the 26th, when crews from all groups were roused from any resulting stupor to attend briefings for operations against enemy troop positions at St Vith in Belgium. The German advance towards Antwerp had run out of steam after its earlier successes, and starved of fuel and ammunition, it was now attempting to withdraw back into Germany. 5 Group contributed twenty-six Lancasters to the force of 296 aircraft for the first joint operation since October. The four 619 Squadron participants departed Strubby between 13.12 and 13.25 with F/L Willitts the senior pilot on duty, and made landfall between Ostend and Dunkerque. They found the target, situated within five miles of the German frontier, to be under clear skies with good visibility, and could identify the aiming point visually and by a red TI. When this became obscured by smoke, the Master Bomber ordered the crews to descend to 10,000 feet and bomb the upwind edge of the smoke. The 619 Squadron crews carried out their attacks from 12,000 to 14,000 feet between 15.32 and 15.34, on red and green TIs, and observed the bombing to be well concentrated. A number of crews reported a four-engine bomber going down but not crashing, and five parachutes were observed.

On the 28th, the 619 Squadron crews of F/Os Dunsmore, Hickmott, McMorran A and McMorran G and Whiteley were told that they would be part of a 5 Group force of sixty-seven Lancasters targeting shipping, specifically the cruiser *Köln*, at Horten in Oslo Fjord. They departed Strubby in company with three Lancasters of 57 Squadron and four of 630 Squadron between 19.38 and 20.17, and reached the target area after an outward flight of four-and-a-half hours. The skies were relatively clear and the visibility good, but a thin layer of alto-cumulus cloud at between 15,000 and 20,000 feet reduced the brightness of the moonlight and cast deceptive shadows on the water to prevent a clear identification of the target. The aiming point was marked by Wanganui flares, but most crews followed the Master Bomber's instructions after establishing their own reference point. A patch of light flak to the north-east of the harbour mole was thought to be concealing a large naval unit, and this area was marked and bombed. Some crews would claim to have attacked a large vessel moving from this area in a southerly direction, and other shipping in the harbour, all in the face of intense shipboard and shore-based light flak. The 619 Squadron quintet bombed from 6,500 to 8,000 feet between 23.47 and 23.56, two of them making two passes, but claimed no direct hits and the operation produced inconclusive results.

The 29th dawned fine and frosty, and, shortly after lunch, 5 Group sent eleven crews on daylight mining sorties in the Onions garden in Oslo harbour. 619 Squadron was not involved, and would conduct its final operations of the year during the early hours of the New Year's Eve. A dozen crews were briefed as part of a 5 Group force of 154 Lancasters to attack an enemy supply line at Houffalize in the Ardennes region of Belgium. They took off between 02.28 and 02.38 with S/L Jordan the senior pilot on duty and on the thirtieth and final sortie of his tour, and found the target area under five to seven-tenths stratus cloud at 5,000 to 6,000 feet, with another layer of eight-tenths with tops at 9,000 feet. This rendered identification something of a challenge, despite which, the marking was punctual and accurate, however, the red TIs were observed only by a proportion of the crews who chanced upon a gap in the clouds directly over the aiming point. Seven of the 619 Squadron participants withheld their bombs, while the remaining five delivered theirs from 9,700 to 11,500 feet between 05.03 and 05.05. A number of crews in the force descended to below the cloud base, and confirmed that the bombing was concentrated around the markers, but it would be deemed necessary to revisit this objective within a short time.

It was dusk when F/Os Franks and Proctor took off from Strubby at 16.26 and 16.33 to head for the Yewtree garden, the channel in the Baltic between Læsø Island and the east coast of North Jutland. The latter were within fifty miles of the pinpoint at Frederikshavn on the mainland coast, when their H2S failed, leaving them with no prospect of delivering their stores accurately. F/O Franks and crew carried out a timed run at 15,000 feet, and deposited their mines into the allotted location at 20.12, before returning home safely to wrap up a very successful, if, testing year for the squadron. During the course of the month the squadron conducted fourteen operations, including those recalled, and dispatched 143 sorties for the loss of two Lancasters and their crews. The New Year beckoned with the scent of victory in the air, however, any thoughts that the enemy defences were spent were misplaced, and, even though they were unable to protect every corner of the Reich, they would continue to provide stubborn opposition for a further three months.

Above: RAF Strubby Watch Office. Below: 619 Squadron, Coningsby. Andy Smith, 'Doc' Folley, 'Jack' McCue sitting on a 4000lb bomb – a cookie.

Coningsby 10th of March 1944 Taffy Evans. Completed 67 sorties by 22nd of May 1944.

F/Sgt Arnold William (Bill) Habergham KIA 19th of July 1944

619 Sqn Coningsby 10th of March 1944 Lancaster PG-X Cpl Kitchen, Cpl Hopkins, Sgt James, LAC Lynch

W/C James Tait

F/O F Molinas. KIA 19th of July 1944

619 Squadron
F/L John Whiteley (Pilot)
F/Sgt John Hurst), W/O Jim Garrett   P/O Ronald Joughin DFC, Sgt Fred Jones
Sgt Bill Adams   Sgt Larry Rigden

F/O Philip Ingleby and F/O Warren Duffy DFC

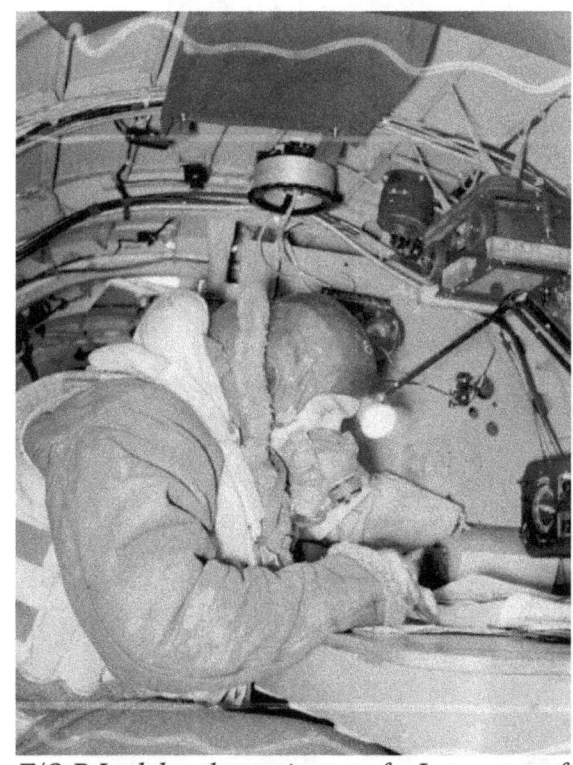

F/O P Ingleby, the navigator of a Lancaster of 619 Squadron based at RAF Coningsby, seated at his table in the aircraft.

P/O Philip Ingleby's grave marker in Coningsby cemetery.

619 Squadron Lancasters

Lancaster LM446 PG-H of 619 Squadron

Gnome-Rhone Factory at Gennevilliers, France. Attacked by 619 Squadron on 9/10th of May 1944

*619 Squadron 'original' crew of Lancaster ME723 PG-X.
Pictured are rear L - R: Sgt Derrick 'Duke' Golding, 'Johnny' Kemp, 'Johnny' Broll.
Front: F/Sgt Roy Withinshaw, Sgt James 'Swift' Durkin, P/O Derek Schofield DFM, George Hexter.
Golding, Withinshaw and Durkin were killed with P/O Schofield while raiding Munich on 25th of April 1944. P/O E N Powell had replaced Sgt Hexter on the sortie and was also killed.*

F/Sgt A Baker and the original grave marker for the crew of the crashed Lancaster ME723 PG-X

Crew of 619 Squadron Lancaster ME723 PG-X.

619 Squadron Lancaster PB346 PG-J lost on the 27th of July 1944 on Givors raid. Crew: Pilot F/O D N McKechnie, Sgt Anthony Barker (FE), Sgt Wilfred Robert Little RCAF (Nav), Sgt Robert Geoffrey Dean (BA), Sgt Richard Arthur Williams (W/O), Sgt Ernest John Courtenay (AG), Sgt Alfred Craven (AG).

619 Squadron Lancaster ME568 PG-F. Crew of W/O Ronald Bennett.
All lost on Trossy raid on the 3rd of August 1944. Crew: W/O Bennett, F/Sgt William Cobb, Sgt Martin Cody, P/O Edwin Charles Thomas Davies, Sgt Ronald Arthur Forrest, F/Sgt Arthur Griffiths, F/Sgt Francis Philip Lyford.

F/Sgt Lyford

F/Sgt Griffiths

The Davis crew pictured during training in early March 1944 in front of a Short Stirling of 1661 Heavy Conversion Unit (HCU) at RAF Winthorpe.

The same crew was lost on a Wesseling raid 21/22nd June 1944 in 619 Squadron Lancaster ME846 PG-C. Those killed were P/O M A H Davis, Sgt G H Moggridge and F/Sgt J E R Bowering RCAF while Sgt W D Belshaw, F/Sgt L E J Taylor, F/Sgt P E Knox RAAF, and Sgt T A Newberry became PoW's.

Sgt John Bell

Sgt Lionel (Lucky) Virgo

The O'Neill Crew. 23rd of June 1944, Dunholme Lodge.
Sgt R R George McQueen, F/O E Y (Ted) O'Neill, Sgt J H MacPherson, F/Sgt Eugene E (Pop) Barritt, F/Sgt F R Alex (Jock) Piggott, Sgt Ray Gorrell, Sgt David Stevenson. Completed tour of operations 28th of October 1944.

F/L R G Churcher DFC.
Flight Commander of 619 Squadron.
(Later G/C Churcher DSO, MVO, DFC*)

619 Squadron April 1944, Coningsby

F/Sgt Jack Forrest. PoW, 7th of June 1944.

P/O John Ernest Lott KIA 7th of June 1944

F/O Guy Herbert Wyand
KIA 7th of June 1944

F/Sgt John Henry Tucker
KIA 7th of June 1944

All of F/L K Roberts' crew.

*F/L Kim Roberts DFC RAAF
KIA 7th of June 1944*

*619 Squadron aircrew
L-R: Unknown, F/S W H Deviell (PoW),
F/Sgt J H Tucker (KIA), Lionel (Lucky) Virgo.*

*S/L R A Squibbs
Killed on Darmstadt raid 12th of September 1944.
All of the crew were killed - Sgt A Furnival, F/Sgt J Singer, F/O J F Parry, Sgt J Davison, Sgt D Greenley and W/O L G Evans RCAF.*

Sgt David Greenley
KIA 12th of September 1944. Aged 19.

```
                                    SECRET      59
From: RAF. Station CONINGSBY.
To:   Headquarters, N°5 Group.
      Copy to Base Intelligence, RAF CONINGSBY

Ref:  OOB/S6069/1/IRT
Date: 26th February 1944

COMBAT REPORT N°33 FOR "E."/619 SQN: 19/20.2.44

CREW; Pilot           Sgt Wadsworth.
      Navigator       F/S Shenton.
      Air Bomber      Sgt Bengston.
      F/Engineer      Sgt Burgess.
      W/Operator      Sgt Brady.
      M.U.Gunner      Sgt Maltby.   N°4. AGS.
                                    N°17.OTU.
      R/Gunner        Sgt Joy.      N°1. AGS,
                                    N°17.OTU.

Target: LEIPZIG

     Lancaster "E." of 619 Squadron over target
area at 0425 hours, height 23,000ft, heading
214° Mag, air speed 160 indicated. Visibility
good. 10/10ths cloud below at 15,000ft, illum
-inated by searchlights, 3/10ths cloud above
at 24,000ft, white fighter flares on starboard.
R/Gunner saw ME 109 on port quarter below at
1,000yds, silhouetted against illuminated cloud,
and reported to pilot. At the same time the W/O
perator reported contact on Visual Monica. E/A
closed to 700yds and R/Gunner ordered the pilot
to corkscrew to port and opened fire. At 500yds
the E/A turned over on its back and fell away
in a vertical dive through clouds. R/Gunner
fired approximately 200 rounds.
E/A did not open fire, and was not seen again.
E/A claimed as damaged.
```

Combat report of Sgt Wadsworth

F/Sgt James Walker Mills (BA)   *F/Sgt Alan Pickstone (W/Op)*
Crew of 619 Squadron Lancaster LL919

P/O Lewis Leslie Feindell (AG)

F/Sgt Ernest George Cass (FE)

Crew of 619 Squadron Lancaster LL919 PG-W. All, except F/Sgt Mills, killed 27th of April 1944 on Schweinfurt raid.

F/L Guy Godfrey Charles Gunzi (Pilot)

F/O Nickolas Vlassie RCAF (Nav)

No.7 Air Observers' School, Portage La Prairie, where Nickolas Vlassie and Archie Carmichael trained March-August 1943. Back row. L-R Russ Wasylkow, Nickolas Vlassie, Jim Cattley. Front: Art Wirth, Wilf Odegaard.

Nickolas Vlassie and Archie Carmichael outside their hut at No5 AOS, RAF Jurby, Isle of Man 1943.

Sgt Kenneth Frank

Frank's photo of himself, Gunzi (top left) Pickstone (centre), others possibly Alan Peets, Feindell, and Don Carter.

Sgt A Peets. 619 Squadron Flew with F/L Gunzi.

F/L Reginald Hutton (FE)

Sgt Don J 'Nick' Carter KIA 20th of September 1944

Dunholme Lodge Airfield. Control Tower and fire tender shelter. (H Watson via Anne Grimshaw)

619 Squadron Lancaster LM446 PG-H. Failed to return from an attack on the Gnome-Rhone aero-engine factory at Gennevilliers, France, on 9/10th of May 1944. It had 215 hours flying time. P/O John Milford Aitken, Sgt Frederick Frank Dring, P/O Kenneth Goodwin, Sgt Roy Ernest Hickling, F/Sgt Sidney Levy, Sgt John Raymond Presland, Sgt Frederick Albert Towse were all killed. W/O L Rhodes became a PoW.

619 Squadron Attack on Gueydon at Brest August 1944

(www.militaer-wissen.de)
The armoured cruiser Gueydon (right) with the armoured cruiser Montcalm (left) and the Armorque (middle) 1940 in the port of Brest.

619 Squadron raid on Limoges, France 8th of February 1944.

*S/L Malcolm 'Mac' Hamilton DFC**

Mailly-Le-Camp
619 Squadron raid on German panzer training centre located in northern France undertaken during the night of 3/4th of May 1944.

A low flying Lancaster is seen through the glare of a burning Mailly-le-Camp.

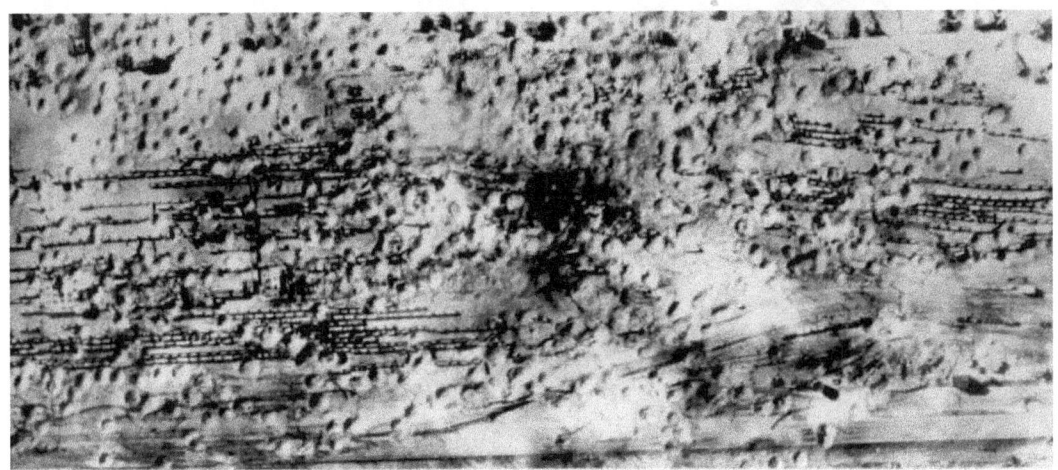

Before and after photos of Juvisy. April 1944.

10.5 cm flak on the Zoo tower, Berlin

619 Squadron attack on Brest

Toulouse, April 1944

F/L L E Tanner KIA 1st of November 1944 　　　*Sgt Marshall Gow Gibson KIA 1st of November 1944*

Both killed on Homberg raid. Also lost were Sgt R J Ward and A P Goddard. Sgts. J R Fletcher, J F Barton and R Ralston were injured and taken into captivity.

Sgt Weir Aged 19　　　Schaefer Crew　　　F/O Meredith, RCAF
Crew: Back - Sgt Swanson, F/O Schaefer RCAF, F/O Awad
Front – Sgt Kielty RCAF, F/O Meredith, Sgt Nisholaiff RCAF.
Except Sgts Kielty and Nisholaiff, all killed 4th of December 1944 on Heilbronn raid in Lancaster LM751 PG-X.

January 1945

The final year of the war began with a flourish, as the Luftwaffe launched its ill-conceived and, ultimately, ill-fated Operation Bodenplatte (Baseplate) at first light on New Year's Day. The intention to destroy the Allied air forces on the ground at the recently liberated airfields in France, Holland and Belgium was only modestly realised, and it cost the German day fighter force around 250 aircraft. Many of the pilots were killed, wounded or fell into Allied hands, and it was a setback from which the Tagjagd would never fully recover, while the Allies could make good their losses within hours from their enormous stockpiles.

5 Group was also active that morning, having roused the crews early from their beds to attend briefings for an attack on the recently repaired Dortmund-Ems Canal near Ladbergen, for which 102 Lancasters and two Mosquitos were made ready. The 54 Base squadrons from Coningsby and Metheringham fell in line behind 83 Squadron, with the 55 Base squadrons from East Kirkby and Spilsby about three miles further back, and a third section, made up of 53 Base units from Waddington, Skellingthorpe and Bardney some twenty miles to the rear. They were allowed to catch up, putting the force two minutes behind schedule at point C, over the North Sea. It was between points C and D that the fighter escort was expected to join them, and, although it was not immediately apparent, it did eventually put in an appearance. The gaggles held together fairly well, although the controller would complain later that the legs were too short to keep them tight, and some aircraft were seen to break formation. When about eight minutes from the target, smoke from a Mosquito-laid red TI could be seen, which was assessed as being on the southern tip of the island between the two branches of the canal. It was clearly visible to all crews, who were able to home in on it without difficulty. A six-gun flak battery greeted their arrival with accurate salvoes, but this did not inhibit the bombing runs, and the impression was of an effective operation. On return, a number of 55 Base crews complained that the gaggle was too tight and put crews at risk from "friendly" bombs. The use of delay fuses prevented an immediate assessment of the results, but photo-reconnaissance revealed later, that the canal had been breached again, and the surrounding fields had become flooded.

Operations for the day were not yet done for 5 Group, which now had an appointment with the Mittelland Canal at Gravenhorst, for which 152 Lancasters and five Mosquitos were made ready. 619 Squadron had not been required for the morning operation, and had nineteen fully laden Lancasters lined up before departing Strubby between 17.00 and 17.20 with W/C Milward the senior pilot on duty. All reached the target area to find that the clear conditions enjoyed during the morning raid nearby, had persisted, and, so accurate were the initial TIs and illumination, delivered visually or by H2S, that the third flare force was not required and was sent home. The main force was called in ahead of H-Hour at around 19.10, and the 619 Squadron element bombed on red TIs from 9,500 to 12,000 feet between 19.10 and 19.22. One of the perils of operating on New Year's Day was the risk of falling victim to trigger-happy American flak gunners, who had been spooked by the German raids at dawn, and now fired at anything that moved, and a number of RAF aircraft and crews would be lost in such "friendly fire" incidents. The employment of predominantly delayed-action bombs again prevented an immediate assessment of results, but a highly successful operation was confirmed later by photo-reconnaissance. The 619 Squadron participants landed at Tain in Scotland, and made their way home on the following morning.

5 Group remained on the ground when Nuremberg and Ludwigshafen were raided by large forces on the night of the 2/3rd, and both operations were hugely destructive. A controversial attack was planned against the small French town of Royan in the early hours of the 5th, in response to requests from Free French forces, which were laying siege. Situated on the east bank at the mouth of the Gironde Estuary, it was occupied by a German garrison, and was in the way of an advance towards the port of Bordeaux. The inhabitants had been offered an opportunity by the German garrison commander to evacuate the area, but around two thousand had declined, and would suffer the consequences. 1, 5 and 8 Groups put together a force of 347 Lancasters and seven Mosquitos, of which seventeen of the former represented 619 Squadron. They departed Strubby between 01.05 and 01.29 with F/L Willitts the senior pilot on duty, each carrying a cookie and sixteen 500 pounders. They were in the first of two waves heading for the unsuspecting target, separated by one hour, and it was approaching 04.00 as they lined up for the bombing run in cloudless skies and excellent visibility. The start of the attack was delayed for two minutes to allow misplaced markers to be corrected, but a red TI went down at 04.01 very close to the aiming point, and another fell in the middle of the town, near the beach, at which point, the Master Bomber called in the main force. The 619 Squadron crews carried out their attacks from 9,500 to 10,000 feet onto Path Finder markers between 04.03 and 04.13, and witnessed a yellow oil fire at 04.08, which began to emit volumes of black smoke. This was just one of a number of large explosions created by the first phase of bombing, and the resultant fires would act as a beacon to the 1 Group force following behind. The attack destroyed about 85% of the town, and between five and eight hundred people lost their lives. In the event, the town was not taken, and it would be mid-April before the garrison surrendered. Four Lancasters failed to return, and among them was 619 Squadron's ND728 in which F/O Gray RAAF and his crew lost their lives.

5 Group was not involved in a major attack on Hannover by more than 650 aircraft on the night of the 5/6th, the first on this northern city since the series in the autumn of 1943. However, a rushed battle order came through to 5 Group stations at 18.30, which would lead to another late briefing and take-off for 131 crews, and it was actually between 00.03 and 00.47 on the 6th that ten 619 Squadron crews departed Strubby bound for a German supply column trapped at Houffalize in the Belgian Ardennes. There were no senior pilots on duty as they made their way south on a clear night above low cloud, which, over the target, formed thin layers of eight to ten-tenths cover between 4,000 and 10,000 feet. The marker force crews were able to identify the aiming point visually, and the first red Mosquito-laid TIs were seen to go down close together, followed by greens at H-3. They were backed up to leave a compact group of reds and greens visible by their glow through the clouds, and the Master Bomber, who was circling at 10,000 feet, called in the main force to bomb. Four of the 619 Squadron crews complied from 9,500 to 12,000 feet between 03.03 and 03.07, while the remainder were among around a third of the force to retain their bombs in accordance with instructions at briefing, if they failed to identify the aiming point. Afterwards, one of the marker crews descended to 3,500 feet between the cloud layers, where they saw two large columns of smoke, the source of which could not be identified. Post-raid reconnaissance confirmed that the target had been bombed with great accuracy, and the success had been gained for the loss of two Lancasters.

Later in the day, 5 Group detailed thirteen Lancaster for mining duties in the Spinach garden off Gdynia and seven for Privet off Danzig. 619 Squadron dispatched the crews of F/Os Dickinson and A McMorran to the former at 16.26 and 16.27 respectively, and they reached the target area to find a layer of ten-tenths cloud with good visibility above, and established their positions by H2S before planting their five vegetables each as briefed from 15,000 feet either side of 20.45.

A major operation against Munich was planned for the 7th, for which a two-wave force of 645 aircraft was drawn from all five of the Lancaster-equipped groups. 5 Group, which was unused to sharing this target, would lead the way with 213 Lancasters and three Mosquitos, leaving the second wave to follow on two hours later, the tanks of the heavy brigade containing sufficient fuel for a nine-hour round trip. The 619 Squadron element of sixteen Lancasters departed Strubby in a remarkably efficient fourteen minutes as dusk was descending between 16.49 and 17.04 with W/C Milward the senior pilot on duty. They encountered broken medium-level cloud at 14,000 feet above the target, with haze or thin cloud below. By this time, the Master Bomber had made a visual identification of the aiming point, and sent the first two primary blind markers in to deliver their TIs at the same time thirty seconds ahead of the planned opening of the attack. The flare force went in immediately afterwards, and illuminated the city very effectively, allowing ground detail to be identified. Red TIs went down west and east of the River Isar, bracketing the aiming point, and the Master Bomber ordered the backers up to drop their TIs between the reds, after which, the next batch of flares formed a circle around the aiming point. The main force was then called in, and the 619 Squadron participants delivered their loads accurately within the specified area from 17,000 to 20,000 feet between 20.32 and 20.44. F/O Davis and crew experienced the frustration of a complete hang-up, and were unable even to jettison the load over the target, although they did manage to dump the cookie, eventually, on the way home. The city was seen to be burning well as the force withdrew, and the glow of fires could be seen from up to 130 miles away. Two hours after the 5 Group attack, in what would become an established pattern, the 1, 3, 6 and 8 Group force arrived to complete the destruction of the central and some industrial districts, and this proved to be the final large-scale attack of the war on Munich. Fourteen Lancasters failed to return, and among them was 619 Squadron's ND957, which disintegrated over Saint-Pierre on the south-eastern outskirts of Paris, killing F/O Flockhart RAAF and his crew.

With the exception of 617 Squadron, 5 Group remained on the ground for the ensuing six days, with snow-clearing providing exercise for all capable of wielding a shovel. The crews were, therefore, no doubt, relieved to be called to briefing on the 13th, when they learned that 5 Group would be operating alone against the Wintershall oil refinery at Politz near Stettin. The plant had sustained damage in the previous attack in December, but production had not been halted, and a force of 218 Lancasters and seven Mosquitos was assembled for the return, of which fifteen of the Lancasters were provided by 619 Squadron. Another dusk departure saw them taking off between 16.50 and 17.04 with F/Ls Smith and Willetts the senior pilots on duty. F/L Smith's rear gunner tested his turret and guns over the North Sea, only to discover that they were unserviceable, and there was no option but to turn back. The rest of the force crossed the North Sea at 1,500 feet in accordance with instructions to not climb until approaching the Danish coast at 19.30, and they arrived in the target area on time to find clear skies with slight haze, by which time the blind marker crews had identified the target by means of H2S, and delivered their green TIs in a line approaching the target shortly after 22.00. The illuminators then dropped their flares, which caused ground detail to stand out, highlighted by the snow on the ground. A blind-bombing attack had been planned, but, because of the excellence of the conditions, Mosquitos were able to go in at low level. The main force was called in, and the 619 Squadron crews bombed from 14,500 to 16,500 feet between 22.17 and 22.29 to help seal the fate of the plant. Photographic reconnaissance confirmed that the site had been severely damaged, and Bomber Command claimed it to be in ruins. PB842 failed to return with the crew of F/O Curran RAAF, and their fate was unknown until news eventually came through that they were enjoying the legendary hospitality of the Swedes in internment. Having bombed the target, they had been attacked by a Me410, which holed a fuel tank before itself being shot down by return fire. They had landed in Sweden, where the Lancaster remained until being scrapped, and returned home in a Dakota in March.

Oil targets would continue to dominate during the remainder of the month, and a two-phase attack was planned for the following night against the I. G. Farbenindustrie A. G. Merseburg-Leuna refinery, which lay some 250 miles from the Dutch frontier and five hundred miles from the bomber bases of eastern England. This was one of many similar sites situated in an arc on the western side of Leipzig from north to south. The first phase would be carried out by 5 Group, which detailed 210 Lancasters and nine Mosquitos, fifteen of the former contributed by 619 Squadron. They took off from Strubby between 16.08 and 16.44 with five captains of flight lieutenant rank leading the way, and headed for the Sussex coast near Brighton to begin the Channel crossing for the southern approach to eastern Germany. They reached the target area to find clear skies but poor vertical visibility due to a layer of haze, which, in the event, was no hindrance to the primary blind markers, whose job was to establish their position over the aiming point by means of H2S. They delivered their TIs from 18,000 feet, after which, the first element of the flare force went in. The Master Bomber called for ground marking only, which was carried out by the low-level Mosquito element, and, by 20.50, he was satisfied and sent the marker aircraft home. The main force crews produced what appeared to be concentrated bombing, the 619 Squadron crews dropping their loads of a cookie and nine 500 pounders each onto red and green TIs from 14,000 to 16,700 feet between 21.00 and 21.07 with a fourteen-second overshoot in accordance with the Master Bomber's instructions. Returning crews reported explosions and smoke rising upwards as they turned for home, leaving behind them a beacon for the second wave of 363 Lancasters and five Mosquitos of 1, 6 and 8 Groups following three hours behind. They would add to the massive destruction, which effectively put the plant out of action for the remainder of the war.

Three oil plants were selected for attention on the night of the 16/17th, at Zeitz, near Liepzig, Wanne-Eickel in the Ruhr, and Brüx in north-western Czechoslovakia (now most in the Czech Republic), some 140 miles due south of Berlin. It was for the last-mentioned that seventeen 619 Squadron crews were briefed as part of a 5 Group force of 224 Lancasters and six Mosquitos, which would be accompanied by seven 101 Squadron ABC Lancasters for RCM duties. They were each carrying a cookie and nine 500 pounders for what would be a nine-hour round trip, and departed Strubby between 17.37 and 17.54 with S/L Purnell the senior pilot on duty. There were ten early returns from the force, and among them were two from Strubby, those of S/L Purnell, because of an unserviceable bomb sight, and F/O Grant after a fire developed in the port-outer and starboard-inner engines. The others reached the target area to encounter nine to ten-tenths low cloud with tops at 3,000 feet, which interfered with the low-level marking system. The four primary blind markers identified the target by means of H2S, and dropped green TIs, and they were followed by the first illuminators, who also relied on H2S to deliver their flares. It seems that a number of Mosquitos managed to get below the cloud base to put red TIs onto the aiming point, and reported that the greens were among the oil tanks. However, the reds were not generally visible through the clouds, and the Master Bomber called for skymarking, while informing flare force 3 that it would not be required. The 619 Squadron participants bombed either on the glow of the red TIs or on the cascading greens from 17,000 to 17,750 feet between 22.31 and 22.41, and observed many explosions and large columns of thick, black smoke emerging through the cloud tops. Photo-reconnaissance would confirm that massive damage had been inflicted upon the plant, and a severe setback delivered to the enemy's oil production.

There would be no further operations for 5 Group during the month, although a number would be posted before being cancelled. The squadron spent the period inducting new crews, attending lectures, training, and, during the last few days, clearing snow from the runways. During the course of the month the squadron operated on eight occasions and dispatched 111 sorties for the loss of three Lancasters, two crews and the temporary loss to internment of a third crew.

February 1945

The weather at the start of February provided difficult conditions for marking and bombing, particularly for 5 Group, and a number of operations would struggle to achieve their aims in the face of thick, low cloud and strong winds. 5 Group was back in harness immediately at the start of the new month following the long lay-off, and 271 Lancaster and eleven Mosquito crews were called to briefings on all 5 Group stations on the 1st to learn that their target was to be the marshalling yards in the town of Siegen, situated some fifty miles east of Cologne. This was a 5 Group show, and was one of three major operations planned for the night, the others, by larger forces, taking place at Ludwigshafen and Mainz further into southern Germany. A high wind during the night had helped to clear some of the snow, and the twenty 619 Squadron Lancasters took off without incident between 15.51 and 16.27 with S/L Purnell the senior pilot on duty, and each carrying either twelve 1,000 pounders or a cookie and sixteen 500 pounders. They all reached the target area shortly after 19.00, and encountered ten-tenths cloud at between 3,000 and 7,000 feet, which caused problems for the flare and marker force, some of which were finding it difficult to obtain a clear H2S image on their screens. Eventually, one of the primary blind markers ran in and dropped green TIs at 19.05 from 15,000 feet, and their glow was visible through the clouds. This prompted the first flares, followed by an attempt to mark at low-level with red TIs, which were not visible through the clouds, and, when the Master Bomber called for skymarking at 19.10, the remaining illuminators were superfluous to requirements and were sent home. The bombing phase was put back by four minutes until 19.20, forcing crews to either orbit or dogleg to waste time if they were still on approach, and then instructions were issued to aim at the skymarkers, which were being driven by the strong wind across the intended aiming point and beyond the target. The glow of red target indicators was faintly visible through the clouds, but this was most likely a decoy fire site prepared by the Germans. It attracted many bomb loads, perhaps some from the 619 Squadron participants, who, in the absence of detail in the ORB, probably bombed in line with the others from 55 Base from 8,000 to 12,000 feet between 19.20 and 19.37, contributing to what became a widely scattered raid. Much of the bombing fell into open and wooded country, and, although the railway station sustained damage, the marshalling yards escaped. *(W/C Milward was about to complete his tour and, probably, had been notified of his posting from the squadron. He took over the record-keeping for the month, but provided only a brief account of each operation, omitting details of individual crews' bombing heights and times.)*

The next briefing revealed the bad news that a tour of operations was to be increased again to thirty-six sorties. Twenty 619 Squadron crews were in attendance at 15.00 on a drizzly afternoon on the 2nd, to be told further, that the night's operation was to be against Karlsruhe in southern Germany. This was to be another 5 Group effort involving 250 Lancasters and eleven Mosquitos, and was again, only one of three major operations taking place. Wiesbaden was to receive its one and only major raid of the war at the hands of almost five hundred aircraft, while a 320-strong predominantly Halifax force dealt with an oil plant at Wanne-Eickel in the Ruhr. The 619 Squadron element departed Strubby between 19.56 and 20.39 with W/C Milward the senior pilot on duty, and headed for the assembly point over Reading. F/O Cowling and crew turned back early with an engine issue, and while attempting to overshoot at base, swung badly and clipped a tree with the tail. The Lancaster remained airborne, and was flown over to Woodbridge, where it landed successfully. F/O Sparkes and crew also returned early because of a defective turret, and, according to the landing time, this occurred well into the outward flight. The winds turned out to be lighter than forecast, and this caused a change in route, which now took the force directly from Reading to the target, straddling the Franco-Belgian frontier all the way to Germany, where they encountered heavy cloud between 3,000 and 15,000 feet. The flare force arrived over the target at 17,500 to 18,500 feet between 23.03 and 23.28, and tried to perform their assigned tasks in difficult conditions, some with malfunctioning H2S boxes. The Mosquito crews tried to establish an aiming point, but the illumination was not getting through to the ground, and, even had they dropped red TIs, it is unlikely that they would have been visible. At 23.11 the Master Bomber called for skymarking and sent the Mosquitos and remaining illuminators home. Based on the 44 (Rhodesia) Squadron records, the bombing took place on the glow of markers, as instructed by the Master Bomber, from 14,000 to 17,000 feet shortly before 23.30. This final raid of the war on Karlsruhe was a complete failure, and cost fourteen Lancasters, four of them from 189 Squadron. F/L Smith and crew failed to return in PB210, which came down somewhere in the target area, and the fact that the pilot alone survived to fall into enemy hands, suggests that the Lancaster broke up in the air, flinging him clear.

While the frontier towns of Goch and Cleves were being pounded by the other groups on the night of the 7/8th, ahead of the advancing British XXX Corps, 5 Group returned to the Dortmund-Ems Canal at Ladbergen with 177 Lancasters and eleven Mosquitos, the heavy brigade carrying delayed action bombs. 619 Squadron made ready eleven Lancasters for the main operation and three others to be occupied by the crews of F/Os Dickinson, Proctor and Runnalls for mining duties in the Forget-me-not garden in Kiel harbour. They departed Strubby first between 19.26 and 19.32, leaving the bombing brigade to follow them into the air later, between 20.56 and 21.11, led by F/L Whiteley. The bombing element all reached the target area to find seven to ten-tenths cloud at between 6,000 and 9,000 feet, and, again, we are reliant up the 44 (Rhodesia) Squadron records to provide us with details. The delivery of the fourteen 1,000 pounders each took place from 9,250 to 11,500 feet between 23.59 and 00.09 onto what were believed to be accurate TIs observed through gaps in the cloud and in accordance with the Master Bomber's instructions. It turned out to be a rare unsuccessful attack on this target, photographic reconnaissance revealing that the bombs had fallen into fields, and had failed to cause any breach. Meanwhile, the gardeners had established their positions by H2S and had delivered their mines into the briefed locations through a layer of thin cloud at 8,000 feet.

Eleven 619 Squadron crews found themselves being briefed on the following day for another long round trip to the Wintershall oil refinery at Politz, as part of a 5 Group force of 227 Lancasters and seven Mosquitos. They were to act as the first wave in a two-phase attack, which would be completed two hours later by 248 Lancasters from 1 and 8 Groups. All but one of the bombing element took off between 17.02 and 17.15 with F/L Whiteley the senior pilot on duty, and were followed into the air between 17.28 and 17.38 by the crews of F/Ls Osborne and May and F/Os Dickinson and Proctor, who were bound for the Geranium garden off the Baltic port of Swinemünde, situated some twenty miles north of Politz. Finally, at 17.40, F/O O'Brien and crew got away, but were unable to make up the time and decided to turn back. The blind markers and the flare force crews went in at 13,000 to 14,500 feet between 21.03 and 21.15 to carry out their assigned tasks in the face of an ineffective smoke screen, and fierce night-fighter activity was evident to the main force crews as they reached the target area to find clear skies and excellent visibility. The 619 Squadron crews identified ground detail in the light of the illuminating flares before delivering their loads onto red TIs in accordance with the Master Bomber's instructions and, based on 44 (Rhodesia) Squadron records, from 9,000 to 12,000 feet, approximately between 21.15 and 21.30. A number of crews from other squadrons reported up to six explosions and smoke rising through 3,000 feet as they turned away to the west, confident in the quality of their work. Ten Lancasters failed to arrive back to home airspace, and among them was 619 Squadron's ME314, which came down over north-eastern Germany or, perhaps, in the Baltic with fatal consequences for F/O Hesketh RAAF and all but his rear gunner, who fell into enemy hands. F/O Dickinson and crew arrived back from their gardening sortie with a fatally wounded rear gunner and seriously wounded wireless operator after being attacked by a night-fighter as they approached the Swedish mainland outbound. They turned back immediately, leaving the remaining three crews to deliver their mines as briefed, for which no details were provided. Later on the 9th, F/L Osborne was promoted to acting squadron leader rank to assume command of B Flight.

Briefings took place on the 13th for the first round of Operation Thunderclap, the Churchill-inspired offensive against Germany's eastern cities, which was devised partly to act in support of the advancing Russians, and also as a demonstration to Stalin of RAF air power, should he turn against the Allies after the war. The historic and culturally significant city of Dresden was selected to open the offensive in another two-phase affair, with a 5 Group force of 246 Lancasters and nine Mosquitos leading the way, to be followed three hours later by 529 Lancasters of 1, 3, 6 and 8 Groups. It had proved to be a successful policy thus far, with the 5 Group low-level marking system and main force attacks providing a beacon for the second force, and should it be required on this night, 8 Group would provide any necessary marking for phase two from high level. The 619 Squadron contingent of thirteen Lancasters took off in just nine minutes from 18.00 with S/L Purnell the senior pilot on duty, and the crews had absolutely no concept of the ramifications of the operation, both in terms of its outcome on the ground, and its hysterical aftermath. Dresden was Germany's seventh largest city, and its built-up areas had mostly remained un-bombed. Those areas, according to American sources, contained more than a hundred factories and fifty thousand workers contributing to the war effort. It was also an important railway hub, to the extent that the marshalling yards had been attacked twice in late 1944 by the USAAF.

The heavy force was two hours out when W/C Maurice Smith of 54 Base, the Master Bomber for the 5 Group attack, lifted off the Woodhall Spa runway at a few minutes before 20.00 hours in Mosquito KB401 AZ-E, a 627 Squadron aircraft, and he was followed away by eight others from

627 Squadron. 619 Squadron's F/L Plenderleith and crew had to contend with a lack of power from the starboard-outer engine, and they abandoned their sortie after little more than an hour. The heavy brigade and the Mosquitos arrived in the target area at the same time to encounter three layers of cloud, between 3,000 and 5,000 feet, 6,000 to 8,000 feet and 15,000 to 16,000 feet, but otherwise good visibility. The first primary blind marker delivered green TIs from 15,000 feet at 22.03, and was followed in by the flare force, which lit the way for the low-level Mosquitos. The main force Lancasters were carrying eight hundred tons of bombs, those from 619 Squadron in the form either of a cookie and twelve 500 pounders or one 2,000 pounder and fourteen cluster bombs, and, based on the records of 44 (Rhodesia) Squadron, these were delivered from 13,500 to 15,000 feet between 22.13 and 22.20 onto the glow of red TIs in accordance with the Master Bomber's instructions. As far as the crews were concerned this was no different from any other attack, and the fires visible for more than a hundred miles into the return journey nothing out of the ordinary.

By the time the second force of 1, 3, 6 and 8 Group Lancasters arrived over Dresden three hours after 5 Group, the skies had cleared, and the fires created by the earlier attack provided the expected reference point. A further eighteen hundred tons of bombs rained down onto the historic and beautiful old city, setting off the same chain of events that had devastated parts of Hamburg in July 1943, and a number of other cities since. Dresden's population had been swelled by masses of refugees fleeing from the eastern front, and many were engulfed in the ensuing firestorm. On the following morning, three hundred American bombers carried out a separate attack under the umbrella of a fighter escort, and completed the destruction. There were claims that RAF aircraft had strafed the streets and open spaces to increase the level of terror, and such accusations abound in the city to this day. In fact, American fighters were responsible, and were trying to add to the general confusion and chaos. Initial propaganda-inspired reports from the Office of the Propaganda Minister, Joseph Goebbels, falsely claimed a death toll of 250,000 people, but an accurate figure of twenty-five thousand has been settled upon since.

The destruction of Dresden has been used by some in this country also as a weapon with which to denigrate Bomber Command and Harris, and label them as war criminals. Curiously, no accusations have been levelled at the Americans. It should also be understood, that Harris had no interest in attacking Dresden, and had to be nagged by Chief-of-the-Air-Staff Portal to fulfil Churchill's wishes. The aircrew simply did the job asked of them, and the Dresden raid was no different from any other attack on a city. The death toll at Hamburg was much higher, and yet, there has been no similar outcry. The legacy of this operation served to deny Harris and the men under his Command their due recognition for the massive part they played in the ultimate victory, and only in recent times has a monument been erected in Green Park in London and a campaign clasp awarded, sadly, far too late for the majority. Churchill, with his eyes set on a peacetime election, betrayed Harris and the Command in a typical politically motivated U-turn, in which he accused Harris of bombing solely for the purpose of inflicting terror. In the post-war honours, Harris was the only commander in the field to be omitted.

Round two of Thunderclap was planned for the following night, when Chemnitz was posted as the target for 717 aircraft drawn from 1, 3, 4, 6 and 8 Groups, while 224 Lancasters and eight Mosquitos of 5 Group targeted an oil refinery in the small town of Rositz, situated twenty-five miles due south of Leipzig and thirty miles north-west of Chemnitz. Fifteen 619 Squadron Lancasters were made ready, and they all departed Strubby safely between 16.46 and 17.03 with

F/Ls May and Willitts the senior pilots on duty. They pushed on across Germany to be greeted by six to ten-tenths thin cloud in the target area in two layers, one at 6,000 to 8,000 feet, and the other at 10,000 to 12,000 feet, but the primary blind marker made a good run on H2S at 15,000 feet at 20.48 to drop green TIs, and the illuminators followed up between 20.51 and 20.58 from a similar height. The main force crews arriving on time carried out support runs with the marker element, before being called in to bomb at 21.07, the 619 Squadron crews carrying out their attacks on red and green TIs, or on their glow, from approximately 6,000 to 11,000 feet between 21.00 and 21.15. Three or four large fires were evident in the oil plant, and black smoke was rising through 5,000 feet as the force turned away. It was established afterwards, that the southern part of the site had been damaged, but it would be necessary to return to finish the job. The Chemnitz raid had been compromised by adverse weather conditions, and it would be March before success was achieved against this target.

An oil refinery at Böhlen was posted as the target on the 19th for a 5 Group force of 264 Lancasters and six Mosquitos. It was another of the collection of similar plants in the Leipzig area and some ten miles north of Rositz, for which 619 Squadron dispatched eighteen Lancasters in a late take-off between 23.51 and 00.13 with the two F/Ls McMorran and F/L Willitts the senior pilots on duty. They all completed the three-and-a-half-hour flight out, and would meet up with the later-departing Mosquito element at the target, which included the Master Bomber for the occasion, 54 Base's W/C Benjamin, who was flying the same Mosquito used by W/C Smith at Dresden six nights earlier. They encountered ten-tenths cloud over the target in two layers at 5,000 to 8,000 feet and 10,000 to 14,000 feet, and this would introduce a challenging element to the operation. The illuminators went in at around 15,000 feet between 04.05 and 04.13, and the VHF chatter suggested that a Mosquito had been able to mark a factory building with a red TI, and that that had been backed up. The main force was called in, before W/C Benjamin's VHF was suddenly cut off, and his Deputy took over. It would be established later, that the Master Bomber's Mosquito had been shot down by flak, and that W/C Benjamin DFC & Bar had died alongside his navigator. The 619 Squadron crews carried out their attacks in accordance with confusing instructions, doing so from approximately 9,000 to 13,000 feet between 04.15 and 04.35, and aiming mostly at the glow in the cloud of red and green TIs. Post-raid reconnaissance revealed only superficial damage to the site, which would have to be attacked again.

The following night, the 20th, proved to be a busy one, with more than five hundred Lancasters targeting Dortmund, while 268 Halifaxes from 4 and 6 Groups provided the heavy elements for raids on Rhenania-Ossag oil refineries in Düsseldorf and Monheim. 5 Group, meanwhile, prepared itself for a further attempt on the Mittelland Canal at Gravenhorst, for which eleven 619 Squadron crews were briefed as part of an overall force of 154 Lancasters and eleven Mosquitos. They departed Strubby between 21.52 and 22.07 with no senior pilots on duty, and all reached the target area to find ten-tenths cloud between them and the aiming point. The primary blind marker succeeded in delivering two green TIs by H2S from 12,000 feet at 00.53, and they fell on the starboard side of the canal. After the flare force went in, the Mosquito element descended to 400 feet, but could not identify the aiming point, and, just before H-Hour, the Master Bomber sent the markers home, to be followed almost immediately by the main force as he abandoned the operation.

The operation was rescheduled for twenty-four hours later, when Duisburg and Worms were also to be attacked by heavy forces of 362 and 349 aircraft respectively. 5 Group detailed 165

Lancasters and twelve Mosquitos, and, among those attending the briefing at Coningsby was G/C Evans-Evans, the station commander, who would be taking the bulk of the 83 Squadron commanding officer's highly experienced crew with him. Evans-Evans was 43 and a larger-than-life character, who had commanded 115 Squadron for a spell earlier in the war during its Wellington era, and had never lost the enthusiasm to be "one of the boys" and take part in operations. A number of years of good living had widened his girth, and it must have been a struggle to fit into the cramped confines of a Lancaster cockpit. The thirteen 619 Squadron participants took off in just ten minutes from 17.04 with S/L Osborne the senior pilot on duty, and reached the target area to find moonlight beaming down from clear skies with some ground haze. One of the primary blind markers was able to deliver his green TIs, doing so two minutes late because of a change in the wind, and they fell about a mile south of the aiming point, quite close to the Wet Triangle meeting point of the Mittelland and Dortmund-Ems Canals. After the flare force had done its job, the Mosquitos delivered their red TIs, which were backed up successfully, before the main force was called in at 20.25. Based on the 44 (Rhodesia) Squadron records, crews released their loads of thirteen 1,000 pounders each from 8,000 to 11,000 feet between 20.34 and 20.41, but could not assess the outcome because of the use of long-delay fuses. The presence of night-fighters was clearly evident by the number of combats taking place, and among nine missing Lancasters was the one belonging to 83 Squadron containing G/C Evans-Evans and seven others. Only the rear gunner survived, and, among those killed was the twenty-two-year-old navigator, S/L Wishart DSO, DFC & Bar, who had completed sixty-one operations in Lancasters with 97 Squadron and eighteen in Mosquitos as navigator to Master Bombers. G/C Ingham was left deeply saddened by the loss of his crew. S/L Osborne was unable to lock his main undercarriage for landing, apparently after damage was caused by a loose bomb in the bomb bay. He flew over to Carnaby, and crash-landed PA255 there without injury to the crew or major damage to the Lancaster.

Later on the 21st, W/C Birch arrived from 50 Squadron, where he had been gaining operational experience before succeeding W/C Milward as commanding officer. 619 Squadron was not involved in the 5 Group operation by seventy-four Lancasters to bomb what was believed to be a U-Boot base at Horten in Oslo Fjord on the night of the 23/24th. Whether or not a U-Boot base existed is uncertain, but no shipping was seen by the crews, and a local report described heavy damage in the port area and a shipyard, and the sinking of a tanker and floating crane. While that was in progress, F/Os Hatten, Hickmott and Proctor joined seven others from the group to sneak in under cover of the main event to mine the waters of the Onions garden in Oslo harbour, a little further north. They had departed Strubby between 17.17 and 17.19, and reached the target area to find clear skies and good visibility, before planting their vegetables into the briefed locations from around 13,000 feet sometime either side of 21.00. On return, the gardeners reported smoke climbing through 8,000 feet over Horten, and large fires visible for eighty miles into the return journey.

Meanwhile, some 770 miles to the south, a force of 366 Lancasters, plus one from the Film Unit, and thirteen Mosquitos drawn from 1, 6 and 8 Groups had been sent against the city of Pforzheim, situated in southern Germany between Karlsruhe to the north-west and Stuttgart to the south-east. This would be the first area raid on the city, which was known as a centre for jewellery and watch manufacture, but was believed by the Allies to be involved in the production of precision instruments in support of Germany's war effort. They were greeted by clear skies and bright moonlight in the target area, and the thin veil of ground haze proved to be no impediment as the first red Oboe TIs went down at 19.52, to be followed quickly by illuminator flares and salvoes of concentrated reds and greens. Fires rapidly took hold until the whole town north of the river looked like a sea of flames, and, by 20.06, the fires were too dazzling for the TIs to be visible, after which, the Master Bomber ordered the smoke to be bombed. The raid lasted twenty-two minutes, during which 1,825 tons of bombs fell into the built-up area, reducing 83% of it to ruins and setting off a firestorm in which 17,600 people lost their lives. This was the highest death toll to result from a single attack on a German city after Hamburg (40,000) and Dresden (25,000). It was during this operation that the final Victoria Cross was earned by a member of RAF Bomber Command. It went posthumously to the Master Bomber from 582 Squadron, Captain Ed Swales of the South African Air Force, who continued to control the attack in a Lancaster severely damaged by a night-fighter, before sacrificing his life to allow his crew to abandon the stricken aircraft.

A daylight attack on the Dortmund-Ems Canal was planned for the afternoon of the 24th, and would involve 166 Lancasters and five Mosquitos, eighteen of the former provided by 617 Squadron with Tallboys on board, while 619 Squadron contributed thirteen, each loaded with fourteen 1,000 pounders. W/C Milward had been on leave, and arrived back at Strubby to learn that he was about to be posted to 5 Lancaster Finishing School (5LFS) at Syerston. Although not originally on the Order of Battle, it seems that he appointed himself gaggle leader and departed Strubby with the others between 14.05 and 14.19. They reached the target with an 11 Group fighter escort to encounter ten-tenths cloud with tops at between 4,000 and 9,000 feet, at which point, the Master Bomber abandoned the operation and sent the force home with its bombs. Once back home at their respective stations, crews complained about the unsatisfactory forming up of Base gaggles, which had been generally chaotic. W/C Milward left the squadron on the 25th at the end of a highly satisfactory tour as commanding officer. During the course of the month the squadron carried out thirteen operations, including those aborted, and dispatched 155 sorties for the loss of two Lancasters and their crews and a rear gunner.

March 1945

The new month would see the Command bludgeon its way across Germany, concentrating on oil, rail and road targets, along with the few towns still boasting a built-up area. The new 5 Group A-O-C, AVM Constantine, visited Strubby on the 1st, and Southern Rhodesian, S/L Palmer, arrived to gain operational experience before being posted to command 44 (Rhodesia) Squadron. Mannheim was raided for the last time in numbers by a large force from 1, 6 and 8 Groups on that day, while 5 Group remained at home. Later, on the 2nd, Cologne was pounded for the final time, first by a force of seven hundred aircraft, which inflicted huge destruction across the city, particularly west of the Rhine, and, later, by a 3 Group force, of which only fifteen bombed because of a faulty G-H station in England. The city ceased to function, thereafter, and was still paralysed when American forces marched in four days later. Just when it seemed that German resistance to air attack might end, March would prove that the defenders were still capable of mounting a challenge, even though they were stretched beyond their capacity to protect every corner of the Reich.

5 Group opened its March account with a return to the Ladbergen aqueduct section of the Dortmund-Ems Canal on the evening of the 3rd, for which 212 Lancasters and ten Mosquitos were made ready. Fifteen 619 Squadron crews attended briefing, thirteen to learn of their part in the main event, while F/L May and F/O Proctor were assigned to mining duties in the Tomato garden at the southern end of Oslo Fjord. The latter pair departed Spilsby first at 17.21, to be followed into the air between 18.41 and 19.08 by the bombing brigade with W/C Birch the senior pilot on duty for the first time, and each crew with thirteen 1,000 pounders beneath their feet. They encountered eight to ten-tenths cloud in the target area at between 3,500 and 6,000 feet, and it was noted that the defences had been strengthened since the last attack, and were throwing up a curtain of intense light flak as high as 15,000 feet. H2S allowed the two 83 Squadron primary blind markers to locate the canal and deliver their green TIs from 14,000 feet at 21.47 and 21.49, and the first illuminators went in a minute later to light the way for the Mosquitos, after which, a large red glow could be seen through the clouds. At 21.59, the Master Bomber called in the main force to bomb on the glow or on sight of the TIs through gaps in the thin cloud, and the 619 Squadron crews complied from around 8,000 to 10,000 feet from 22.00 onwards. They contributed to the breaching of both branches, which rendered the waterway unnavigable and out of action for the remainder of the war. Meanwhile, the gardeners had found clear skies and good visibility over Oslo Fjord, and delivered their mines into the briefed locations from 10,000 feet between 20.51 and 21.05. F/O Proctor and crew returned from the north with a dead engine courtesy of flak, and F/O Dickinson also lost one to a similar cause at Ladbergen. W/C Birch and crew reported that they had shot down a V-1, which was probably bound for Antwerp.

The Luftwaffe mounted Operation Gisella on this night, sending some two hundred intruders to catch the bombers as they prepared to land, and they succeeded in shooting down twenty for the loss of three of their own. The Strubby crews were warned, but all got down safely, and the aerodrome was shot up later without sustaining any damage.

Eighteen 619 Squadron crews attended briefing on the 5th, to learn that 5 Group would be sending 248 Lancasters and ten Mosquitos back to Böhlen, for another crack at the synthetic oil refinery. A simultaneous operation by a Thunderclap force of 760 aircraft would attempt to redress the recent failure at Chemnitz, some thirty-five miles to the south. Take-off from Strubby was accomplished without incident between 17.09 and 17.27 with a whole host of flight lieutenants representing the senior pilots on duty, and all reached the target area, some after climbing above 15,000 feet to escape icing conditions. Ten-tenths cloud lay over the target in layers between 2,000 and 11,000 feet, but uncertainty concerning the prevailing conditions on arrival had been planned for and two marking plans prepared, low-level and skymarking, and the lead primary blind marker made his first run at 14,000 feet to drop green TIs at 21.40. He did not see them burst because of the cloud, but thought that the illuminator flares were well-placed. Some of the Coningsby crews experienced H2S difficulties, and not all were able to pinpoint on Leipzig for the run-in. This meant that they were unsure of their position, and, when the Master Bomber called for Wanganui flares at 21.45, they withheld them, rather than risk dropping them inaccurately and attracting some of the bombing. A large explosion was witnessed at 21.50, and, three minutes later, Wanganui flares were observed by the approaching main force crews. Seventeen of the 619 Squadron crews delivered their cookie and eleven 500 pounders each from around 10,000 to 14,000 feet either side of 22.00, observing another large explosion at 21.57, before the Master Bomber called a halt at 22.01 and sent everyone home, leaving evidence of fires and smoke behind them. F/L Johnston and crew failed to identify the aiming point and, deciding not to bomb indiscriminately, returned their load to store. Post-raid reconnaissance revealed extensive damage to the coal-drying plant, and some hits in other areas of the site, but it was still not a knockout blow. Meanwhile, the Thunderclap force had succeeded in inflicting severe fire damage in central and southern districts of Chemnitz.

The target posted on 5 Group stations on the 6th was the town and port area of Sassnitz, located on the Baltic island of Rügen, about thirty miles north of Peenemünde, a region with memories of heavy casualties sustained by 5 Group in August 1943. The two-fold purpose of the operation was to destroy the port installations and facilities, and sink shipping to render it unusable as a refuge for escaping Kriegsmarine units. 150 Lancasters and seven Mosquitos were made ready, ten of the former by 619 Squadron, which also loaded three others with mines destined for the Willow garden on the approaches to Sassnitz. The two elements departed Strubby together between 18.35 and 18.44 with S/L Purnell the senior pilot on duty, but F/O Sparkes and crew were back in the circuit within two hours with a feathered starboard-outer engine. The others reached the target area to find five to nine-tenths drifting cloud with tops in places at 8,000 feet. An 83 Squadron blind marker made a run at 22.50 to drop green TIs over the port from 12,000 feet, and the flare force maintained illumination of the town and outer harbour for the next twenty-five minutes. Apart from a short break, when cloud slid across the aiming point, the markers remained visible to the main force crews, and those from 619 Squadron bombed on red TIs from an average of 9,000 feet either side of 23.00, some after orbiting to await a clear view of the ground. Bombing activity ceased at H+18, and those with bombs still aboard took them home. Three large ships identified in the harbour were attacked, and, according to post-raid reconnaissance, sunk, and there was also extensive damage in the northern part of the town. Meanwhile, F/L A McMorran and F/Os Proctor and Whittaker had encountered five to seven-tenths cloud with tops at 9,000 feet, and dropped their six mines each into the allotted location in the harbour from 6,000 and 13,000 feet just after 23.00. When F/Os Hickmott and Proctor returned to base, they were declared tour-expired.

It was back to the oil campaign for 5 Group on the following night, for an attack on a refinery at Harburg, south of Hamburg, for which a force of 234 Lancasters and seven Mosquitos was made ready. They would not be alone over Germany, however, as more than a thousand other aircraft would be engaged against similar targets at Dessau and Hemmingstedt and in minor and support operations. 619 Squadron provided sixteen Lancasters, which took off between 18.16 and 18.30 with Capt Meter SAAF probably outranking the plethora of pilot on duty of flight lieutenant rank. The force arrived over the target to find eight-tenths thin cloud and red and yellow target indicators clearly visible, which they bombed in accordance with the Master Bomber's instructions with a seven-second overshoot from 11,000 to 13,000 feet either side of 22.00. Bomb bursts were clearly seen, along with explosions and black smoke rising through 10,000 feet, and all but two from 619 Squadron returned safely to Strubby, confident in the success of the operation. NG286 and PB699 were brought down in the target area with no survivors from the crew of F/O Sparkes RNZAF in the latter, while four escaped with their lives in the former to spend a short time in captivity. Their captain, F/L G McMorran lost his life with two others, and this left his younger brother to continue the fight with 619 Squadron. 5 Group crews distinguished themselves on this night by claiming the destruction of seven enemy fighters, one of them, a Me410 shot down by F/O Pennells and crew. Post-raid reconnaissance confirmed further damage to this previously attacked target, with oil storage tanks taking the most hits, and revealed that a rubber factory had also been severely damaged.

An all-time record was set on the 11th, when 1,079 aircraft, the largest Bomber Command force ever for a single target, was assembled to attack Essen for the last time. 5 Group contributed 199 Lancasters and a single Mosquito, 619 Squadron loading fourteen Lancasters with a cookie and sixteen 500 pounders each, and dispatching them between 12.02 and 12.18 with W/C Birch the senior pilot on duty. By the time that F/O Hooker and crew had reached the Brussels area, they had reason to abort their sortie, for which the squadron ORB provided no detail, and, while trying to land at Evere, LM207 was damaged beyond repair without injury to the occupants. The others found the target city covered by ten-tenths cloud with tops at 6,000 feet, which required the Path Finder element to employ skymarkers in the form of red and blue smoke puffs, and these were bombed by the 619 Squadron crews from around 15,000 to 19,000 feet between 15.15 and 15.30. More than 4,600 tons of bombs were dropped into the already ravaged city and former industrial powerhouse, and left it with smoke rising through 10,000 feet as the force turned away. It would still be in a state of paralysis when the American ground forces captured it unopposed on the 10th of April. Operations were not yet over for the 11th, as 5 Group sent eleven Lancasters that night to mine the approaches to Oslo harbour in the Onions III garden. F/L May and F/Os Grant and Whittaker departed Strubby between 17.46 and 17.53, and found the target area to be under clear skies with good visibility. They identified the drop zone by H2S, before making timed runs to deliver their stores from 12,000 feet between 21.15 and 21.22.

A little over twenty-four hours later, the short-lived record was surpassed by the departure from their stations in the early afternoon of 1,108 aircraft, which had Dortmund as their destination. This time 5 Group provided 211 Lancasters, sixteen of them from 619 Squadron, which departed Strubby between 13.26 and 13.55 led by pilots of flight lieutenant rank. Each was carrying a cookie and sixteen 500 pounders, which arrived over the eastern Ruhr to find it still under a blanket of ten-tenths cloud, this time with tops at 6,000 feet. The Path Finders marked the target with green and blue smoke puffs, and the main force was directed by the Master Bomber to aim for the blues, which the 619 Squadron crews strived to do from around 13,000 to 17,000 feet in the minutes leading to 17.00. Returning crews spoke of brown smoke climbing through the clouds to 8,000 feet from the northern end of the city, and also a ring of smoke encircling the area. In fact, the smoke was so dense, that it remained visible for 120 miles into the return flight. A new record of 4,800 tons of bombs was delivered, and photo-reconnaissance revealed that the central and southern districts of the city had received the greatest weight, and had been left in chaos with all industry silenced permanently and railway tracks torn up.

The Group's next objective was the Wintershall oil refinery at Lützkendorf, another site to the west of Leipzig and south-west of Leuna in the Geiseltal. *(Lützkendorf no longer exists on a map of Germany, and is now known as either Mücheln or Krumpa).* The briefing of 244 Lancaster and eleven Mosquito crews took place on the 14th, fifteen of the former representing 619 Squadron, and they departed Strubby between 16.56 and 17.05 with S/L Purnell the senior pilot on duty. They headed out over the Wash and the bulge of East Anglia en route to the Scheldt Estuary, but F/O Cowling turned back early for an undisclosed reason. The remaining Lancasters crossed Belgium to swing south of Cologne, before pointing their snouts to the east for the long leg to the target. They were met on arrival by conditions described variously as ten-tenths cloud, no cloud, thin layer of cloud, thin banks of stratus with tops at 12,000 feet, a little medium cloud, poor visibility and good visibility, but there was unanimity with regard to the haze. Ahead, the primary blind markers could be seen delivering their green TIs at 21.49, followed by the illuminators immediately afterwards between 21.51 and 22.00 to drop flares and bombs. Finally, the low-level Mosquitos did their job to accurately mark the aiming point before the main force crews were called in, and the 619 Squadron participants bombed on red and green TIs in accordance with the Master Bomber's instructions from around 8,000 to 11000 feet either side of 22.00. Returning crews claimed an accurate attack, reporting explosions and fires, and thick black smoke drifting across the plant and ascending through 7,000 feet, which rendered impossible a detailed assessment. Night-fighters were very much in evidence over the target and during the return flight, but the 619 Squadron crews managed to evade contact and were diverted on return. A hefty eighteen Lancasters failed to return, 7.4% of those dispatched, and post-raid reconnaissance revealed a partially successful operation, which meant that a further visit would be required.

Fifteen 619 Squadron crews assembled in the briefing room at 14.00 on the 16th, to learn that they were to attack the virgin target of Würzburg, a small city on the River Main, situated some sixty miles south-east of Frankfurt in southern Germany. While this operation was in progress, a similar-sized force, drawn from 1 and 8 Groups, would be delivering the final attack of the war on Nuremberg, fifty miles to the south-east. A 5 Group force of 225 Lancasters and eleven Mosquitos was made ready for an early-evening take-off, and the 619 Squadron element got away between 17.51 and 18.01 with W/C Birch the senior pilot on duty and S/L Palmer undertaking his first sortie. The latter was back in the circuit five hours later with a dead port-outer engine, by which time the other crews were also on their way home, having all reached the target area to find clear skies with ground haze. The marking and flare forces had carried out their assigned tasks between 21.25 and 21.34, leaving the way clear for the main force crews to exploit the favourable bombing conditions. The 619 Squadron crews found red and yellow target indicators marking the aiming point, and complied with the Master Bomber's call for a sixteen-second overshoot, to deliver their loads of a cookie and incendiaries each from around 10,000 to 12,000 feet shortly after 21.30. All but one returned to Strubby, apparently without incident to report a successful operation, but had to wait for the reconnaissance reports to discover the extent of the destruction. The bombing had lasted just seventeen minutes, during which period 1,127 tons of bombs had fallen into the historic old cathedral city, destroying an estimated 89% of the built-up area and killing four to five thousand people. Among six missing Lancasters was 619 Squadron's NG503, in which F/O Farrow RCAF and his predominantly RCAF crew lost their lives. The Nuremberg operation had also been highly destructive, but had cost 1 Group twenty-four Lancasters, thus proving, that the enemy defences were not yet spent and could still give the Command a bloody nose.

There was still business to attend to at the Böhlen oil refinery, and 5 Group prepared a force of 236 Lancasters and eleven Mosquitos on the 20th, to deal what was hoped to be the knockout blow. Briefings began at 20.00, and, at Strubby, was attended by fifteen 619 Squadron crews, with S/L Palmer the most senior pilot present. A small-scale diversionary raid on Halle, situated some twenty miles to the north-west of Leipzig, involved a number of 55 Base crews, but none from 619 Squadron. They took off between 23.45 and 23.58, each carrying a cookie and eleven 500 pounders, and set out on the now familiar path to eastern Germany. They lost the services of F/O Gampe and crew to an unknown cause, leaving the others to arrive in the target area, where conditions were fairly good, with three to six-tenths cloud topping out at 6,000 to 8,000 feet. The bomber stream arrived early because of stronger-than-forecast winds, and the main force had to orbit while the first primary blind marker crew delivered green TIs at 03.33. They fell 750 yards south of the plant, to be followed at H-16 by a yellow TI bursting two miles short of the target. A cluster of illuminator flares ignited ahead, revealing that a smoke screen had been activated and was generating much smoke to create difficulties for the Mosquito low-level markers, despite which, they deposited red TIs on the button, and the main force was called in. A few dummy TIs attracted a number of bomb loads, but the 619 Squadron crews complied with the instructions of the Master Bomber to bomb on specific reds and yellows from around 11,000 to 12,500 feet between 03.44 and 04.00. The main weight of the attack was concentrated around the target, and numerous explosions were witnessed, as was smoke rising through 5,000 feet as they turned away. The operation put the oil plant out of action, and it was still idle when American forces moved in a few weeks later. The success cost nine Lancasters and their crews, among them PD425, in which S/L Palmer, died with four of his second-tour crew, which meant that he would not realise the honour of commanding 44 (Rhodesia) Squadron.

It was after 22.00 on the 21st that 151 Lancaster and eight Mosquito crews of 5 Group were informed that the Deutsche Erdölwerke synthetic oil refinery at Hamburg was to be their target that night. 619 Squadron loaded a dozen Lancasters with a cookie and sixteen 500 pounders each, and sent them into the air between 01.28 and 01.43 with S/L Purnell the senior pilot on duty. They pinpointed on the Danish coast to approach the target from the north, and found thin stratus cloud at around 2,000 feet, through which the primary blind marker dropped green TIs on H2S from 14,000 feet at 03.55. The first illuminators went in thirty seconds later, and continued to light up the aiming point until 04.01, by which time the Mosquitos had marked, allowing the main force to be called in at 04.05. The 619 Squadron crews bombed from around 15,000 to 18,000 feet between 04.00 and 04.15, observing many fires and a large explosion at 04.11 that produced red flame and black smoke. Another was reported at 04.16, and it was clear to the homebound crews that the attack had been successful, a fact confirmed by post-raid reconnaissance, which revealed that twenty storage tanks had been destroyed in exchange for the loss of just four Lancasters.

The 55 Base squadrons were not involved in 5 Group's operations against railway bridges at Nienburg and Bremen on the 22nd and 23rd, but they were called to briefing on the afternoon of the 23rd to learn of their part in a raid that night on the town of Wesel. This had the misfortune to lie close to the Rhine and in the path of the advancing British 21st Army Group, which, since the 16th of February, had caused it to be systematically reduced to rubble by repeated air attacks, and now had one final onslaught to face, having already endured one by 3 Group earlier in the day. 195 Lancasters and eleven Mosquitos were made ready, the fourteen representing 619 Squadron departing Strubby between 19.18 and 19.45 with W/C Birch the senior pilot on duty. They found the target under clear skies with slight ground haze, and were able to identify it visually, observing the aiming point to be well-marked by red and green TIs, which were bombed from 8,000 to 12,000 feet between 22.30 and 22.40 in accordance with the Master Bomber's instructions. It was noticed, that, despite the Master Bomber ending the attack at H+8, bombing had continued. Post-raid reconnaissance confirmed the effectiveness of the raid, which left only 3% of Wesel's buildings standing, and, after the war, it would claim justifiably to be the most completely destroyed town in Germany.

W/C Balme arrived on attachment on the 29th to gain operational experience before moving on to command 227 Squadron, which, a week hence, would take up residence at Strubby. During the course of the month the squadron took part in fourteen operations and dispatched 167 sorties for the loss of four Lancasters and their crews. Fewer than four weeks of operations remained ahead of the crews before the bombing war finally came to an end.

April 1945

There would be a gentle introduction to April for 5 Group, with no operations until the 4th, the day on which 227 Squadron arrived to take up residence. It would not be involved with the rest of the "Independent Air Force" in that day's operation against what was believed to be a military barracks at Nordhausen, situated in the Harz Mountains between Hannover to the north-west and Leipzig to the south-east. It had been attacked on the previous day by 1 Group, and was, in fact, a camp for forced workers at the V-2 factory that had been constructed in tunnels under the mountains after the destruction of Peenemünde. There, the workers endured the most appalling conditions and brutal treatment as an increasingly desperate regime sought to change the course of the war. The 5 Group attack, by 243 Lancasters, was to be divided between the barracks and the town, ninety-three to the former and 150 to the latter. The 55 Base squadrons were assigned to the former, and each of their Lancasters was loaded with a cookie and sixteen 500 pounders. The 619 Squadron element of eighteen departed Strubby between 06.12 and 06.25 with S/L Osborne the senior pilot on duty, and arrived at the target to encounter five-to-seven-tenths cloud with tops as high as 7,000 feet, through which they were able to establish a visual reference until smoke began to obscure the barracks. Five of the Strubby crews arrived early and did not bomb, but the others carried out their attacks from 13,000 to 16,000 feet between 09.10 to 09.20. Those assigned to the barracks, but thwarted by the smoke, directed their attention upon the town, and, although some of the early bombing of the town was seen to undershoot, the Master Bomber corrected this by calling for a five-second overshoot, and, thereafter, the markers were soon obscured also by smoke. At debriefing, the crews were able to report a concentrated attack on both aiming points, claiming severe damage, but, tragically and inevitably, heavy casualties were suffered by the unfortunate slave workers.

The only sizeable effort on the night of the 7/8th was by 175 Lancasters and eleven Mosquitos of 5 Group, which had a benzol plant at Molbis, near Leipzig, as their target. Situated south of the city, and less than two miles east of Böhlen, it was becoming a familiar destination for 5 Group via a well-trodden route across Belgium to pass south of Cologne. 619 Squadron made ready fourteen Lancasters, which departed Strubby between 18.01 and 18.43 with S/L Purnell the senior pilot on duty. They found themselves delayed by wrongly forecast head winds, and, although they would reach the target area, not all would do so in time to participate in the attack. Two 83 Squadron primary blind markers formed the tip of the spear, and identified Zeitz on H2S, before making the ten-mile north-easterly run from there to the target. Green TIs were released from 15,000 feet at 22.48, and the flare force followed up between 22.50 and 22.57 to enable the low-level Mosquitos to drop red and green TIs among the chimneys of the plant. The approaching main force crews were greeted by clear skies with ground haze, or, perhaps, a smoke screen in operation, but the highly accurate and visible marking was an invitation for them to plaster the aiming point with high explosives. In the event, only F/O Pennells and crew of the 619 Squadron contingent was too late to bomb with the others on red and green TIs from around 11,000 to 14,000 feet between 23.05

and 23.15. Photo-reconnaissance confirmed the operation to have been a complete success, which ended all production at the plant. When F/O Runnalls landed at 02.37, he was unaware that later in the day, the length of a tour would be reduced from thirty-six to thirty-three sorties, and he and his crew would be declared tour-expired.

Two major operations were scheduled for the 8th, the larger one involving 440 aircraft from 4, 6 and 8 Groups to be directed against Hamburg's shipyards, where the new Type XXI U-Boots were under construction. 5 Group, meanwhile, would take on the Lützkendorf refinery, following a failed attempt on the 4th by 1 and 8 Groups to conclusively end production at the site. A force of 231 Lancasters and eleven Mosquitos was put together, of which the seventeen 619 Squadron participants departed Strubby between 17.52 and 18.20 with S/L Osborne the senior pilot on duty. They all reached the target area, where conditions were as they had been twenty-four hours earlier, with clear skies and either ground haze or generated smoke. The primary blind markers ran in at 14,000 feet at 22.33 to deliver green TIs, and the illuminators followed between 22.35 and 22.42, after which, the main force was called in. The 619 Squadron crews attacked in accordance with the Master Bomber's instructions to bomb the southerly red and yellow TIs after an eleven second overshoot. They ran in at around 11,000 to 14,000 feet between 22.45 and 22.55, and all returned safely to diversion airfields, confident that it would not be necessary to return to that particular target. They described their experiences to the Intelligence Section at debriefing, reporting many explosions, including a large one at 22.47, which was surpassed in size by another one two minutes later, and flames were said to have reached up to 3,000 feet. F/O Taylor and crew claimed the destruction of a Me110, which was seen to spin down in flames and impact the ground. The complete destruction of the site was confirmed by photo-reconnaissance, and the plant would remain out of action for what remained of the war.

55 Base sat out a modest 5 Group raid on oil storage tanks and U-Boot pens at Hamburg in daylight on the 9th, and, when its crews were called to briefing on the 10th, it was to discover that they would be going back to the Leipzig area for the third successive operation, this time to hit a stretch of railway track linked to the Wahren marshalling yards, situated to the north-west of the city. A larger operation on this night, involving more than three hundred aircraft from 1 and 8 Groups, was to be directed at the Plauen marshalling yards to the south-west of Dresden, and the two forces would adopt a similar route until shortly before reaching Leipzig. 5 Group contributed all seventy-six Lancasters for Leipzig and eleven Mosquitos, with 8 Group providing the other eight Oboe Mosquitos, which, now that mobile Oboe stations had been set up on the Continent, could operate over the whole of Germany. The 619 Squadron element of eleven took off between 18.19 and 18.33, each carrying eleven 1,000 pounders, and reached the target area to find clear skies and excellent conditions for bombing. There were many ineffective searchlights, and flak was light, probably because of a heavy night-fighter presence. The Oboe Mosquitos dropped green TIs as a reference for the 83 Squadron crews, which provided the illumination between 22.51 and 22.57 for the low-level Mosquito element. They placed their red TIs accurately onto the aiming point, before the main force bombed the southernmost red TI in accordance with the Master Bomber's instructions. Based yet again on the 44 (Rhodesia) Squadron records, they carried out their attacks from 11,500 to 14,000 feet either side of 23.00, and all but one returned home to make their reports. SW254 crashed at Löberitz, some fifteen miles north-east of Halle, killing F/L Albert McMorran RCAF and all but his bomb-aimer, who fell into enemy hands. It will be recalled that his elder brother, F/L George McMorran, had lost his life a month earlier. Photographic-reconnaissance

would confirm serious damage to the eastern half of the targeted stretch of track.

A major attack on Kiel by elements of 3, 6 and 8 Groups was planned for the night of the 13/14th, while 5 Group took advantage of that activity to send eighteen Lancasters to lay mines in the Forget-me-not garden in Kiel harbour. The crews of F/L Lavigne, F/Os Hatten and Leriger and W/O Potter departed Strubby between 20.37 and 20.40, and reached the target area to encounter six to ten-tenths stratus with tops up to 7,000 feet, through which the Lavigne and Leriger crews delivered their vegetables by H2S from an undisclosed altitude at some time around 23.30. F/O Hatten and W/O Potter returned their mines to store after one of them failed to identify the drop zone through the cloud and the other suffered H2S failure.

5 Group was used to being handed the most distant targets, and, as the final days of the bombing war approached, it found itself facing three long-range trips on consecutive nights, all to railway targets. The first of these was at Pilsen in Czechoslovakia, for which a force of 222 Lancasters and eleven Mosquitos was made ready. The fourteen 619 Squadron crews were joined at the early evening briefing by fourteen from 227 Squadron, and made their way to the runway at around 23.30 with W/C Birch the senior pilot on duty. The 619 Squadron element took off between 23.22 and 23.53, but lost the services of F/O Hunter and crew to port-inner engine failure. The others pressed on and found clear skies in the target area with only slight haze, and, ahead, watched the first primary blind marker deliver green TIs at 03.38, before the flare forces followed between 03.51 and 03.56. The main force was called in at 03.58, and the 619 Squadron participants bombed from around 13,000 to 16,000 feet either side of 04.00, aiming at the north-westerly red and yellow TIs with an eight-second overshoot in accordance with the Master Bomber's instructions. Returning crews reported a large explosion at 04.00, followed by oily smoke, and it was concluded that the raid had been successful.

There was good news to celebrate on the 17th, when the length of a tour was reduced yet again to thirty sorties, releasing many crews to contemplate a long future. The target posted for ninety 5 Group Lancasters and eleven Mosquitos that night was the marshalling yards at Cham, on Germany's border with Czechoslovakia, for which seventeen 619 Squadron crews were briefed. They departed Strubby between 23.16 and 00.10 with S/L Purnell the senior pilot on duty, and the Lancasters loaded with a mixture of 1,000 and 500 pounders. F/L Willitts and crew were back in the circuit within two-and-a-half hours carrying a dead port-outer engine, and it seems that F/L Lavigne and crew experienced a similar problem, probably when close to the target, and continued on to deliver an attack. It took more than four hours to reach the target area, where they were greeted by clear skies with slight ground haze. The primary blind marker dropped the first green TIs on H2S from 14,000 feet at 03.47, and the flare forces went in between 03.51 and 03.54 to light the way for the Mosquito low-level markers. Their efforts were seen to be very concentrated, but the use of delay-fused bombs meant that no immediate assessment would be possible. The 619 Squadron crews bombed in accordance with the Master Bomber's instructions from around 9,000 to 11,000 feet, aiming at the north-westerly red TIs either side of 04.00. Photo-reconnaissance later confirmed that tracks had been torn up and rolling stock damaged, and it was another success for the group.

5 Group was not involved when a force of over nine hundred aircraft reduced the island of Heligoland to the appearance of a cratered moonscape on the 18th, and the 55 Base squadrons also

sat out a raid that night by 113 Lancasters and ten Mosquitos of 5 Group that put out of action the railway yards at Komotau (now Chomutov), also in Czechoslovakia. This proved to be the last raid in the communications offensive, which had begun more than a year earlier in preparation for D-Day. Strubby was not called into action again until the 23rd, when 5 Group sent 148 Lancasters to attack the railway yards and port area of Flensburg on the eastern coast of the Schleswig-Holstein peninsula. The twelve 619 Squadron crews took off between 15.15 and 15.30 with W/C Birch the senior pilot on duty, and led the 55 Base formation, which fell in behind that of 53 Base. They reached the target area to encounter ten-tenths cloud with tops at 4,500 feet, which persuaded the Master Bomber to send the force home with their bomb loads intact. On landing, F/O Hatten and crew were declared tour-expired.

5 Group operated for the final time on the 25th, with an operation in the morning against the SS barracks at Hitler's Eaglesnest retreat at Berchtesgaden in the Bavarian mountains, and later that night on an oil refinery at Tonsberg in Norway. 5 Group supported the former with eighty-eight Lancasters and a single Mosquito in an overall 1, 5 and 8 Group force of 359 Lancasters and sixteen Mosquitos. The six 619 Squadron participants departed Strubby between 04.13 and 04.32 with S/L Osborne the senior pilot on duty, and all arrived in the target area to find clear skies, despite which, it proved difficult to identify the barracks in the absence of visible markers, and the Master Bomber's instructions were not getting through. However, a nearby lake and the town stood out clearly, and the 619 Squadron crews were able to establish their position before carrying out their attacks from around 15,000 to 16,000 feet either side of 09.00. It was difficult to assess the accuracy of this operation, but it appeared to be effective, and no local report emerged to provide clarity. LM756 failed to return with the crew of F/O De Marco RCAF, who were on their twenty-ninth sortie and so close to surviving the war. The Lancaster crashed in the general target area, killing the pilot and three others, and it is believed that the three survivors were soon in Allied hands.

That night, 5 Group conducted its and Bomber Command's final offensive operation of the war involving heavy bombers, when sending 107 Lancasters and seven Mosquitos to attack a target, believed to be oil-related, at Tonsberg, situated close to the western shore of Oslo Fjord, a dozen or so miles south of the recently attacked Horten. At the same time, fourteen 5 Group Lancasters carried out the final gardening sorties of the war nearby in Oslo Fjord, and it was for the latter that 619 Squadron dispatched the crews of F/Ls Johnston and Wilkinson, F/O Reid and W/O Potter from Strubby between 20.15 and 20.19. They all reached the target area to find a layer of eight to ten-tenths cloud, and the crews of F/L Johnston and W/O Potter delivered their mines as briefed, while the Wilkinson and Reid crews experienced equipment issues that prevented them from releasing theirs. F/L Johnston and crew were declared tour-expired with this operation, and, when F/L Wilkinson and crew touched down in RA588 at 02.56, they had the honour of bringing to a close the operational career of 619 Squadron. Operations were posted over the ensuing days, but cancelled, and, meanwhile, Operation Exodus was under way to repatriate prisoners of war, a process which would continue into the summer.

During the course of this final month of the bombing war, 619 Squadron took part in ten operations and dispatched 117 sorties for the loss of two Lancasters and their crews. The squadron began to support Operation Exodus in early May, but there is no mention of participation in Operation Manna, the supply of food to the starving Dutch people still under occupation, which began during the final few days of April and continued until the cessation of hostilities on the 8th of May. 619

Squadron was one of many arriving relatively late on the operational scene, and was never awarded an official crest and motto. This does not diminish the part it played in the drive to victory, and its record stands as a testament to those gallant men and women who served it in the air and on the ground.

F/O E J Mortis, wireless operator on Lancaster PB210 PG-V. lost on the Karlsruhe raid 2nd of February 1945.

619 Squadron Pilot Royce Bateman

'B' Flight Wireless Operators, 619 Squadron.
RAF Strubby, c.February/March 1945.
Back row: F/Sgt C H Andrew RNZAF, - - - - Sgt P C Marshall
Middle row: F/Sgt C D Tosswill RAAF, - - - Sgt Ross, - F/Sgt G I Malowy (RAAF)
Front row: - - F/O J Crisp, F/L E Belcher ('B' Flight Signals Leader) - - -.

F/O W T DeMarco crew
W/O G V Walker KIA, F/O DeMarco (KIA) P/O N H Johnston (KIA), J Spears (PoW),
A H Sharman, Sgt E W Norman (KIA), F Cowie.

619 Squadron RAF Strubby 1944. Lancaster PG-D.
Lost while raiding Berchtesgaden 25th of April 1945. L-R: N H Johnson RCAF (KIA), F Cole, G V Walker RCAF (KIA), F/O W T DeMarco RCAF (KIA), A H Sharman, J Spears RCAF, E W Norman (KIA).

619 Squadron. RAF Strubby 1945.
W/O Porters (Gillie) Crew:
Sid Turner. 'Taffy' Evans, 'Jock' Prittard, Bill Smith, Eric Worth, Alec Jamieson, Jimmy Vincent, Jack Shane.

619 Squadron Lancaster PB842 PG-Y and 460 Squadron PB379 AR-E interned in Sweden, 1945

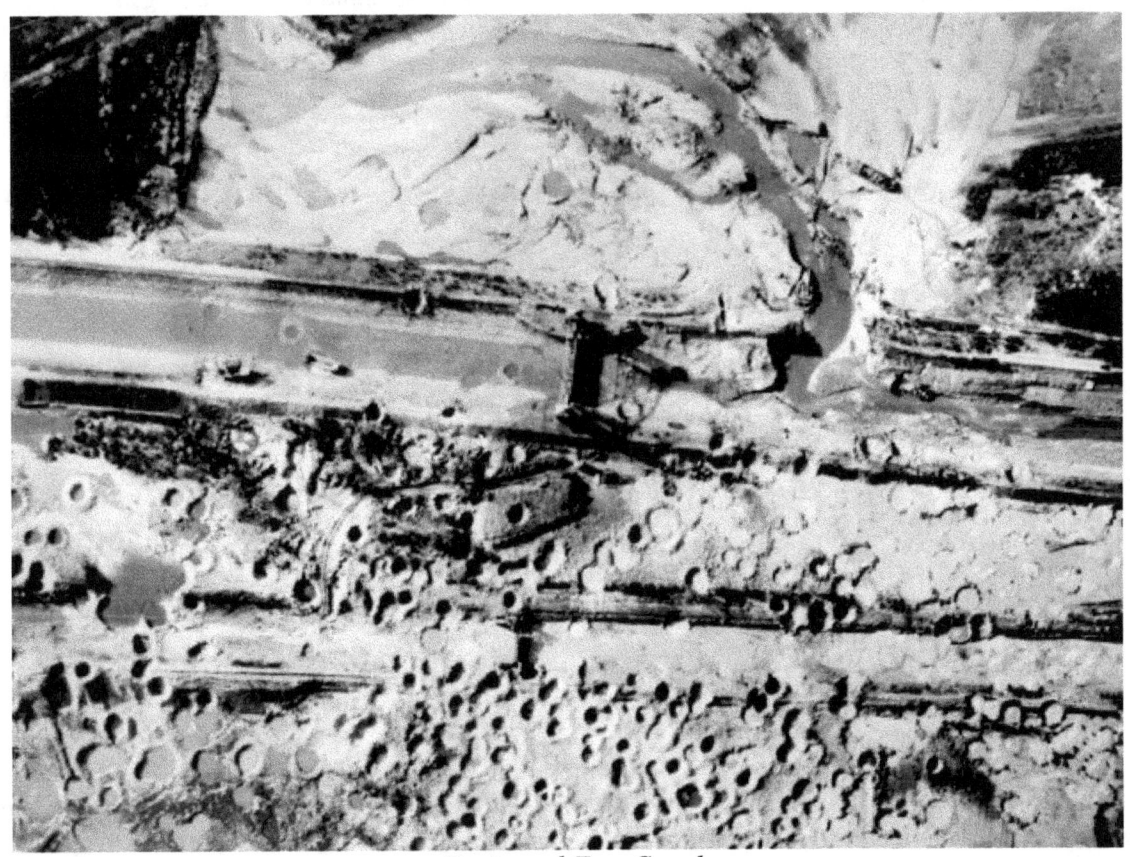
Dortmund-Ems Canal

F/L John Faulkner (AG)
RAF Strubby 1945
W/C Birch crew

G/C A C "Tiny" Evans-Evans
Station Commander of Coningsby
when he was KIA 21st of February 1945

619 Squadron   (www.veterans.gc.ca)
Albert Elmore McMorran (left) and his brother George Melvin McMorran (right) Canadian Brothers, who were both killed, serving in Bomber Command - Elmore on the 11th of April 1945 and Melvin a month earlier on the 8th of March 1945.

Elmore McMorran

Melvin McMorran

619 Sqn Lancaster PG-N at Strubby 1945. F/O Hooper's crew

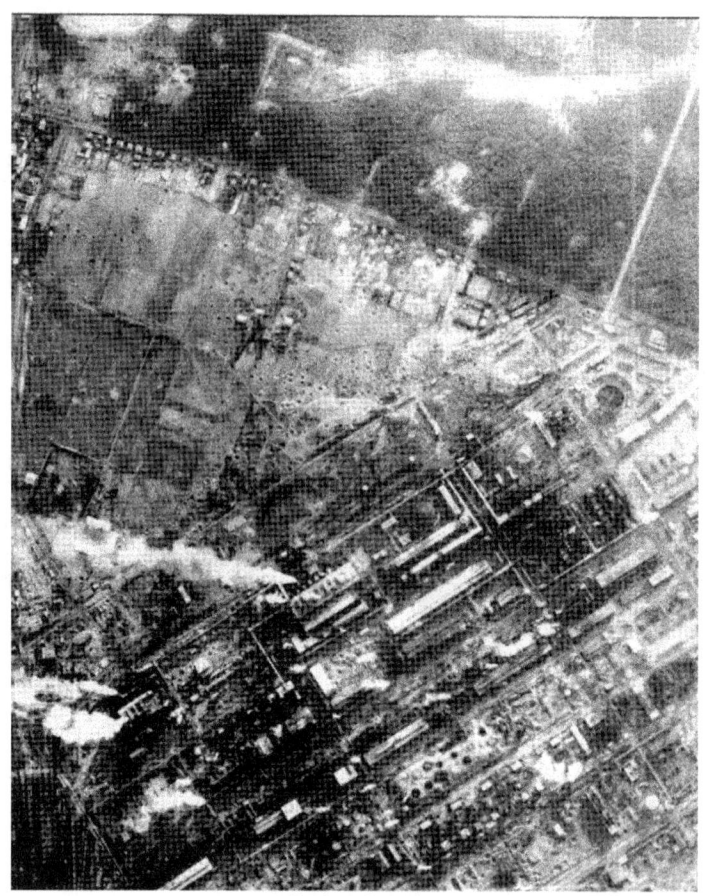
Politz Raid

F/Sgt H Insley   *W/O L J Symonds*   *Sgt R Brown*

All missing after raid on Royan, France on the 4/5th January 1945 and commemorated on the Runnymede Memorial. Also lost were pilot F/O D Gray, Sgt A Johnson, F/Sgt E A Morley. Sgt W H Bartholomew was injured.

Above and below: 619 Squadron F/O Knape and Crew
F/O Knape, Sgt Pearce, Sgt Mills, F/Sgt Appleby, Sgt Haddock, Sgt Davies, Sgt Cashmore

F/Sgt T H Appleby

619 Squadron. S/L S Osborne's crew.
Back: F/O D J Davis, O'Niell, F/O H C Devenish, unknown.
S/L Sidney Osborne bottom centre, and Sgt Ian Fraser (FE) with life vest

Berchtesgaden, Germany. 25th of April 1945. Targets were attacked by Lancaster aircraft of RAF Bomber Command including 619 Squadron in daylight. A bomb burst near Hitler's chalet, bottom left.

Unidentified aircrew believed to have served with 619 Squadron

619 Squadron Lancaster RA521 PG-D

619 SQUADRON

NO MOTTO   Code **PG**

Stations

WOODHALL SPA	18.04.43. to 09.01.44.
CONINGSBY	09.01.44. to 17.04.44.
DUNHOLME LODGE	17.04.44. to 28.09.44.
STRUBBY	28.09.44. to 30.06.45.

Commanding Officers

WING COMMANDER I J McGHIE DFC	18.04.43. to 18.08.43.
WING COMMANDER W ABERCROMBY DFC	18.08.43. to 04.12.43.
WING COMMANDER J R JEUDWINE OBE	04.12.43. to 23.05.44.
WING COMMANDER J R MALING AFC	23.05.44. to 26.07.44.
WING COMMANDER R A MILWARD DFC	28.07.44. to 25.02.45.
WING COMMANDER S G BIRCH	25.02.45. to 14.06.45.

Aircraft

LANCASTER I/III	04.43. to 07.45.

Operational Record

OPERATIONS	SORTIES	AIRCRAFT FTR	% LOSSES
240	3011	77	2.6

Category of Operations

BOMBING	MINING
223	17

Aircraft Histories

LANCASTER.   **From April 1943.**

W4127 PG-D	From 1660 Conversion Unit. FTR La Chappelle 20/21.4.44.
W4921	From 617 Squadron. To 1654 Conversion Unit.
W4929	From 617 Squadron. To 1661 Conversion Unit.
DV238	To 49 Squadron.
DV326 PG-P	Completed ten Berlin operations. To 5 Lancaster Finishing School.
DV328 PG-L	FTR Berlin (eleventh Berlin operation.) 24/25.3.44.
DV330 PG-O	FTR Berlin 15/16.2.44.
DV335 PG-H	To 46 Maintenance Unit.
DV336 PG-U	Crashed near Elvington on return from Berlin 27.11.43.
DV381 PG-B	FTR Berlin 26/27.11.43.
ED597	From 49 Squadron. Crashed on take-off from Coningsby while training, and damaged beyond repair 17.3.44.
ED602 PG-X	From 49 Squadron. FTR Karlsruhe 26/27.9.44.
ED756	From 617 Squadron. To 1654 Conversion Unit.
ED839 PG-C	From 97 Squadron. Crashed on take-off from Woodhall Spa when bound for Hannover 8.10.43.
ED859 PG-G/V	From 156 Squadron. FTR Wesseling 21/22.6.44.
ED866 PG-E	From 97 Squadron. To 5 Lancaster Finishing School.
ED977 PG-A	FTR Stettin 5/6.1.44.
ED978 PG-B	FTR Düsseldorf 11/12.6.43.
ED979	FTR Cologne 28/29.6.43.
ED980	FTR Oberhausen 14/15.6.43.
ED981 PG-V	FTR Berlin 23/24.8.43.
ED982 PG-D	FTR Peenemünde 17/18.8.43.
ED983 PG-W	Crashed in Lincolnshire on return from Bochum 30.9.43.
EE106 PG-C/E	FTR Antheor Viaduct 16/17.9.43.
EE109 PG-F	FTR Hannover 18/19.10.43.
EE110 PG-U	Crashed in Bristol Channel on return from Hagen 1/2.10.43.
EE111 PG-S	Abandoned over Yorkshire coast on return from Berlin 27.11.43.
EE112 PG-T	FTR Nuremberg 10/11.8.43.
EE113	FTR from air-test 9.6.43.
EE114 PG-B	FTR Leipzig 20/21.10.43.
EE115 PG-G	FTR Berlin 31.8/1.9.43.
EE116 PG-Q	FTR Aachen 11/12.4.44.
EE117 PG-L	FTR Peenemünde 17/18.8.43.
EE118	To 156 Squadron.
EE134 PG-X/Y	From 49 Squadron. To 5 Lancaster Finishing School.
EE147 PG-P	From 617 Squadron. FTR Peenemünde 17/18.8.43.
EE149 PG-U	From 617 Squadron. Written off on return from Gelsenkirchen 25/26.6.43.
EE150 PG-F	From 617 Squadron.. Crash-landed on approach to Woodhall Spa on return from Berlin 17.12.43.

EE168 PG-R	From 97 Squadron. Crashed in Yorkshire on return from Berlin 27.11.43.
EE170 PG-N	From 617 Squadron. FTR Berlin 2/3.12.43.
EE198 PG-H	FTR Krefeld 21/22.6.43.
HK803	From 9 Squadron. To 463 Squadron.
JA844 PG-J	Collided over Sussex with ED361 (207 Squadron) on return from Milan 13.8.43.
JA847 PG-C	FTR Berlin 2/3.12.43.
JA848 PG-R	FTR Berlin 31.8/1.9.43.
JA867 PG-X	FTR Berlin 16/17.12.43.
JA898	To 617 Squadron.
JB123 PG-D	FTR Berlin 2/3.1.44 on tenth Berlin operation.
JB125	To 5 Lancaster Finishing School.
JB131 PG-T	To 5 Lancaster Finishing School after ten Berlin operations.
JB133 PG-L	FTR Mannheim 5/6.9.43.
JB134 PG-Y/G	FTR Mailly-Le-Camp 3/4.5.44. after 12 Berlin operations.
JB186 PG-G/O	From 156Squadron. FTR Revigny 18/19.7.44.
LL778 PG-A	To 5 Lancaster Finishing School.
LL783 PG-G/C	FTR Caen 6/7.6.44.
LL784 PG-M/W	FTR Aachen 11/12.4.44.
LL808 PG-D	FTR Wesseling 21/22.6.44.
LL904 PG-S	FTR Schweinfurt 26/27.4.44.
LL919 PG-W	FTR Schweinfurt 26/27.4.44.
LL969 PG-G	FTR Revigny 18/19.7.44.
LL977 PG-H	FTR Wesseling 21/22.6.44.
LM191 PG-O	From 49 Squadron. FTR Darmstadt 11/12.9.44.
LM207	From 49 Squadron. Crashed while landing at Brussels-Evere on return from Essen 11.3.45.
LM209 PG-H	FTR Darmstadt 11/12.9.44.
LM309	From 617 Squadron. To 463 Squadron via 1661 & 1660 Conversion Units.
LM378 PG-J	FTR Revigny 18/19.7.44.
LM418 PG-R/S	Crash-landed at Woodbridge on return from Nuremberg 31.3.44.
LM419 PG-N	FTR Schweinfurt 24/25.2.44.
LM420 PG-R	To 5 Lancaster Finishing School.
LM423 PG-H	FTR Berlin 2/3.1.44.
LM446 PG-H	FTR Gennevilliers 9/10.5.44.
LM484 PG-M/H	FTR Givors 26/27.7.44.
LM536 PG-Q	FTR Stuttgart 28/29.7.44.
LM630 PG-D	
LM640 PG-L	FTR Revigny 18/19.7.44.
LM643 PG-E	FTR Donges 24/25.7.44.
LM656 PG-M	FTR Königsberg 29/30.8.44.
LM657 PG-R/Q	
LM737 PG-A	
LM742 PG-S	FTR Mittelland Canal at Gravenhorst 7.11.44.
LM751 PG-X	FTR Heilbronn 4/5.12.44.
LM756 PG-F	From 227 Squadron. FTR Berchtesgaden 25.4.45.

ME314 PG-W	FTR Politz 9.2.45.
ME472 PG-J	To 207 Squadron.
ME568 PG-F	FTR Trossy-St-Maximin 3.8.44.
ME569 PG-X	To 1668 Conversion Unit.
ME723 PG-X	FTR Munich 24/25.4.44.
ME745 PG-L	FTR St-Leu-d'Esserent 7/8.7.44.
ME747 PG-Q	Crashed into the North Sea during an exercise 23.4.44.
ME787 PG-J	From 49 Squadron.
ME846 PG-E/G/C	FTR Wesseling 21/22.6.44.
ME855 PG-X	FTR Braunschweig (Brunswick) 12/13.8.44.
ME866 PG-W	FTR Châtellerault 9/10.8.44.
ND728 PG-N	FTR Royan 4/5.1.45.
ND730 PG-O	FTR Salbris 7/8.5.44.
ND792	From 49 Squadron. Crashed while landing at Strubby during training 4.2.45.
ND932 PG-U	FTR Heilbronn 4/5.12.44.
ND935 PG-Z/K	FTR Stuttgart 25/26.7.44.
ND957 PG-M	From 49 Squadron. Broke up in the air on return from Munich 7/8.1.45.
ND986 PG-S	FTR Wesseling 21/22.6.44.
NE151 PG-W	FTR Wesseling 21/22.6.44.
NF929	From 9 Squadron.
NG198	
NG286 PG-Y	From 207 Squadron. FTR Harburg 7/8.3.45.
NG483	
NG503 PG-W	FTR Würzburg 16/17.3.45.
NN695 PG-X	Shot down over Norfolk by intruder returning from Duisburg 21/22.5.44.
NN723 PG-G/H/J	From 57 Squadron. FTR Mittelland Canal at Gravenhorst 5/6.11.44.
NN751 PG-H	
NN768	To 44 Squadron.
NX574 PG-E	
PA180 PG-G	
PA198	
PA255 PG-V	
PA277	
PB205	From 44 (Rhodesia) Squadron. To 1661 Conversion Unit.
PB208 PG-S	FTR Kiel 23/24.7.44.
PB210 PG-U/V	FTR Karlsruhe 2/3.2.45.
PB245 PG-L/Z	FTR Revigny 18/19.7.44.
PB261 PG-L	From SIU. To 57 Squadron.
PB297	From SIU. To 57 Squadron.
PB346 PB-J	From 44 (Rhodesia) Squadron. FTR Givors 26/27.7.44.
PB356 PG-G	FTR Harburg 11/12.11.44.
PB404 PG-F	To 227 Squadron.
PB405 PG-S	FTR Mönchengladbach 19/20.9.44.
PB481	From 7 Squadron. To 5 Lancaster Finishing School.
PB540 PG-Z	Crash-landed at Woodbridge on return from Homburg 1.11.44.

PB590 PG-Z/V	
PB696	From 9 Squadron.
PB699 PG-Z	From 207 Squadron. FTR Harburg 7/8.3.45.
PB751	To 44 (Rhodesia) Squadron.
PB758 PG-S	To 1661 Conversion Unit.
PB782	
PB842 PG-Y	FTR Politz 13/14.1.45.
PB852	To 57 Squadron.
PB862	To 1660 Conversion Unit.
PD425 PG-T	From 1661 Conversion Unit. FTR Böhlen 20/21.3.45.
PD441 PG-B	From 1661 Conversion Unit.
RA519 PG-U	
RA521 PG-D	
RA527 PG-M	
RA588 PG-W	
RA590 PG-Y	
RF234 PG-T	From 44 (Rhodesia) Squadron.
RF239 PG-K	
SW254 PG-S	From 1661 Conversion Unit. FTR Leipzig 10/11.4.45.

HEAVIEST SINGLE LOSS.

21/22.06.44. Wesseling. 6 Lancasters FTR.

Roll of Honour

Rank	Name	Surname	Date
F/Sgt	Glenn Prosper	ADAMS	27.09.44.
Sgt	Jack	ADSETTS	29.06.43.
P/O	John Milford	AITKEN	10.05.44.
F/O	Francis Victor	ANDERSON	02.10.43.
Sgt	Alfred	ARCHER	12.09.44.
Sgt	William	ARCHIBALD	27.11.43.
Sgt	George William	ARLETT	03.12.43.
Sgt	John	ATKINSON	21.04.44.
P/O	Allan Daniel	AUMELL	24.07.44.
F/O	Philip Peter	AWAD	04.12.44.
F/Sgt	Alfred	BAKER	25.04.44.
F/O	Frederick John	BAKER	22.05.44.
F/O	Geoffrey Anthony	BAKER	22.06.44.
F/O	Charles Francis (Paddy)	BALE	02.10.43.
P/O	Sigmund Bernard	BANDUR	22.05.44.
Sgt	Leslie	BANKS	16.12.43.
Sgt	Tom Brown	BARRIE	18.08.43.
F/O	Albert Bramwell	BEARCROFT	03.01.44.
F/O	Albert Henry James	BEGERNIE	19.07.44
Sgt	Thomas	BELL	06.01.44.
F/Sgt	John	BENGSTON	04.05.44.
W/O	Ronald	BENNETT	03.08.44.
P/O	Leonard William	BENNETT	11.11.44.
Sgt	Edward Stanley	BICKNELL	06.11.44.
Sgt	John Anthony Geoffrey	BILLINGHAM	30.09.43.
F/Sgt	Harry Vincent	BIRCH	27.11.43.
F/Sgt	Peter Noble	BLACK	08.03.45.
F/O	Alec Hayward	BLAZER	11.08.43.
F/Sgt	Derek Webb	BLUNDELL	27.11.43.
Sgt	Edmund Douglas	BONE	12.09.44.
Sgt	Jack	BOOTH	08.05.44.
Sgt	Harry	BOWDEN	02.02.45.
W/O	Graham Westwood	BOWER	01.09.43.
F/O	John Frank	BOWER	02.12.43.
P/O	John Ernest Ralph	BOWERING	22.06.44.
Sgt	Henry George	BRADY	04.05.44.
Sgt	Frederic Charles	BRIGHT	19.07.44.
F/O	Aubrey Ginders	BRITTEN	19.07.44.

Sgt	Basil Hubert	BRODIE	06.11.44.
F/Sgt	James	BROLL	24.07.44.
P/O	John	BROOMFIELD	24.04.44.
Sgt	Richard	BROWN	22.06.44.
Sgt	Ronald	BROWN	05.01.45.
F/Sgt	Edward	BRUNT	25.04.44.
Sgt	Joseph	BRYCE	08.03.45.
F/Sgt	John Arthur	BUCKLEY	22.06.44.
Sgt	Daniel	BURDEN	03.01.44.
Sgt	John Raymond	BURGESS	04.05.44.
Sgt	Frederick	BURTON	22.06.43.
F/O	Peter Ross	BUTLER	12.04.44.
F/Sgt	Dennis Raymond	BUTLER	29.07.44.
Sgt	William Harry	CADE	24.08.43.
F/Sgt	John Gordon	CAMPBELL	24.03.44.
F/Sgt	Elmer Kenneth	CARLSON	12.09.44.
Sgt	Reginald William	CARPENTER	06.01.44.
Sgt	Donald John	CARTER	20.09.44.
F/Sgt	Ernest George	CASS	27.04.44.
Sgt	Alfred	CASTLE	24.08.43.
P/O	John William	CHAMBERS	11.04.45.
F/O	Stanley Victor	CHAMBERS	04.12.44.
Sgt	Alfred Charles Richard	CHAPMAN	18.08.43.
Sgt	Kenneth William	CHESHIRE	03.01.44.
Sgt	Donald Walter	CHICK	27.04.44
P/O	Elmo Foster	CHRISTY	10.08.44.
F/O	Philip Charles	CLAPHAM	11.11.44.
F/Sgt	William	COBB	03.08.44.
Sgt	Martin	CODY	03.08.44.
Sgt	John Percival Victor	COLE	16.02.44.
F/O	Phillip James	COLEMAN	16.02.44.
Sgt	Edward Leslie	COLLEY	10.08.44.
Sgt	Patrick Joseph	COOK	09.06.43.
F/Sgt	Charles Smith	COOK	27.11.43.
Sgt	Joseph	COOKSEY	03.01.44.
Sgt	Raymond Lester	COOPER	30.09.43.
Sgt	Daniel	CORBITT	16.12.43.
Sgt	Hedley John	COSSEY	22.06.44.
Sgt	John Charles	COVERLEY	30.08.44.
Sgt	Douglas Graham	COX	18.08.43.
F/L	John Kevin	COX	03.01.44.

Rank	Name	Surname	Date
Sgt	Richard Belton	COX	19.07.44
P/O	Kent Elliott	CRAWFORD	22.06.44.
Sgt	Reginald Herbert	CROOKS	01.09.43.
F/Sgt	Richard	CROSSLEY	18.08.43.
Sgt	Arthur Ernest	CURTIS	19.07.44
Sgt	John	CUTTING	22.06.44.
Sgt	Alan Charles	DALMAN	22.06.44.
F/L	Edward	DAMPIER-CROSSLEY	11.08.43.
F/O	Gordon Daniel	DANIELSON	30.08.44.
Sgt	William Arthur	DAVIES	22.06.43.
Sgt	Robert Thomas Edward	DAVIES	30.09.43.
P/O	Edwin Charles Thomas	DAVIES	03.08.44.
F/O	Lewis George	DAVIS	17.08.43.
P/O	Mark Anthony Hamilton	DAVIS	22.06.44.
Sgt	James	DAVISON	12.09.44.
F/Sgt	Frank	DAWSON	11.08.43.
F/O	Alfred George	DAY	06.01.44
F/O	Henry Andrew	De VRIES	16.12.43.
F/O	Terence	De VRIES	30.08.44.
Sgt	Douglas	DEMAINE	20.10.43.
F/O	Wilfred Tarquinas	De MARCO	25.04.45.
Sgt	Harry James	DEPOTEX	12.09.44.
Sgt	Robert Douglas	DEUGARD	18.08.43.
Sgt	Allan	DICKSON	24.07.44.
Sgt	George Walter	DILLNUTT	20.10.43.
F/O	Cyril Bernard	DOCKREY	12.09.44.
F/O	Norman Wilfred	DONNELLEY	19.07.44.
Sgt	William John	DOUGLAS	09.06.43.
Sgt	Frederick Frank	DRING	10.05.44.
Sgt	Frank Charles	DRYDEN	31.08.43.
Sgt	John Hubert	DUNCAN	03.12.43.
Sgt	James Alexander	DURKIN	25.04.44
P/O	Leo	EAUDE	18.10.43.
F/O	Frederick Eric	ELEY	30.08.44.
Sgt	Ernest George	EMSLEY	24.04.44.
Sgt	Paul	ENGEL	02.10.43.
F/Sgt	Lloyd Francis	ENGLISH	18.08.43.
W/O	Ernest Stanley Ivor	EVANS	03.01.44.
W/O	Lloyd George	EVANS	12.09.44.
F/O	Cyril Edward	EYLES	08.03.45.
F/O	Basil Walter	EYNON	08.03.45.

Rank	Name	Surname	Date
F/O	Thomas Edison	FARROW	17.03.45.
P/O	Lewis Leslie	FEINDELL	27.04.44.
F/O	Robert Nicholas	FERGUSON	08.03.45.
P/O	Christopher	FIRTH	20.10.43.
P/O	Clarence Clyde	FLEWELLING	22.06.44.
F/O	Colin Kelvin	FLOCKHART	07.01.45.
Sgt	Ronald Arthur	FORREST	03.08.44.
Sgt	Ronald Victor Stuart	FORSDICK	06.09.43.
F/O	Harry	FORSHAW	15.06.43.
F/Sgt	Joseph Arthur	FOWLER	27.11.43.
Sgt	Patrick	FOX	09.06.43.
Sgt	Clarence Bedbrook	FRANCIS	18.08.43.
Sgt	Kenneth	FRANK	27.04.44.
P/O	William Frederick	FRASER	30.08.44.
P/O	Peter Henry	FRENCH	21.04.44.
Sgt	Terence Frederick	FROGLEY	19.07.44.
P/O	Cyril	FULLER	18.10.43.
S/L	Frederick Edgar	FULLER	08.05.44.
Sgt	Thomas Henry	FULLWOOD	09.02.45.
Sgt	Albert	FURNIVAL	12.09.44.
W/OII	Thomas Francis	GALBRAITH	27.07.44.
F/Sgt	John Douglas	GALLIARD	04.12.44.
F/O	Keith Alexander	GALLOWAY	22.06.44.
F/Sgt	John Albert	GARBUTT	19.07.44.
Sgt	Leslie	GARDNER	24.08.43.
F/O	Dennis Frederick	GAY	30.08.44.
Sgt	Jack	GEDDES	19.07.44.
F/O	Max	GENNIS	16.12.43.
Sgt	Marshall Gow	GIBSON	01.11.44.
Sgt	Robert Gifford	GIDDINGS	12.04.44.
Sgt	Joseph Harry	GILLIVER	27.07.44.
F/O	William McCall	GIRDWOOD	22.06.43.
F/Sgt	James George Leslie	GLAZEBROOK	25.02.44.
F/Sgt	Charles Albert	GODDARD	06.09.43.
Sgt	Arthur Parvin	GODDARD	01.11.44.
Sgt	Hyman	GOLDBERG	27.04.44.
Sgt	Derrick Walter	GOLDING	25.04.44.
P/O	Peter Mylrea	GOLDSMITH	18.08.43
F/Sgt	Robert Wallace	GOLLOGLY	31.08.43.
P/O	Kenneth	GOODWIN	10.05.44.
Sgt	Colin William	GOODWIN	22.06.44.

Sgt	Raymond Archibald	GRACE	29.06.43.
F/L	William Forster	GRAHAM	21.03.45.
Sgt	Edward	GRAHAM	27.07.44.
F/O	Donald Irving	GRANT	19.07.44
Sgt	Bernard Francis	GRATWICKE	24.03.44.
Sgt	Percival Stanley	GRAVES	07.01.45.
Sgt	Douglas Murray	GRAY	09.06.43.
F/Sgt	John	GRAY	16.12.43.
F/O	Dean	GRAY	05.01.45.
Sgt	David	GREENLEY	12.09.44.
F/Sgt	Arthur	GRIFFITHS	03.08.44.
P/O	George Alan	GRIGG	24.07.44.
F/L	Guy Godfrey Charles (Nip)	GUNZI	27.04.44.
Sgt	Ivor Ronald Frank	HABERFIELD	11.04.44.
F/Sgt	Arnold William	HABERGHAM	19.07.44.
F/Sgt	Frank Horace	HALL	29.07.44.
F/O	Lawrence Ambrose	HALL	10.08.44.
P/O	John Lawrence	HALPIN	22.06.44.
Sgt	Alan John	HANDFORD	22.06.44.
P/O	Edward Thompson	HARGREAVES	03.12.43.
Sgt	Kenneth Wilfred	HARMER	22.05.44.
F/O	Eric	HARPER	29.06.43.
Sgt	John	HARPER	26.07.44.
F/Sgt	James Arthur	HARRISON	06.11.44.
P/O	Rupert Thomas William	HARWOOD	19.07.44
F/Sgt	James	HAY	24.03.44.
F/O	John Anthony Foch	HEFFERNAN	03.01.44.
F/O	Harold Thomas	HESKETH	08.02.45.
Sgt	Roy Ernest	HICKLING	10.05.44.
F/Sgt	John	HILL	08.05.44.
Sgt	Raymond	HILLIER	12.04.44.
Sgt	William Frederick	HINETT	19.07.44.
Sgt	Frederick	HODSON	01.09.43.
Sgt	Robert John	HOGG	06.11.44.
P/O	Aldrene Gail	HOLKE	08.05.44.
Sgt	William Dennis	HOLLIDAY	06.01.44.
P/O	James	HORNE	18.10.43.
W/OII	James Chandler	HORNE	27.04.44.
F/Sgt	Peter John	HORSHAM	18.08.43.
Sgt	Bernard	HOWE	22.06.43.
P/O	Thomas Edward George	HOWE	22.06.44.

Sgt	John Thomas	HUBBARD	18.08.43.
F/O	Roy Albert	HUDSON	09.02.45.
Sgt	Walter Henry	HUMPHREY	18.08.43.
Sgt	Kenneth William Percival	HUNT	24.04.44.
Sgt	Edward Hope	HUNTER	29.07.44.
F/Sgt	Howard	INSLEY	05.01.45.
F/Sgt	Eric Kenneth	IRELAND	17.03.45
F/L	Fred	JACKSON	11.04.45.
F/O	Frank Martin	JACKSON	11.04.45.
Sgt	Anthony Leslie	JAMIESON	22.06.44.
Sgt	Arrol	JOHNSON	05.01.45.
P/O	Peter	JOHNSON	22.06.44.
P/O	James Kitchener	JOHNSON	19.07.44.
Sgt	William	JOHNSON	20.09.44.
F/O	Jack Dennison	JOHNSTON	17.03.45.
P/O	Norman Hubert	JOHNSTON	25.04.45
Sgt	John Oswald	JOHNSTON	22.06.44.
Sgt	David Vincent	JONES	13.08.43.
Sgt	Rhys	JONES	01.09.43.
Sgt	Myrddin	JONES	20.10.43.
Sgt	Donald Valentine	JORDAN	22.06.43.
F/O	Derek McLean	JOSS	01.10.43.
Sgt	Frederick Henry	JOY	04.05.44.
Sgt	Henry Cyril	KEATLEY	30.08.44.
F/O	Leslie Charles	KEELING	03.01.44.
F/Sgt	Robert Wilfred	KEIGHTLEY	07.01.45.
F/O	John	KELLETT	27.11.43.
P/O	John Reid	KELLUM	26.07.44.
Sgt	Leslie	KENNEDY	06.11.44.
F/Sgt	Douglas William Anthony	KERSEY	24.04.44.
Sgt	William	KERSHAW	06.09.43.
F/O	Thomas Edward	KERSLAKE	27.09.44.
F/Sgt	Earl David	KIDD	22.06.44.
Sgt	Herbert Edward	KILBURN	31.08.43.
F/Sgt	Walter William Nelson	KNIGHTS	27.11.43.
F/O	Joseph John	KOMMES	25.07.44.
F/Sgt	Elmer Nels	KULLBERG	22.06.44.
F/Sgt	Victor Walter	LAMBERT	07.03.45.
Sgt	Henry George	LANG	12.04.44.
P/O	George James	LANGRIDGE	27.04.44.
F/Sgt	William Henry Garrett	LEBATT	19.07.44

Rank	Name	Surname	Date
Sgt	Andrew Christie	LEITCH	02.12.43.
F/O	Leslie William	LEONARD	20.09.44.
Sgt	Thomas Luther	LETCHFORD	07.01.45.
F/Sgt	Sidney	LEVY	10.05.44.
F/O	Joseph Vincent	LEYLAND	24.03.44.
Sgt	Lawrence Edward	LILLEY	29.07.44.
Sgt	Samuel Wardley	LING	19.07.44.
F/Sgt	Robert Harrison	LITTLE	16.02.44.
F/Sgt	David Robert	LLOYD	08.03.45.
F/O	Robert	LOGAN	19.07.44.
P/O	Glen Benson	LONEY	16.12.43.
Sgt	William Arthur	LOOSE	22.06.44.
Sgt	Max	LOOSLI	19.07.44.
F/O	Norman Albert	LORANGER	08.05.44.
F/O	William Charles John	LORD	03.01.44.
P/O	John Ernest	LOTT	07.06.44.
Sgt	Joseph	LOWE	02.10.43.
Sgt	Peter Charles	LOWE	27.09.44.
Sgt	George Henry	LUCAS	25.07.44.
F/Sgt	Francis Philip	LYFORD	03.08.44.
Sgt	Martin John	LYNCH	27.11.43.
F/Sgt	John William Charles	MABBUTT	20.09.44.
F/Sgt	James Livingston	MacDONALD	08.02.45.
P/O	Keith Mitchell	MacDONALD	03.01.44.
F/O	Alexander	MACKAY	29.06.43.
Sgt	Jeremy Ernest	MACKINTOSH	19.07.44.
F/O	Elmer Joseph Alexander	MacNAIR	12.09.44.
Sgt	John	MACPHERSON	17.03.45.
Sgt	Leslie Thomas Christian	MADDAFORD	13.08.43.
Sgt	Jack Harrison	MALTBY	04.05.44.
F/Sgt	Joseph Frederick	MARA	19.07.44.
Sgt	Arnold	MARPER	19.07.44.
F/Sgt	Stanley John James	MATON	07.03.45.
F/L	Charles Wylie	McBRIDE	17.03.45.
F/O	Norman Edward Henry	McCONNELL	11.11.44.
P/O	Kenneth	McCULLOCH	15.06.43.
F/Sgt	Bernard	McDONAGH	08.07.44.
F/Sgt	Alphonsus Mary Bonaventure	McDONALD	27.09.44.
W/C	Irwin John	McGHIE	18.08.43.
Sgt	William	McGILL	01.09.43.
S/L	John William Eunson Duncan	McGILVRAY	11.04.44.

F/O	Allan Charles	McKAY	30.09.43.
Sgt	Ronald Alexander	McKAY	22.05.44.
F/O	Leslie John	McKINNON	22.06.44.
F/O	John MacArthur	McLEAN	11.08.43.
F/O	Reginald Willis	McMANAMAN	02.12.43.
F/L	George Melvin Stark	McMORRAN	08.03.45.
F/L	Albert Elmore	McMORRAN	11.04.45.
P/O	Donald Cameron	McNIE	02.02.45.
P/O	Eric	MEARIS	30.09.43.
P/O	Kenneth James	MEARS	27.11.43.
Sgt	Ronald Lawrence	MEASOR	31.08.43.
F/O	Frederick Leonard	MEREDITH	04.12.44.
Sgt	Keith Addingley	METCALF	06.09.43.
P/O	Frederick Gerard	METCALFE	31.08.43.
F/Sgt	Harold	MINO	17.03.45.
Sgt	Leonard	MINSHULL	24.03.44.
Sgt	William Arthur	MITCHELL	18.08.43.
Sgt	George Harry	MOGGRIDGE	22.06.44.
Sgt	Alexander	MOIR	27.09.44.
F/O	Frank Francis	MOLINAS	19.07.44.
Sgt	Terence	MONAGHAN	02.10.43.
F/O	Stephen Bickford	MORCOM	19.07.44.
F/Sgt	Leonard	MORGAN	19.07.44.
F/Sgt	Eric Andrew	MORLEY	05.01.45.
F/O	Ewart Laverne	MORRISON	19.07.44.
F/O	Edward James	MORTIS	02.02.45.
F/Sgt	Kenneth George	MORTLOCK	02.10.43.
F/Sgt	Clifford Keith	MORTON	06.11.44.
F/O	Peter Clement	MOXHAM	11.08.43.
P/O	Joseph Francis Edward	MOYLE	08.02.45.
Sgt	Thomas	MULLEN	19.07.44
W/O	Alexander Armstrong	MUNRO	11.04.44.
F/Sgt	Anthony Frederick	MURDOCH	07.01.45
F/Sgt	Terence Peter	MURPHY	29.06.43.
F/Sgt	David Matthew	MURPHY	25.07.44
F/Sgt	Paul Antoine	MUSSO	01.09.43.
Sgt	William George	MYCOCK	31.08.43.
F/Sgt	Alfred	MYRES	19.07.44.
Sgt	Arthur	NAYLOR	04.05.44.
Sgt	Eric Ernest	NICHOLLS	06.09.43.
Sgt	George	NIXON	11.11.44.

Rank	Name	Surname	Date
Sgt	Edward William	NORMAN	25.04.45.
Sgt	Alick Clem	NORRIS	06.11.44.
P/O	Owen Arthur	O'LEARY	18.08.43.
F/O	Ronald William	ORBELL	25.07.44
Sgt	Alfred George	OSBORNE	20.10.43.
S/L	Colin Murray	PALMER	21.03.45.
F/O	John	PARKER	24.07.44.
Sgt	William James	PARKES	22.06.43.
P/O	Herbert	PARROTT	26.07.44
F/O	Richard Charles	PARRY	16.02.44.
F/O	James Francis	PARRY	12.09.44.
Sgt	Archie	PASCOE	04.12.44.
F/O	William Henry Charles	PATEMAN	16.02.44.
W/O	John	PATERSON	29.07.44.
P/O	George Barnes Penny	PATTERSON	11.08.43.
Sgt	Johnston Irwin Stewart (Jack)	PATTERSON	08.07.44
Sgt	Reginald	PATTERSON	11.11.44.
Sgt	Cyril George	PAYNE	03.01.44.
P/O	Alfred John	PEARCE	18.08.43.
F/Sgt	Jack Gordon	PEARCE	27.07.44.
F/Sgt	Leslie	PEARSE	27.11.43.
P/O	Charles Thomas William	PERRING	11.04.45.
F/O	Raymond Wilbur	PETTIGREW	27.09.44
F/Sgt	Alan	PICKSTONE	27.04.44.
F/O	Cyril Keith	PLUNKETT	08.05.44.
F/Sgt	Albert William	POPE	10.08.44.
F/O	Joseph Reginald	POTTS	12.09.44.
P/O	Eric Nash	POWELL	25.04.44.
Sgt	John Raymond	PRESLAND	10.05.44.
F/O	Elmont Gasper	PREST	18.08.43.
F/Sgt	Arthur Philip	PRICE	09.06.43.
Sgt	Ronald Watkin	PRICE	07.01.45.
P/O	John Leonard	PRITCHARD	11.04.44.
F/Sgt	Robert	PRUNKLE	04.12.44.
P/O	Geoffrey Norman	RACKLEY	22.06.44.
Sgt	James William	RANDALL	21.04.44.
F/L	Leonard Charles	RAW	21.03.45.
F/L	Ronald David	RAYMENT	27.11.43.
F/O	Robert Hall	REDSHAW	22.05.44.
Sgt	Charles John	REED	04.12.44.
Sgt	Reginald Charles	REID	08.05.44.

Rank	Name	Surname	Date
F/Sgt	Edward Albert	REX	02.02.45.
Sgt	Kenneth Frederick	RICE	22.06.44.
Sgt	Norman MacKenzie	RICE	24.07.44.
F/Sgt	Stanley Douglas Gordon	RICE	29.07.44.
Sgt	Norman Conrad	RICHARDS	15.06.43.
F/Sgt	John Thomas	RICHARDS	27.11.43.
Sgt	Leslie Joseph	RICHARDSON	22.05.44.
F/Sgt	John Charles	RICHARDSON	11.11.44.
F/O	Frederick James	RICKETTS	21.03.45.
Sgt	Norman Evans	RIVERS	29.06.43.
F/L	Kimberley	ROBERTS	07.06.44.
Sgt	William Arthur	ROBINSON	09.06.43.
F/Sgt	Robert	RODGER	29.07.44.
F/Sgt	Len	ROTHWELL	27.07.44.
Sgt	Patrick Joseph	RUANE	15.06.43.
F/O	Robert Mons	RUMBLE	16.02.44.
P/O	Gordon Geoffrey	SALT	27.11.43.
Sgt	John George Douglas	SANDERS	11.11.44.
F/O	Robert Harry	SCHAEFER	04.12.44.
P/O	Derek	SCHOFIELD	25.04.44.
Sgt	James Waugh	SCOTT	03.12.43.
Sgt	James Rattray	SCOTT	25.07.44
P/O	Ira Walter	SHANTZ	04.12.44.
F/Sgt	William Arthur	SHARP	24.07.44.
Sgt	John Hatfield	SHAW	18.08.43.
Sgt	Henry Frederick	SHEARSBY	12.04.44.
F/Sgt	Arthur Clifford	SHENTON	04.05.44.
W/O	Charles Henry	SHERIDAN	22.06.44.
Sgt	Francis William	SHIRLEY	09.06.43.
Sgt	Stephen	SINCLAIR	25.07.44
F/Sgt	John	SINGER	12.09.44.
F/Sgt	Robert	SMELLIE	10.08.44.
F/Sgt	Eric Alfred	SMITH	07.01.45.
Sgt	Henry Eadsporth	SMITH	27.09.44.
Sgt	Ronald	SMITHERS	03.12.43.
Sgt	Henry Roy	SNELL	24.08.43.
F/O	Cecil Paul	SPARKES	08.03.45.
Sgt	Richard Stephen	SPRACKMAN	18.10.43.
S/L	Reginald Arthur	SQUIBBS	12.09.44.
F/Sgt	Albert Christopher	ST LEGER	09.02.45.
P/O	Victor George	STABELL	18.08.43.

Sgt	Ernest	STANLEY	22.06.43.
P/O	Reginald	STEVENS	18.10.43.
F/Sgt	Joseph Kenneth	STOBBS	20.09.44.
F/Sgt	Mark	STUART	06.01.44.
Sgt	Francis	SUMNER	06.09.43.
Sgt	John Rennie	SUTHERLAND	20.09.44.
Sgt	John Lonsdale	SWANSON	04.12.44.
W/O	Leslie James	SYMONDS	05.01.45.
F/L	Llewellyn Elvet	TANNER	01.11.44
W/O	John Frederick Russell	TATE	19.07.44.
Sgt	Archibald William	TAYLOR	10.08.44.
F/Sgt	Rex Bernard	TEMPLETON	06.11.44
Sgt	Reginald James	THAIR	27.07.44.
F/Sgt	William John	THOMAS	19.07.44.
W/O	Ford Arnold	THOMPSON	18.08.43.
P/O	Paul	THOMPSON	24.03.44.
Sgt	Robert	THOMPSON	21.04.44.
F/O	John William	THOMPSON	27.09.44.
F/O	Jack Stewart	THOMSON	21.04.44.
F/O	Lloyd	TILLEY	17.03.45.
Sgt	Lionel	TIMMS	15.06.43.
F/O	Edmund Thomas	TINKER	21.04.44.
Sgt	Robert Edward	TOFTS	15.06.43.
Sgt	Frederick Albert	TOWSE	10.05.44.
Sgt	Roy	TRAHAIR	18.10.43.
Sgt	Frederick Liege	TUCKER	24.04.44.
F/Sgt	John Henry	TUCKER	07.06.44.
F/Sgt	Philip	TURNER	02.02.45.
F/O	Ronald George	TURVEY	27.07.44.
Sgt	Thomas	UNDERDOWN	18.08.43.
F/Sgt	Ralph Hughes	VAN CAMP	15.06.43.
F/Sgt	James	VAUGHTON	22.06.44.
F/Sgt	Frederick Ernest William	VEAL	24.04.44.
F/O	Nickolas	VLASSIE	27.04.44.
P/O	Douglas Arnold	WADSWORTH	04.05.44.
Sgt	William	WALCH	25.02.44.
F/Sgt	John Harvey William	WALKER	29.06.43.
W/O	Gordon Victor	WALKER	25.04.45.
Sgt	Archibald James	WALKER	22.06.44.
Sgt	Kenneth Richard	WALLACE	24.08.43.
Sgt	Jack Ronald	WALLIS	22.06.44.

Rank	Name	Surname	Date
P/O	James Francis	WARD	03.12.43.
Sgt	Arthur Roy	WARD	22.06.44.
Sgt	John Ronald	WARD	25.07.44
Sgt	Robert James	WARD	01.11.44.
Sgt	John	WARDLE	11.08.43.
F/O	John Michael	WARREN	18.08.43.
Sgt	Edwin Ernest	WATSON	06.01.44.
Sgt	John Ernest	WATSON	27.04.44.
W/O	James	WEBSTER	20.09.44.
P/O	John Layard Butler	WEBSTER	06.11.44.
Sgt	George Myron	WEIGHELL	20.10.43.
Sgt	Leslie George	WEIR	04.12.44.
Sgt	John James	WEMYSS	09.06.43.
F/L	Richard Edward	WESSON	06.01.44.
F/Sgt	Robert Ford	WHINFIELD	27.04.44.
F/L	Kenneth William	WHITEFIELD	11.11.44.
F/Sgt	Samuel	WHITEHURST	19.07.44
F/Sgt	John Edward Gifford	WHITTOME	22.06.44.
F/Sgt	Reginald Amesbury	WICKHAM	27.04.44.
Sgt	Aubrey Ralph	WILCHER	27.11.43.
F/Sgt	Geoffrey Talbot	WILKS	23.04.44.
F/O	Erle Keith	WILLIAMS	25.02.44.
F/Sgt	Leslie Edward	WILLIAMS	07.06.44.
F/L	Bruce Arthur	WILLIAMSON	11.04.45.
F/Sgt	Robert Arthur	WILLIS	13.08.44.
Sgt	George Arthur	WILSON	18.10.43.
F/O	Harry James	WILSON	19.07.44.
Sgt	Peter Charles	WISEMAN	21.03.45.
F/Sgt	Roy	WITHINSHAW	25.04.44.
F/O	Peter Michael	WOOD	12.04.44.
Sgt	Edward Frederick	WOOD	06.11.44.
Sgt	John Harold	WOODCOCK	08.05.44.
W/OII	Charles Notley Dawson	WRIGHT	20.10.43.
F/O	Guy Herbert	WYAND	07.06.44.

Key to Abbreviations

A&AEE	Aeroplane and Armaments Experimental Establishment.
AA	Anti-Aircraft fire.
AACU	Anti-Aircraft Cooperation Unit.
AAS	Air Armament School.
AASF	Advance Air Striking Force.
AAU	Aircraft Assembly Unit.
ACM	Air Chief Marshal.
ACSEA	Air Command South-East Asia.
AFDU	Air Fighting Development Unit.
AFEE	Airborne Forces Experimental Unit.
AFTDU	Airborne Forces Tactical Development Unit.
AGS	Air Gunners School.
AMDP	Air Members for Development and Production.
AOC	Air Officer Commanding.
AOS	Air Observers School.
ASRTU	Air-Sea Rescue Training Unit.
ATTDU	Air Transport Tactical Development Unit.
AVM	Air Vice-Marshal.
BAT	Beam Approach Training.
BCBS	Bomber Command Bombing School.
BCDU	Bomber Command Development Unit.
BCFU	Bomber Command Film Unit.
BCIS	Bomber Command Instructors School.
BDU	Bombing Development Unit.
BSTU	Bomber Support Training Unit.
CF	Conversion Flight.
CFS	Central Flying School.
CGS	Central Gunnery School.
C-in-C	Commander in Chief.
CNS	Central Navigation School.
CO	Commanding Officer.
CRD	Controller of Research and Development.
CU	Conversion Unit.
DGRD	Director General for Research and Development.
EAAS	Empire Air Armament School.
EANS	Empire Air Navigation School.
ECDU	Electronic Countermeasures Development Unit.
ECFS	Empire Central Flying School.
ETPS	Empire Test Pilots School.
F/L	Flight Lieutenant.
Flt	Flight.
F/O	Flying Officer.
FPP	Ferry Pilots School.

F/S	Flight Sergeant.
FTR	Failed to Return.
FTU	Ferry Training Unit.
G/C	Group Captain.
Gp	Group.
HCU	Heavy Conversion Unit.
HGCU	Heavy Glider Conversion Unit.
LFS	Lancaster Finishing School.
MAC	Mediterranean Air Command.
MTU	Mosquito Training Unit.
MU	Maintenance Unit.
NTU	Navigation Training Unit.
OADU	Overseas Aircraft Delivery Unit.
OAPU	Overseas Aircraft Preparation Unit.
OTU	Operational Training Unit.
P/O	Pilot Officer.
PTS	Parachute Training School.
RAE	Royal Aircraft Establishment.
SGR	School of General Reconnaissance.
Sgt	Sergeant.
SHAEF	Supreme Headquarters Allied Expeditionary Force.
SIU	Signals Intelligence Unit.
S/L	Squadron Leader.
SOC	Struck off Charge.
SOE	Special Operations Executive.
Sqn	Squadron.
TF	Training Flight.
TFU	Telecommunications Flying Unit.
W/C	Wing Commander.
Wg	Wing.
WIDU	Wireless Intelligence Development Unit.
W/O	Warrant Officer.

www.ingramcontent.com/pod-product-compliance
Lightning Source LLC
Chambersburg PA
CBHW080538170426
43195CB00016B/2607